**Date Du**

*E*ducation
and
the
Economics of
Human
Capital

# Education

COLLIER-MACMILLAN LIMITED

LONDON

EDITED BY

# RONALD A. WYKSTRA

ASSOCIATE PROFESSOR OF ECONOMICS
COLORADO STATE UNIVERSITY

*and*

*the*

*Economics of*

*Human*

*Capital*

 THE FREE PRESS

NEW YORK

*Copyright* © 1971 *by The Free Press*
*A Division of The Macmillan Company*

Printed in the United States of America

*The Free Press*
*A Division of The Macmillan Company*
*866 Third Avenue, New York, New York* 10022

*Collier-Macmillan Canada Ltd., Toronto, Ontario*

*Library of Congress Catalog Card Number:* 75–153078

*printing number*
1   2   3   4   5   6   7   8   9   10

# contents

v

*part three*

## Selected Issues in the Economics of Education

# *preface*

Human resource development has become a primary public policy issue within the last decade. Although human capital formation through educational investment did not seriously attract the analytical scrutiny of economists until recently, the magnitude of educational expenditures and the relations between education and economic growth have prompted a great deal of research recently. This volume is concerned with some of the economic implications of expenditures on education as one form of investment in human resources.

The selections chosen stress the macroeconomic problem of economic growth and development and the microeconomic problem of investment efficiency in the formation of human capital through education—subjects rapidly being incorporated into the disciplines of education and economics. Three questions constitute the core of this inquiry.

1. What is the relationship between economic growth and human capital formation through educational expenditures?

2. What decision-making guidelines are applicable to human capital investment analysis, much of which occurs outside the price-directed market system?

3.  What are the returns earned from investment in education
    and how do manpower development and educational
    planning relate to these returns?

These inquiries into human capital are directly related to
several fields in economics including macroeconomic theory,
economic growth and development, the economics of education,
labor economics, and manpower economics. Thus, a collection of
selected papers on the subject of human capital is timely. The selections presented here sample the many excellent articles on the
subject of investment in education as one dimension to human
capital formation. Other articles of interest are cited in the biblio-
graphies provided by the contributors to this volume.

Appreciation is extended to Theodore W. Schultz, Professor
of Economics at the University of Chicago, Campbell R. McConnell,
Professor of Economics at the University of Nebraska, and my
colleagues at Colorado State University, particularly Edward K.
Smith and Richard G. Walsh, for their helpful suggestions. My wife
patiently assisted in the many chores necessary to bring this volume
to press. A major indebtedness is owed the authors of these papers
whose analytical commitment to the economics of human captial
formation made this collection possible. I wish to thank those to
whom I am obligated and obsolve them of all responsibilities for
any remaining errors of omission or commission that are mine
alone. Formal acknowledgement of authors, publishers, and sources
is given at the beginning of each selection.

R. A. W.

# RONALD A. WYKSTRA

# *Introduction*

I n their search for a fuller explanation of economic growth, economists have turned their attention to the quality as well as the quantity of labor and physical capital. Contemporary research on the long-run economic growth of modern economies has indicated that less than half of the growth rate in output can be explained by changes in quantities of the conventional factors of production, i.e., capital and labor. To measure only the quantities of inputs is to ignore other sources of growth such as scale economies, qualitative changes in inputs, and improved organization among factors of production.The common label given to these less readily identifiable sources of growth is technological change or increased productivity. This difference in output growth compared to growth in labor and

Notes to this Introduction will be found on pages 269–270.

capital inputs has also been referred to as a *residual of ignorance*, because it reflects our lack of knowledge concerning economic growth.

Substantial efforts have been devoted to developing a concept of human capital as well as analyzing its qualitative and quantitative characteristics, particularly in relation to economic growth and development and the efficient allocation of resources to human capital formation. Let us first examine the historical origins of the human capital concept and then illustrate how education and human capital formation are related to economic growth and efficiency in resource allocation.

## DEVELOPMENT OF THE HUMAN CAPITAL CONCEPT

The word *capital* generally refers to the reproductive power of natural and man-made producer goods. Capital resources typically are factors of production which must themselves be produced at some cost and are subject to changing value with use or disuse.[1] The treatment of human beings as a capital component that is integral to economic development is by no means a novel idea, as is demonstrated in the literature of the early classical economists.[2] Nevertheless, the discipline of economics failed to incorporate fully the human capital component into the stream of economic thought.

The concept of human capital remained underdeveloped until very recent times despite much evidence of awareness on the part of economists that education and human resources were analogous to real capital in some ways. Historically, interest in human capital stemmed from a desire to draw attention to the value of preservation of life, the need to develop systems of compensation for injury or death, interest in the development of equitable tax systems, curiosity about the impact of educational investments on the distribution of earnings, and attempts at identification of the costs of war. In addition, interest in human capital was sparked by the topic's implications for sources of wealth and the power of nations, the "proper" role of government, and education as a source of socioeconomic control and class stratification.[3] Some classical economists recognized that human beings received inadequate amounts of education for the total welfare of the state as well as for the individual. Like Parson Malthus, Adam Smith's concern for human capital was so oriented to economic wealth and development.

Those few classical economists who argued vigorously that human beings should be viewed in a capital context defended the proposition by noting that (1) there were costs associated with the development and formation of human capital (largely education), (2) the output of skilled human resources added incrementally to the national product, and (3) expenditures on human resources which increased the national product also increased national wealth. For the most part, however, reluctance characterized the view that human resources could be treated explicitly as a form of capital. Sir William Petty's estimate of the stock of human capital by capitalization of income represents an exception to the implicit and more general awareness displayed in the writings of Adam Smith, Alfred Marshall, J. S. Mill, *et al.* Toward the turn of the century, J. S. Nicholson utilized Petty's capitalized earning method of valuing human beings and arrived at an estimate of human capital that was five times the value of estimated physical capital.[4] More recently, S. J. Strumlin utilized a sample of workers in the USSR in one of the first attempts to measure the rate of return from investment in education.[5] The work of J. R. Walsh, who estimated the present value of future returns from a college education, is also notable among efforts in the early twentieth century.[6]

The prevailing tradition among economists remained that of recognizing only the standard factors of production—labor and physical capital. Failure to deal directly with human capital partially reflects the difficulty of isolating investment and consumption as two components of educational expenditures. The moral implications of viewing human beings as capital also appear to have discouraged more complete acceptance of the human capital concept. Finally, lack of interest may also have been a result of the development of governments which became stabilizing forces that encouraged the development of human capital.

Human capital formation is affected primarily by investments in formal education, improved health, on-the-job training, manpower rehabilitation, and mobility or migration. Factors unrelated to investment expenditures (*e.g.*, labor force participation or age-sex changes in manpower supply) also influence the stock and formation of human capital. The renewed interest in human capital formation that exists today reflects two general concerns of economists and educators: the economic efficiency implications of rapidly growing expenditures in the education industry and the relation of human capital to economic growth and development.

In slightly more than a decade, direct expenditures on formal education in the United States nearly tripled from a 1955/56 outlay of $16.8 billion to an estimated $70 billion for fiscal 1970/71.[7] School enrollment increased 83 per cent from 1940 to 1966 while aggregate expenditures increased fivefold from a 1940 level of $9.4 billion.[8] Theodore W. Schultz has estimated that foregone earnings by 10.7 million enrollees in high school and college approximated $12.4 billion in 1956.[9] With high school and college enrollment approximating 20 million students as the 1970s begin, the direct and indirect (the opportunity cost of substituting learning for work) costs of formal education approximate $100 billion, two-thirds of which represents direct costs. Indeed, direct expenditures alone grew at 6 per cent annually throughout the 1960s, which suggests that aggregate direct expenditures may reach $100 billion midway in the 1970s. This is a sizable industry by most standards. Consequently, the efficiency implications of investment in formal education constitutes a focal point in the study of the formation of human capital. The earlier described *residual of ignorance*, a significant demonstration of our inability to identify the sources of economic growth and development, is equally as important a reason for examining investment in education more closely.

## EDUCATION, HUMAN CAPITAL AND ECONOMIC GROWTH

Estimating the value of the stock of human capital at different points in time constitutes one approach to economic growth analysis.

The major contribution in the area of estimating the educational stock of human capital remains that of Theodore W. Schultz, who developed such data for the United States.[10] The procedure used by Schultz to estimate the stock value of human capital involved the summation of past expenditures on education adjusted for a variety of intervening factors, such as length of the school year. Alternatively, one can discount future earnings capacity in arriving at an estimate of the human capital stock.[11] The discounted earnings approach raises numerous unresolved issues including future mortality, the implied assumption that earnings reflect marginal productivity, the proper rate of discount, and the treatment of human capital appreciation or depreciation. The production cost approach also raises difficulties that require careful consideration. Such difficulties include the extent to which the costs of education constitute investment rather than consumption expenditures and the appropriateness of including foregone earnings as a cost component. Although both approaches to measuring the stock of human capital are subject to limitations, identification of the relative importance of human capital stocks improves our understanding of capital-output relationships and the process of economic growth. At the same time numerous noneconomic and qualitative variables related to the quality of human resources are not easily identifiable. For this reason it is important to remain cognizant of the limitations of measuring human capital stocks.

The residual or production function approach to analysis of human capital consists of delineating the form and magnitude of relations between inputs (labor and capital), outputs (national income), and whatever unexplained growth in output might remain. In some instances the character of the production function has been postulated, whereas in other studies the growth rates of inputs and outputs are measured and compared to estimate the residual—a procedure used by Denison.[12] The residual nature of unexplained economic growth is discouraging because of its relative size as well as the heterogeneity of the numerous unspecified growth-inducing components it masks. Use of this method is limited in that the interplay of technology and physical factors of production remains unidentified and is typically assumed away. Nevertheless, the production function approach has made important contributions, particularly by identifying how much is unknown. The omnipresent existence of so large a growth residual reminds all concerned that economic growth entails much more than the accumulation of savings and investment in physical capital.[13] This unexplained residual, typically labeled productivity or technological change, also embodies much more than education and human capital. The subject matter of education and human capital formation represents *one* of the time-worn "givens" that had to be dropped, however, in an effort to understand more fully the process of economic growth and development.

## Economic Growth and the Residual

Typically, economic growth is measured by changes in national income at full employment and constant prices. This definition of economic growth sets aside some baffling and important issues, but it does give us a reasonably clear starting point for analyzing factors that operate in a growing economy.[14] The sources of growth in output as measured by real national income are numerous. A nonexhaustive list of factors that influence the productive capacity of a nation would include: (1) the quantity and quality of labor, (2) the quantity and quality of physical capital, (3) the quantity and quality of natural resources, (4) the level of technology used in combining factors of production, (5) the degree of competition which may influence the productive efficiency of firms, (6) the cultural incentives and attitudes toward work and punctuality, and (7) the socioeconomic structure of institutions in a society. Analysis of the economic growth process depicts growth in potential output or national income ($Yg$) as a function of capital ($Kg$), labor ($Lg$), and an error term ($R$) commonly termed productivity or technological change. The technological change component is a catchall residual of ignorance representative of the gross effects of all factors enumerated above except the *quantity* of labor and capital. Thus, the percentage rate of growth in output ($Yg$) is:

$$Yg = f(Lg, Kg)$$
$$Yg = XLg + ZKg + R \qquad (1)$$
$$\frac{\Delta Y}{Y} = X\frac{\Delta L}{L} + Z\frac{\Delta K}{K} + R,$$

where $R$ is residually determined as the difference in the percentage growth in output and the percentage growth in weighted inputs. The weighting coefficient $X$ depicts two things: the output elasticity of labor—some percentage change in output due to a change of one per cent in labor inputs ($\%\Delta Y \div \%\Delta L$); and the share of real national income earned by labor, $WL/PY$, where $P$ denotes the aggregate price level and $W$ represents wages.[15] Similarly, $Z$ denotes the output elasticity of physical capital and the share of income earned by capital resources.

If all income is earned by capital and labor, it is obvious that $X + Z = 1.0$. Empirical evidence suggests that the values $X = \frac{3}{4}$ and $Z = \frac{1}{4}$ are reasonably realistic. Thus, if the stocks of labor and capital grow at the rate of 2 per cent and $R = 0$, output will also grow by 2 per cent as equation (2) indicates.[16]

$$Yg = XLg + ZKg + R$$
$$Yg = \tfrac{3}{4} \times 2\% + \tfrac{1}{4} \times 2\% + 0 \qquad (2)$$
$$Yg = 2\%$$

Our ultimate interest is in $R$, because the conventional theory of economic growth tends to disguise a variety of growth-inducing factors, including the effect of education on human resources, in the $R$ component. Moreover, no matter what $R$ embodies as a residual, empirical studies repeatedly indicate that labor and capital quantities account for substantially less than half of the observed growth in output.

Annual average data closely approximating twentieth century growth trends (1909 to 1957) in the American economy indicate that growth rates depicted in equation (3) are reasonable empirical approximations.[17]

$$Yg = XLg + ZKg + R$$
$$Yg = \tfrac{3}{4} \times 0.9\% + \tfrac{1}{4} \times 2.4\% + R$$
$$2.9\% = .68\% + .60\% + R, \text{ or} \tag{3}$$
$$R = 1.62\%$$

A residual of ignorance of this magnitude (1.6 of 2.9 per cent) may be a serious constraint to more effective economic growth policy. Concern for per capita output growth and the capital investment policy implications embodied in equation (3) suggest that the matter requires careful attention. Under such circumstances it certainly behooves economists to be concerned with elements traveling in the disguise of technological change or productivity increases. (This is the precise concern of the selections contained in Part I of this book.)

Capital-widening investment occurs if physical capital stocks grow less rapidly than labor (and the population), whereas capital-deepening investment occurs when growth in physical capital exceeds growth in labor inputs. Capital-deepening investment in the absence of a positive residual factor demonstrates the importance of $R$. This can be illustrated by again using data that approximate the long-term growth record of the American economy taken from equation (3). Solving for the required physical capital growth rate (assuming $XLg = .68$ and $R = 0$) reveals the hypothetical $Kg$ required:

$$Yg = XLg + ZKg + R$$
$$ZKg = Yg - (XLg + R)$$
$$\tfrac{1}{4}Kg = 2.9\% - .68\% \tag{4}$$
$$Kg = 8.9\%$$

In the absence of $R$, required physical capital growth would be 8.9 per cent instead of the approximately 2.4 per cent that did occur. Capital-deepening investments of this order of magnitude are not likely to be realized; thus, the positive intervention of $R$ added significantly to the feasibility of a 2.9 per cent annual growth rate in output. Even if the stock of physical capital had increased at more than twice its historical rate (e.g., $Kg = 5\%$) and $R$ remained zero, total output would have grown less than 2 per cent per year in contrast to the observed 2.9 per cent.[18] In short, the burden upon physical capital formation is lessened considerably because of the unknown $R$. Furthermore, higher levels of investment in physical capital increase the capital — labor ratio and can generate diminishing returns to capital. To date, diminishing returns to capital have been offset by a positive $R$ that has increased the productivity of capital. In brief, whatever $R$ is, it is very important to a viable economy.

**Economic Growth Theory**

Before examining the human capital efficiency issue, it is appropriate to remind ourselves of the traditional role assigned to savings and net investment (physical capital formation) in the theory of economic growth. Growth in output viewed naïvely is a product of savings and/or investment (*i.e.*, accumulation of physical capital) and the productivity of capital.[19] The net investment growth rate ($\Delta I/I$) and growth in physical capital formation ($\Delta K/K$) are equivalent, where the investment-income ratio ($I/Y$) equals the savings-income ratio ($S/Y$) when the economy is in full employment equilibrium. The ratio ($S/Y$) will be recognized as the propensity to save, henceforth denoted as $s$, where the average and marginal propensities are assumed to be equal and constant. Equal average and marginal productivity of capital is given by $\Delta Y/\Delta K = Y/K$, henceforth $\sigma$. Change in output capacity ($\Delta Y^c$) is the product of changes in the capital stock due to current investment ($I$) and the productivity of capital ($\sigma$). Full employment growth requires that the change in demand for output ($\Delta Y^d$) must equal the change in output capacity, where $\Delta Y^d$ is the product of the multiplier ($1/s$) and net increments to current investment ($\Delta I$). Thus:

$$\Delta Y^c = \Delta Y^d$$

$$I\sigma = \frac{1}{s} \Delta I$$

$$\sigma s = \frac{\Delta I}{I}, \text{ and}$$

$$\sigma s = \frac{\Delta K}{K}, \text{ our } Kg \text{ of earlier expressions.}^{[20]}$$

(5)

Full employment growth in output, therefore, requires that an economy grow at the rate $\Delta K/K = (Kg) = \sigma s$. For example, assume that the average propensity to save is 9 per cent of national income ($s = 9/100$), and it takes \$3 of capital to produce \$1 of additional output ($\sigma = 1/3$). Growth in equilibrium output ($Yg$) is one-third the rate of net capital formation: ($Kg = \sigma s = \frac{1}{3} \times 9\% = 3\%$).[21]

The relationships in equation (5) indicate that the propensity to save and net investment are of considerable importance to economic growth. Although savings and physical capital formation are important, increases in *physical* capital formation are only a part, and perhaps a very small part, of the process of economic growth. Continuing in a naïve vein for the moment by ignoring human capital and other growth sources embodied in $R$, equation (6) demonstrates the relatively insignificant role of physical capital investment.

If $s$ increases from 9.0% to $s = 13.5\%$ ($\Delta s = 4.5\%$) and $XLg$, $Z$, $\sigma$, and $R$ are unchanged, the incremental growth in output ($\Delta Yg$) resulting from a 50 per cent increase in savings shown earlier in equation (3) is less than half of one per cent.

$$\Delta Yg = Z \times \sigma \times \Delta s$$

$$\Delta Yg = \tfrac{1}{4} \times \tfrac{1}{3} \times 4.5\% \qquad\qquad (6)$$

$$\Delta Yg = .375\%$$

In summary, the formation of physical capital through savings and net investment does not play the dominant role suggested by a naïve interpretation of economic growth theory depicted in equation (5).

Additional refinements in growth theory have followed the recognition of these circumstances. Some of these refinements suggest that input quantities ($K$ and $L$) are not independent of technological change, which is now buried in $R$ as equation (1) implies. Robert M. Solow has observed that technology may be embodied in new physical capital investment; *i.e.*, the "quality" of the physical capital stock changes with both replacement investment and with net capital formation.[22] For example, if $100 of new capital is half again as efficient as $100 of retired capital equipment, such replacement investment is the equivalent of adding half again that amount (*i.e.*, a total of $150) to the capital stock. Furthermore, *net* investment that embodies improved technology lowers the age of the total capital stock and therefore represents improved technology. Kenneth J. Arrow has noted that technological change is a function of learning by doing and is thus embodied in qualitative changes in factors of production.[23] Nicholas Kaldor and Joan Robinson tend to emphasize the effects of income distribution and stress lifetime consumption and savings patterns.[24] The thrust of human capital analysis in relation to growth represents similar embodiment concepts at work, in this instance, on the human factor of production. Analyses of the process of economic growth in the past have stressed, perhaps excessively, readily observed economic magnitudes, such as dollar savings and investment in physical capital. The development and measurement of human capital represents an alternative emphasis in the continuing reassessment of the process of economic growth.

## RETURNS FROM INVESTMENT IN EDUCATION

The goal of economic efficiency is predicated upon the notion that resources are scarce—a condition which is presumed to induce a community to behave in such a manner as to squeeze the most it can out of its limited resources. Given some total amount of claims on productive resources, it is appropriate to study the optimal allocation of educational expenditures among competing alternative programs. For that matter evaluation of the allocation of all resources managed within the public sector in such diverse areas as transportation, health, crime, and defense is also legitimate for analogous reasons. Let us briefly examine the rationale, methodology, and problems embodied in viewing investment in education in an economic efficiency context.

## The Efficiency Rationale

Decision making and resource allocation in the private sector of the economy is guided, at least in a general sense, through market-established prices. By studying the conditions under which market prices are established, economists have been able to draw some tentative (and often very restrictive) conclusions about the efficient allocation of resources in the private sector. On the basis of that information, public policy is formulated for the purpose of achieving economic goals, one of which is economic efficiency.

Benefit-cost or rate-of-return analysis of government expenditure programs in defense, health, or education is nothing more than an attempt to evaluate the allocative efficiency of resources devoted to such public enterprises. In most instances public enterprise exists because the good or service in question is a collective good where it is difficult or impossible to apply user prices. Inability to establish a price may reflect the fact that the benefits (costs) of a social good accrue to other than the immediate user, a condition described as *external economies (diseconomies)*.[25] Fire protection, highways, and control of communicable diseases are some of the many examples of externalities. In many other instances the collectivity feature of social goods is complemented by the fact that social goods are not readily supplied by the private sector because they demand a scale of operation beyond that feasible in the private sector (*e.g.*, highways). The general character of the benefit-cost framework, which originated in the field of water and natural resource economics, is similar to comparisons of profits and costs in business firms except that social instead of private market values are at stake. This one exception generates a host of complex issues in determining the returns to investment in public goods like education. Full evaluation of an irrigation project, for example, must take account of more than direct construction outlays as costs and more than increased agricultural output and electrical power as benefits. Water diversion from other areas or displacement of families may represent other external costs. Similarly, enhanced community development potential may also represent an important benefit.

Bearing such indirect social factors in mind, one might use the present value approach, where aggregate future benefits in terms of present monetary values are compared to aggregate costs also in terms of present monetary values. This process involves discounting—subtracting from future benefit flows the equivalent of what a comparable investment might earn elsewhere—a process which we discuss in detail later. One decision rule would be selection of any program where the ratio of presently valued benefits to costs exceeds unity. An analogous procedure is to subtract aggregate social costs from gross social benefits, yielding current net benefits which are then discounted to their present value. Any positive value then suggests that a program is worthwhile. Still another alternative is to compute the rate of return on investment, usually expressed as the ratio of net benefits to costs per year. The internal rate of return is simply that interest rate which makes the discounted value of aggregate benefits and costs equal. In this latter instance the decision rule is to invest in those programs yielding the largest percentage return, provided the rate of return exceeds some cut-off rate which represents the social opportunity cost of investment funds.[26]

## Methodology

Four methodological steps are involved in implementing what might appear on the surface to be a reasonably straightforward cost and return comparison. The first of these involves the theoretical criterion which defines an optimum. An optimum is attained when marginal benefits are equal to or greater than marginal costs. More specifically, the optimum return ($r$) on program ($h$) subject to no budget constraint exists where:

$$\text{Maximum Net Returns} = \begin{array}{c}\text{Marginal}\\\text{Benefit of}\\\text{Program } h\end{array} - \begin{array}{c}\text{Marginal}\\\text{Cost of}\\\text{Program } h\end{array} = 0; \qquad (7)$$

thus,

$$\frac{\text{Marginal Benefits}}{\text{Marginal Costs}} = 1.0.$$

which is                    $dBh/dh - dCh/dh = 0;$

thus,                       $$\frac{dBh/dh}{dCh/dh} = 1.0. \tag{8}$$

If budget constraints do exist, as is the usual case, maximum returns are identified for all investment options when equal marginal benefit-marginal cost ratios prevail for all programs. In other words, the ratio of marginal benefits for programs $i \ldots j$ are proportional to the marginal cost ratios for programs $i \ldots j$.[27] Delineation of marginal benefits and costs sometimes represents a difficult problem as some of the selections in Part II of this book point out.

A second area of concern in benefit-cost analysis is to identify and measure fully all costs and benefits. Investment in education may generate *private* benefits by enhancing the earning potential of an individual. This *direct* private benefit may be augmented by other less apparent *indirect* benefits. Additional schooling may enhance future options to acquire even more skills and hurdle certain types of job-entry barriers (*e.g.*, a college degree for hopeful corporate managers).[28] Some benefits (or costs) may be *noneconomic*—the case if education broadens one's understanding of the life process or contributes to greater job satisfaction. The direct-indirect and economic-noneconomic distinction also applies to *social* benefits. Social benefits such as reduced unemployment from job retraining may be approximated without undue difficulty, but the value to society of less poverty or juvenile delinquency is more difficult to estimate. Costs, like benefits, may appear in any combination of this private-social, direct-indirect, and economic-noneconomic classification scheme. Part of the costs of voyaging to the moon may be the noneconomic and indirect cost of rising tensions in urban ghettoes. These distinctions are difficult to evaluate fully because identification is sometimes subtle, quantification may be impossible, and measurement in the form of economic magnitudes is not always feasible. Moreover, interdependence among social benefits and costs are hazardous to delineate.

Still another and third step is to decide between the use of present value, benefit-cost, or rates of return as the appropriate decision criterion. Assuming that marginal values are obtained for relevant combinations of private-social, direct-indirect, and economic-noneconomic variables, these three decision criteria must reflect the time-value of money. Discounting a future stream of values (*e.g.*, earnings for $t$ years into the future) is necessary because there is a time preference for money. Present returns are more valuable than future returns because funds earn a positive return over time. Consequently, future sums must be reduced to a present value—a process accomplished by deducting the interest-earnings equivalent from the lifetime return to educational investment. Essentially, discounting merely involves a reversal of compounding interest into the future. Ignoring momentarily certain relevant questions concerning the appropriate interest rate ($r$) used to discount an infinite future sum, the present value ($B_v$) for investments having current costs of ($C$) is $B_v = B/r$, where $B$ is understood to represent marginal net annual returns. Thus, if $r = 10$ per cent and $B = \$100$ annually, $B_v = \$1,000$—the maximum current cost ($C$) that could be paid for receipt of \$100 annually in perpetuity. Rearranging the notions embodied in this expression and assuming that $C = \$1,000$ also reveals that $r = B/C$ ($.10 = \$100/\$1,000$). Obviously, if $C < \$1,000$, the rate of return is greater than 10 per cent. Moreover, a larger $r$ implies a lower $B_v$; *i.e.*, a lesser value is placed on a payment of $\$B$ annually. This definition of discounting is of restricted usefulness because all costs are assumed to be incurred in the current period and benefits are assumed to prevail forever. Nonetheless, it does serve to establish the *general* relationships between $r$, $B_v$, $B$ and $C$. Now, let us examine the present value, benefit-cost, and rate of return criteria.

### The Present Value Approach

Suppose we wish to determine the worth of an investment in program $h$ which yields marginal *net* benefits (gross benefits less costs over the asset life) of $b$, where $b$ and $r$ may vary over a finite time period ($t$). The formula for the present value of marginal net benefits is:

$$B_v^h = \sum_{t=1}^{t} \frac{b_t^h}{(1 + r)^t} \tag{9}$$

Individual time periods exhibiting different values for $r$ can thus be accommodated and changes in gross benefits and costs from which $B_v^h$ is derived can also vary. Assuming that $r$ properly reflects the social opportunity cost of capital and that competing programs do not exist, investment in program $h$ is advisable if $B_v^h$ is positive. If another program $g$ is competing for the same scarce resources, the gain (or loss) from selecting $h$ is given as $B_v^h - B_v^g$.

### Benefit-Cost Ratios

The second decision criterion is selection of projects where the ratio of *gross* benefits ($B$) to costs ($C$) at the margin is at least equal to unity. As before, discounting is appropriate, in which case the decision rule is to invest in a program if, after discounting:

$$\frac{B_v^h}{C_v^h} \geq 1.0 \tag{10}$$

Comparison of alternative programs simply requires selection of program $h$ provided that:

$$\frac{B_v^h}{C_v^h} \geq \ldots \frac{B_v^g}{C_v^g} \geq 1.0 \tag{11}$$

### Internal Rate of Return Criterion

A third criterion appears to be the most popular comparison basis insofar as human capital is concerned. This approach consists of calculation of the internal rate of return ($r^*$), which is expressed as a percentage that can be compared to any interest rate representative of the social opportunity cost of public capital. The rate of return is that interest rate which equates the present value of costs and benefits. Under the restrictive assumptions of infinite returns, the rate of return used for discounting was expressed earlier as $r = B/C$. Under finite time conditions and constant gross benefits ($B$) and costs ($C$) per period for program $h$, the internal rate-of-return is implied by selection of a rate of return $r^*$ that equates costs and returns:

$$C_v^h = \sum_{t=1}^{t} \frac{B_t^h}{(1 + r^*)^t} \tag{12}$$

In short, the internal rate of return is a discount rate such that the present value of benefits and costs are equal. The decision criterion is to select programs yielding the highest relative $r^*$, provided that $r^*$ exceeds the social opportunity cost of public capital.[29]

A variety of criticisms, which cannot be dealt with in detail here, have been leveled against analyses of the type just described.[30] Nevertheless, to ignore these problems represents an inexcusable error, as several of the contributors to this volume recognize in their articles. Therefore, brief comment on some of the more common methodological, measurement, and conceptual difficulties is in order.

### Measurement and Comparison Problems

Controversy exists over the most appropriate of the three above-mentioned decision criteria to use. There are good reasons for dispute, because it is quite possible that present values, benefit-cost ratios, and internal rates of return will all identify different programs as preferable. Probably the best single treatment of such problems as well as the one work acknowledged by many as being responsible for the flurry of human capital research that appeared in the 1960s is Gary Becker's *Human Capital*.[31] As Becker and others have noted, the internal rate of return will vary over time if benefits and costs change from time period to time period. The present-value technique suffers in that use of different discount rates at varying points in time for similar programs produces variance in ranking of projects. It is also possible to invest in one program which produces a smaller present return than a combination of programs because of budget constraints using the benefit-cost criterion. There is simply no way of predetermining the "best" criterion for all comparisons. As the authors of some of the following selections suggest, the criterion used for any specific program evaluation must use the method which best fits the comparative circumstances.

Some of the more important conceptual and data limitations which arise in applying economic analysis to investment in education are as follows:

1. Economic analysis and the efficiency deity may mask many of the nonmonetary considerations which motivate private behavior as well as social goals prompting investment in education. Treating people as "capital" to be produced may distort a useful and purposeful dimension of life, and in any event does not necessarily represent the multiple objectives which characterize educational investments.

2. Investment in education, or human capital in the general sense, is only one of many interdependent variables which increase economic welfare. Multicollinearity between independent variables such as motivation, customs, socioeconomic status, and ability, precludes accurate identification of the average contribution of education much less the marginal returns generated by education.

3. Selection of a "proper" discount rate or the "relevant" rate of return is ambiguous—a problem particularly acute where the social rate of discount is needed.

4. Quantification of social, indirect, and noneconomic values is almost impossible. Educational quality, poverty and slums, income redistribution, or an alteration in national defense posture due to greater emphasis on education illustrate some of the valuation problems involved.

5. Uncertainty prevails in terms of future benefits, costs, interest rates, and time periods in both the private and social context. The relative attractiveness of occupations may change over time as technological conditions are altered. Disadvantaged Americans may invest less in education because of a higher time preference for money due in part to different perceptions of risk and uncertainty.

6. Unlike investments in physical capital, human capital expenditures represent consumption as well as investment outlays, again in an unknown magnitude.

7. Different forms of human capital investment provide for more or less mobility and liquidity. The depreciation or appreciation characteristics of human resources also may

be important to investment in education, yet these relations are seldom dealt with.

Although considerably more could be said about the conceptual and methodological issues touched upon in this brief introduction, we leave that task to the selections that follow.

# part one

# Education,
## Human Capital,
## and
## Economic Growth

# THEODORE W. SCHULTZ

# *Investment in*
# *Human*
# *Capital*

*T*he growth record of developed nations clearly reveals that
increases in output have exceeded the rise in conventionally
*measured inputs. Theodore W. Schultz, Professor of Economics at*
*the University of Chicago, cogently calls for an explicit recognition*
*of investment in human beings in this selection, his Presidential Address*
*to the American Economic Association. He suggests that human*
*capital may be responsible for much of the rapid rise in real income of*
*this century. Foregone earnings, direct expenditures on education,*

Reprinted from Theodore W. Schultz, "Investment in Human Capital," *The
American Economic Review* 51 (March 1961), pp. 1–17, with permission of the
author and publisher.

Notes to this essay are on pages 273–276; References are on 266–267.

*the costs of migration, on-the-job training expenses, and health care
expenditures constitute investment outlays in human capital that have
grown rapidly in recent decades. Recognition of investment in human
beings as generating a form of human capital raises important theoretical and public policy issues for developed and developing nations.
Several economic problems and policy matters are noted by Schultz,
including tax discrimination against human capital, depreciation of
human capital with nonuse, and inadequate access to financial markets
for human capital investments.*

Although it is obvious that people acquire useful skills and
knowledge, it is not obvious that these skills and knowledge are a
form of capital, that this capital is in substantial part a product of
deliberate investment, that it has grown in Western societies at a
much faster rate than conventional (nonhuman) capital, and that its
growth may well be the most distinctive feature of the economic
system. It has been widely observed that increases in national output
have been large compared with the increases of land, man-hours,
and physical reproducible capital. Investment in human capital is
probably the major explanation for this difference.

Much of what we call consumption constitutes investment in
human capital. Direct expenditures on education, health, and
internal migration to take advantage of better job opportunities are
clear examples. Earnings foregone by mature students attending
school and by workers acquiring on-the-job training are equally
clear examples. Yet nowhere do these enter into our national
accounts. The use of leisure time to improve skills and knowledge is
widespread and it too is unrecorded. In these and similar ways the
*quality* of human effort can be greatly improved and its productivity
enhanced. I shall contend that such investment in human capital
accounts for most of the impressive rise in the real earnings per
worker.

I shall comment, first, on the reasons why economists have
shied away from the explicit analysis of investment in human
capital, and then, on the capacity of such investment to explain

many a puzzle about economic growth. Mainly, however, I shall concentrate on the scope and substance of human capital and its formation. In closing I shall consider some social and policy implications.

## I. SHYING AWAY FROM INVESTMENT IN MAN

Economists have long known that people are an important part of the wealth of nations. Measured by what labor contributes to output, the productive capacity of human beings is now vastly larger than all other forms of wealth taken together. What economists have not stressed is the simple truth that people invest in themselves and that these investments are very large. Although economists are seldom timid in entering on abstract analysis and are often proud of being impractical, they have not been bold in coming to grips with this form of investment. Whenever they come even close, they proceed gingerly as if they were stepping into deep water. No doubt there are reasons for being wary. Deep-seated moral and philosophical issues are ever present. Free men are first and foremost the end to be served by economic endeavor; they are not property or marketable assets. And not least, it has been all too convenient in marginal productivity analysis to treat labor as if it were a unique bundle of innate abilities that are wholly free of capital.

The mere thought of investment in human beings is offensive to some among us.[1] Our values and beliefs inhibit us from looking upon human beings as capital goods, except in slavery, and this we abhor. We are not unaffected by the long struggle to rid society of indentured service and to evolve political and legal institutions to keep men free from bondage. These are achievements that we prize highly. Hence, to treat human beings as wealth that can be augmented by investment runs counter to deeply held values. It seems to reduce man once again to a mere material component, to something akin to property. And for man to look upon himself as a capital good, even if it did not impair his freedom, may seem to debase him. No less a person than J. S. Mill at one time insisted that the people of a country should not be looked upon as wealth because wealth existed only for the sake of people [15]. But surely Mill was wrong; there is nothing in the concept of human wealth contrary to his idea that it exists only for the advantage of people. By investing in themselves, people can enlarge the range of choice available to them. It is one way free men can enhance their welfare.

Among the few who have looked upon human beings as capital, there are three distinguished names. The philosopher-economist Adam Smith boldly included all of the acquired and useful abilities of all of the inhabitants of a country as a part of capital. So did H. von Thünen, who then went on to argue that the concept of capital applied to man did not degrade him or impair his freedom and dignity, but on the contrary that the failure to apply the concept was especially pernicious in wars; ". . . for here . . . one will sacrifice in a battle a hundred human beings in the prime of their lives without a thought in order to save one gun." The reason is that, ". . . the purchase of a cannon causes an outlay of public funds, whereas human beings are to be had for nothing by means of a mere conscription decree" [20]. Irving Fisher also clearly and cogently presented an all-inclusive concept of capital [6]. Yet the main stream of thought has held that it is neither appropriate nor practical to apply the concept of capital to human beings. Marshall [11], whose great prestige goes far to explain why this view was accepted, held that while human beings are incontestably capital from an abstract and mathematical point of view, it would be out of touch with the market place to treat them as capital in practical analyses. Investment in human beings has accordingly seldom been incorporated in the formal core of economics, even though many economists, including Marshall, have seen its relevance at one point or another in what they have written.

The failure to treat human resources explicitly as a form of capital, as a produced means of production, as the product of investment, has fostered the retention of the classical notion of labor as a capacity to do manual work requiring little knowledge and skill, a capacity with which, according to this notion, laborers are endowed about equally. This notion of labor was wrong in the classical period and it is patently wrong now. Counting individuals who can and want to work and treating such a count as a measure of the quantity of an economic factor is no more meaningful than it would be to count the number of all manner of machines to determine their economic importance either as a stock of capital or as a flow of productive services.

Laborers have become capitalists not from a diffusion of the ownership of corporation stocks, as folklore would have it, but from the acquisition of knowledge and skill that have economic value [9]. This knowledge and skill are in great part the product of investment and, combined with other human investment, predominantly account for the productive superiority of the technically advanced countries. To omit them in studying economic growth is like trying to explain Soviet ideology without Marx.

## II. ECONOMIC GROWTH FROM HUMAN CAPITAL

Many paradoxes and puzzles about our dynamic, growing economy can be resolved once human investment is taken into account. Let me begin by sketching some that are minor though not trivial.

When farm people take nonfarm jobs they earn substantially less than industrial workers of the same race, age, and sex. Similarly nonwhite urban males earn much less than white males even after allowance is made for the effects of differences in unemployment, age, city size and region [21]. Because these differentials in earnings correspond closely to corresponding differentials in education, they strongly suggest that the one is a consequence of the other. Negroes who operate farms, whether as tenants or as owners, earn much less than whites on comparable farms.[2] Fortunately, crops and livestock are not vulnerable to the blight of discrimination. The large differences in earnings seem rather to reflect mainly the differences in health and education. Workers in the South on the average earn appreciably less than in the North or West and they also have on the average less education. Most migratory farm workers earn very little indeed by

comparison with other workers. Many of them have virtually no
schooling, are in poor health, are unskilled, and have little ability to
do useful work. To urge that the differences in the amount of human
investment may explain these differences in earnings seems elementary. Of more recent vintage are observations showing younger
workers at a competitive advantage; for example, young men
entering the labor force are said to have an advantage over unemployed older workers in obtaining satisfactory jobs. Most of these
young people possess twelve years of school, most of the older
workers six years or less. The observed advantage of these younger
workers may therefore result not from inflexibilities in social security
or in retirement programs, or from sociological preference of
employers, but from real differences in productivity connected with
one form of human investment, i.e., education. And yet another
example, the curve relating income to age tends to be steeper for
skilled than for unskilled persons. Investment in on-the-job training
seems a likely explanation, as I shall note later.

Economic growth requires much internal migration of workers
to adjust to changing job opportunities [10]. Young men and women
move more readily than older workers. Surely this makes economic
sense when one recognizes that the costs of such migration are a form
of human investment. Young people have more years ahead of them
than older workers during which they can realize on such an investment. Hence it takes less of a wage differential to make it economically advantageous for them to move; or, to put it differently, young
people can expect a higher return on their investment in migration
than older people. This differential may explain selective migration
without requiring an appeal to sociological differences between
young and old people.

The examples so far given are for investment in human beings
that yield a return over a long period. This is true equally of investment in education, training, and migration of young people. Not all
investments in human beings are of this kind; some are more nearly
akin to current inputs as for example expenditures on food and
shelter in some countries where work is mainly the application of
brute human force, calling for energy and stamina, and where the

intake of food is far from enough to do a full day's work. On the "hungry" steppes and in the teeming valleys of Asia, millions of adult males have so meager a diet that they cannot do more than a few hours of hard work. To call them underemployed does not seem pertinent. Under such circumstances it is certainly meaningful to treat food partly as consumption and partly as a current "producer good," as some Indian economists have done [3]. Let us not forget that Western economists during the early decades of industrialization and even in the time of Marshall and Pigou often connected additional food for workers with increases in labor productivity.

Let me now pass on to three major perplexing questions closely connected with the riddle of economic growth. First, consider the long-period behavior of the capital-income ratio. We were taught that a country which amassed more reproducible capital relative to its land and labor would employ such capital in greater "depth" because of its growing abundance and cheapness. But apparently this is not what happens. On the contrary, the estimates now available show that less of such capital tends to be employed relative to income as economic growth proceeds. Are we to infer that the ratio of capital to income has no relevance in explaining either poverty or opulence? Or that a rise of this ratio is not a prerequisite to economic growth? These questions raise fundamental issues bearing on motives and preferences for holding wealth as well as on the motives for particular investments and the stock of capital thereby accumulated. For my purpose all that needs to be said is that these estimates of capital-income ratios refer to only a part of all capital. They exclude in particular, and most unfortunately, any human capital. Yet human capital has surely been increasing at a rate substantially greater than reproducible (nonhuman) capital. We cannot, therefore, infer from these estimates that the stock of *all* capital has been decreasing relative to income. On the contrary, if we accept the not implausible assumption that the motives and preferences of people, the technical opportunities open to them, and the uncertainty associated with economic growth during particular periods were leading people to maintain roughly a constant ratio between *all* capital and income, the decline in the estimated capital-income ratio[3] is simply a signal that human capital has been increasing relatively not only to conventional capital but also to income.

The bumper crop of estimates that show national income increasing faster than national resources raises a second and not unrelated puzzle. The income of the United States has been increasing at a much higher rate than the combined amount of land, man-hours worked and the stock of reproducible capital used to produce the income. Moreover, the discrepancy between the two rates has become larger from one business cycle to the next during recent decades [5]. To call this discrepancy a measure of "resource productivity" gives a name to our ignorance but does not dispel it. If we accept these estimates, the connections between national resources and national income have become loose and tenuous over time. Unless this discrepancy can be resolved, received theory of production applied to inputs and outputs as currently measured is a toy and not a tool for studying economic growth.

Two sets of forces probably account for the discrepancy, if we neglect entirely the index number and aggregation problems that bedevil all estimates of such global aggregates as total output and total input. One is returns to scale; the second, the large improvements in the quality of inputs that have occurred but have been omitted from the input estimates. Our economy has undoubtedly been experiencing increasing returns to scale at some points offset by decreasing returns at others. If we can succeed in identifying and measuring the net gains, they may turn out to have been substantial. The improvements in the quality of inputs that have not been adequately allowed for are no doubt partly in material (nonhuman) capital. My own conception, however, is that both this defect and the omission of economies of scale are minor sources of discrepancy between the rates of growth of inputs and outputs compared to the improvements in human capacity that have been omitted.

A small step takes us from these two puzzles raised by existing estimates to a third which brings us to the heart of the matter, namely the essentially unexplained large increase in real earnings of workers. Can this be a windfall? Or a quasi-rent pending the adjustment in the supply of labor? Or, a pure rent reflecting the fixed amount of labor? It seems far more reasonable that it represents rather a return to the investment that has been made in human beings. The observed growth in productivity per unit of labor is simply a consequence of holding the unit of labor constant over time although in fact this unit of labor has been increasing as a result of a steadily growing amount of human capital per worker. As I read our record, the human capital component has become very large as a consequence of human investment.

Another aspect of the same basic question, which admits of the same resolution, is the rapid postwar recovery of countries that had suffered severe destruction of plant and equipment during the war. The toll from bombing was all too visible in the factories laid flat, the railroad yards, bridges, and harbors wrecked, and the cities in ruin. Structures, equipment and inventories were all heaps of rubble. Not so visible, yet large, was the toll from the wartime depletion of the physical plant that escaped destruction by bombs. Economists were called upon to assess the implications of these wartime losses for recovery. In retrospect, it is clear that they over-estimated the prospective retarding effects of these losses. Having had a small hand in this effort, I have had a special reason for looking back and wondering why the judgments that we formed soon after the war proved to be so far from the mark. The explanation that now is clear is that we gave altogether too much weight to nonhuman capital in making these assessments. We fell into this error, I am convinced, because we did not have a concept of *all* capital and, therefore, failed to take account of human capital and the important part that it plays in production in a modern economy.

Let me close this section with a comment on poor countries, for which there are virtually no solid estimates. I have been impressed by repeatedly expressed judgments, especially by those who have a responsibility in making capital available to poor countries, about the low rate at which these countries can absorb additional capital. New capital from outside can be put to good use, it is said, only when it is added "slowly and gradually." But this experience is at variance with the widely held impression that countries are poor fundamentally because they are starved for capital and that additional capital is truly the key to their more rapid economic growth. The reconciliation is again, I believe, to be found in emphasis on particular forms of capital. The new capital available to these countries from outside as a rule goes into the formation of structures, equipment and sometimes also into inventories. But it is generally not available for additional investment in man. Consequently, human capabilities do not stay abreast of physical capital, and they do become limiting factors in economic growth. It should come as no surprise, therefore, that the absorption rate of capital to augment particular nonhuman resources is necessarily low. The Horvat [8] formulation of the optimum rate of investment which treats knowledge and skill as a critical investment variable in determining the rate of economic growth is both relevant and important.

## III. SCOPE AND SUBSTANCE
## OF THESE INVESTMENTS

What are human investments? Can they be distinguished from consumption? Is it at all feasible to identify and measure them? What do they contribute to income? Granted that they seem amorphous compared to brick and mortar, and hard to get at compared to the investment accounts of corporations, they assuredly are not a fragment; they are rather like the contents of Pandora's box, full of difficulties and hope.

Human resources obviously have both quantitative and qualitative dimensions. The number of people, the proportion who enter upon useful work, and hours worked are essentially quantitative characteristics. To make my task tolerably manageable, I shall neglect these and consider only such quality components as skill, knowledge, and similar attributes that affect particular human capabilities to do productive work. In so far as expenditures to enhance such capabilities also increase the value productivity of human effort (labor), they will yield a positive rate of return.[4]

How can we estimate the magnitude of human investment? The practice followed in connection with physical capital goods is to estimate the magnitude of capital formation by expenditures made to produce the capital goods. This practice would suffice also for the formation of human capital. However, for human capital there is an additional problem that is less pressing for physical capital goods: how to distinguish between expenditures for consumption and for investment. This distinction bristles with both conceptual and practical difficulties. We can think of three classes of expenditures: expenditures that satisfy consumer preferences and in no way enhance the capabilities under discussion—these represent pure consumption; expenditures that enhance capabilities and do not satisfy any preferences underlying consumption—these represent pure investment; and expenditures that have both effects. Most relevant activities clearly are in the third class, partly consumption and partly investment, which is why the task of identifying each component is so formidable and why the measurement of capital formation by expenditures is less useful for human investment than for investment in physical goods. In principle there is an alternative method for estimating human investment, namely by its yield rather than by its cost. While any capability produced by human investment becomes a part of the human agent and hence cannot be sold; it is nevertheless "in touch with the market place" by affecting the wages and salaries the human agent can earn. The resulting increase in earnings is the yield on the investment.[5]

Despite the difficulty of exact measurement at this stage of our understanding of human investment, many insights can be gained by examining some of the more important activities that improve human capabilities. I shall concentrate on five major categories: (1) health facilities and services, broadly conceived to include all expenditures that affect the life expectancy, strength and stamina, and the vigor and vitality of a people; (2) on-the-job training, including old-style apprenticeship organized by firms; (3) formally organized education at the elementary, secondary, and higher levels; (4) study programs for adults that are not organized by firms, including extension programs notably in agriculture; (5) migration of individuals and families to adjust to changing job opportunities. Except for education, not much is known about these activities that is germane here. I shall refrain from commenting on study programs for adults, although in agriculture the extension services of the several states play an important role in transmitting new knowledge and in developing skills of farmers [17]. Nor shall I elaborate further on internal migration related to economic growth.

Health activities have both quantity and quality implications. Such speculations as economists have engaged in about the effects of improvements in health,[6] has been predominantly in connection with population growth, which is to say with quantity. But surely health measures also enhance the quality of human resources. So also may additional food and better shelter, especially in underdeveloped countries.

The change in the role of food as people become richer sheds light on one of the conceptual problems already referred to. I have pointed out that extra food in some poor countries has the attribute of a "producer good." This attribute of food, however, diminishes as the consumption of food rises, and there comes a point at which any further increase in food becomes pure consumption.[7] Clothing, housing and perhaps medical services may be similar.

My comment about on-the-job training will consist of a conjecture on the amount of such training, a note on the decline of apprenticeship, and then a useful economic theorem on who bears the costs of such training. Surprisingly little is known about on-the-job training in modern industry. About all that can be said is that the expansion of education has not eliminated it. It seems likely, however, that some of the training formerly undertaken by firms has been discontinued and other training programs have been instituted to adjust both to the rise in the education of workers and to changes in the demands for new skills. The amount invested annually in such training can only be a guess. H. F. Clark places it near to equal to the amount spent on formal education.[8] Even if it were only one-half as large, it would represent currently an annual gross investment of about $15 billion. Elsewhere, too, it is thought to be important. For example, some observers have been impressed by the amount of such training under way in plants in the Soviet Union.[9] Meanwhile, apprenticeship has all but disappeared, partly because it is now inefficient and partly because schools now perform many of its functions. Its disappearance has been hastened no doubt by the difficulty of enforcing apprenticeship agreements. Legally they have come to smack of indentured service. The underlying economic factors and behavior are clear enough. The apprentice is prepared to serve during the initial period when his productivity is less than the cost of his keep and of his training. Later, however, unless he is legally restrained, he will seek other employment when his productivity begins to exceed the cost of keep and training, which is the period during which a master would expect to recoup on his earlier outlay.

To study on-the-job training Gary Becker [1] advances the theorem that in competitive markets employees pay all the costs of their training and none of these costs are ultimately borne by the firm. Becker points out several implications. The notion that expenditures on training by a firm generate external economies for other firms is not consistent with this theorem. The theorem also indicates one force favoring the transfer from on-the-job training to attending school. Since on-the-job training reduces the net earnings of workers at the beginning and raises them later on, this theorem also provides an explanation for the "steeper slope of the curve relating income to age," for skilled than unskilled workers, referred to earlier.[10] What all this adds up to is that the stage is set to undertake meaningful economic studies of on-the-job training.

Happily we reach firmer ground in regard to education. Investment in education has risen at a rapid rate and by itself may well account for a substantial part of the otherwise unexplained rise in earnings. I shall do no more than summarize some preliminary results about the total costs of education including income foregone by students, the apparent relation of these costs to consumer income and to alternative investments, the rise of the stock of education in the labor force, returns to education, and the contribution that the increase in the stock of education may have made to earnings and to national income.

It is not difficult to estimate the conventional costs of education consisting of the costs of the services of teachers, librarians, administrators, of maintaining and operating the educational plant, and interest on the capital embodied in the educational plant. It is far more difficult to estimate another component of total cost, the income foregone by students. Yet this component should be included and it is far from negligible. In the United States, for example, well over half of the costs of higher education consists of income foregone by students. As early as 1900, this income foregone accounted for about one-fourth of the total costs of elementary, secondary and higher education. By 1956, it represented over two-fifths of all costs. The rising significance of foregone income has been a major factor in the marked upward trend in the total real costs of education which, measured in current prices, increased from $400 million in 1900 to $28.7 billion in 1956 [18]. The percentage rise in educational costs was about three and a half times as large as in consumer income, which would imply a high income elasticity of the demand for education, if education were regarded as pure consumption.[11] Educational costs also rose about three and a half times as rapidly as did the gross formation of physical capital in dollars. If we were to treat education as pure investment this result would suggest that the returns to education were relatively more attractive than those to nonhuman capital.[12]

Much schooling is acquired by persons who are not treated as income earners in most economic analysis, particularly, of course, women. To analyze the effect of growth in schooling on earnings, it is therefore necessary to distinguish between the stock of education in the population and the amount in the labor force. Years of school completed are far from satisfactory as a measure because of the marked increases that have taken place in the number of days of school attendance of enrolled students and because much more of the education of workers consists of high school and higher education than formerly. My preliminary estimates suggest that the stock of education in the labor force rose about eight and a half times between 1900 and 1956, whereas the stock of reproducible capital rose four and a half times, both in 1956 prices. These estimates are, of course, subject to many qualifications.[13] Nevertheless, both the magnitude and the rate of increase of this form of human capital have been such that they could be an important key to the riddle of economic growth.[14]

The exciting work under way is on the return to education. In spite of the flood of high school and college graduates, the return has not become trivial. Even the lower limits of the estimates show that the return to such education has been in the neighborhood of the return to nonhuman capital. This is what most of these estimates show when they treat as costs all of the public and private expenditures on education and also the income foregone while attending school, and when they treat all of these costs as investment, allocating none to consumption.[15] But surely a part of these costs are consumption in the sense that education creates a form of consumer capital[16] which has the attribute of improving the taste and the quality of consumption of students throughout the rest of their lives. If one were to allocate a substantial fraction of the total costs of this education to consumption, say one-half, this would, of course, double the observed rate of return to what would then become the investment component in education that enhances the productivity of man.

Fortunately, the problem of allocating the costs of education in the labor force between consumption and investment does not arise to plague us when we turn to the contribution that education makes to earnings and to national income because a change in allocation only alters the rate of return, not the total return. I noted at the outset that the unexplained increases in U. S. national income have been especially large in recent decades. On one set of assumptions, the unexplained part amounts to nearly three-fifths of the total increase between 1929 and 1956.[17] How much of this unexplained increase in income represents a return to education in the labor force? A lower limit suggests that about three-tenths of it, and an upper limit does not rule out that more than one-half of it came from this source.[18] These estimates also imply that between 36 and 70 per cent of the hitherto unexplained rise in the earnings of labor is explained by returns to the additional education of workers.


## IV. A CONCLUDING NOTE ON POLICY

One proceeds at his own peril in discussing social implications and policy. The conventional hedge is to camouflage one's values and to wear the mantle of academic innocence. Let me proceed unprotected!

1. Our tax laws everywhere discriminate against human capital. Although the stock of such capital has become large and even though it is obvious that human capital, like other forms of reproducible capital, depreciates, becomes obsolete, and entails maintenance, our tax laws are all but blind on these matters.

2. Human capital deteriorates when it is idle because unemployment impairs the skills that workers have acquired. Losses in earnings can be cushioned by appropriate payments but these do not keep idleness from taking its toll from human capital.

3. There are many hindrances to the free choice of professions. Racial discrimination and religious discrimination are still widespread. Professional associations and governmental bodies also hinder entry; for example, into medicine. Such purposeful interference keeps the investment in this form of human capital substantially below its optimum [7].

4. It is indeed elementary to stress the greater imperfections of the capital market in providing funds for investment in human beings than for investment in physical goods. Much could be done to reduce these imperfections by reforms in tax and banking laws and by changes in banking practices. Long-term private and public loans to students are warranted.

5. Internal migration, notably the movement of farm people into industry, made necessary by the dynamics of our economic progress, requires substantial investments. In general, families in which the husbands and wives are already in the late thirties cannot afford to make these investments because the remaining payoff period for them is too short. Yet society would gain if more of them would pull stakes and move because, in addition to the increase in productivity currently, the children of these families would be better located for employment when they were ready to enter the labor market. The case for making some of these investments on public account is by no means weak. Our farm programs have failed miserably these many years in not coming to grips with the costs and returns from off-farm migration.

6. The low earnings of particular people have long been a matter of public concern. Policy all too frequently concentrates only

on the effects, ignoring the causes. No small part of the low earnings
of many Negroes, Puerto Ricans, Mexican nationals, indigenous
migratory farm workers, poor farm people and some of our older
workers, reflects the failure to have invested in their health and
education. Past mistakes are, of course, bygones, but for the sake of
the next generation we can ill afford to continue making the same
mistakes over again.

7. Is there a substantial underinvestment in human beings
other than in these depressed groups? [2] This is an important
question for economists. The evidence at hand is fragmentary. Nor
will the answer be easily won. There undoubtedly have been over-
investments in some skills, for example, too many locomotive
firemen and engineers, too many people trained to be farmers, and
too many agricultural economists! Our schools are not free of loafers
and some students lack the necessary talents. Nevertheless, underinvestment in knowledge and skill, relative to the amounts invested
in nonhuman capital would appear to be the rule and not the exception for a number of reasons. The strong and increasing demands for
this knowledge and skill in laborers are of fairly recent origin and it
takes time to respond to them. In responding to these demands, we
are heavily dependent upon cultural and political processes, and
these are slow and the lags are long compared to the behavior of
markets serving the formation of nonhuman capital. Where the
capital market does serve human investments, it is subject to more
imperfections than in financing physical capital. I have already
stressed the fact that our tax laws discriminate in favor of nonhuman
capital. Then, too, many individuals face serious uncertainty in
assessing their innate talents when it comes to investing in themselves,
especially through higher education. Nor is it easy either for public
decisions or private behavior to untangle and properly assess the
consumption and the investment components. The fact that the
return to high school and to higher education has been about as
large as the return to conventional forms of capital when all of the
costs of such education including income foregone by students are
allocated to the investment component, creates a strong presumption
that there has been underinvestment since, surely, much education

is cultural and in that sense it is consumption. It is no wonder, in view of these circumstances, that there should be substantial under-investment in human beings, even though we take pride, and properly so, in the support that we have given to education and to other activities that contribute to such investments.

8. Should the returns from public investment in human capital accrue to the individuals in whom it is made?[19] The policy issues implicit in this question run deep and they are full of perplexities pertaining both to resource allocation and to welfare. Physical capital that is formed by public investment is not transferred as a rule to particular individuals as a gift. It would greatly simplify the allocative process if public investment in human capital were placed on the same footing. What then is the logical basis for treating public investment in human capital differently? Presumably it turns on ideas about welfare. A strong welfare goal of our community is to reduce the unequal distribution of personal income among individuals and families. Our community has relied heavily on progressive income and inheritance taxation. Given public revenue from these sources, it may well be true that public investment in human capital, notably that entering into general education, is an effective and efficient set of expenditures for attaining this goal. Let me stress, however, that the state of knowledge about these issues is woefully meager.

9. My last policy comment is on assistance to underdeveloped countries to help them achieve economic growth. Here, even more than in domestic affairs, investment in human beings is likely to be underrated and neglected. It is inherent in the intellectual climate in which leaders and spokesmen of many of these countries find themselves. Our export of growth doctrines has contributed. These typically assign the stellar role to the formation of nonhuman capital, and take as an obvious fact the superabundance of human resources. Steel mills are the real symbol of industrialization. After all, the early industrialization of England did not depend on investments in the labor force. New funds and agencies are being authorized to transfer capital for physical goods to these countries. The World Bank and our Export-Import Bank have already had much ex-

perience. Then, too, measures have been taken to pave the way for
the investment of more private (nonhuman) capital abroad. This
one-sided effort is under way in spite of the fact that the knowledge
and skills required to take on and use efficiently the superior techniques of production, the most valuable resource that we could make
available to them, is in very short supply in these underdeveloped
countries. Some growth of course can be had from the increase in
more conventional capital even though the labor that is available is
lacking both in skill and knowledge. But the rate of growth will be
seriously limited. It simply is not possible to have the fruits of a
modern agriculture and the abundance of modern industry without
making large investments in human beings.

Truly, the most distinctive feature of our economic system is
the growth in human capital. Without it there would be only hard,
manual work and poverty except for those who have income from
property. There is an early morning scene in Faulkner's *Intruder in
the Dust*, of a poor, solitary cultivator at work in a field. Let me para-
phrase that line, "The man without skills and knowledge leaning
terrifically against nothing."

EDWARD F. DENISON

# Education,
# Economic Growth,
# and Gaps in Information

*M*uch *more needs to be known about the interrelations among economic variables which contribute to growth. Edward F. Denison's primary concern is to account more fully for the economic growth rate of the American economy and to draw attention to differences in the growth of potential and actual national product. By identifying the sources of past economic growth, the author hopes to encourage a more vigorous public policy designed to achieve full employment of all resources and to realize full growth potentials.*

Reprinted from Edward F. Denison, "Education, Economic Growth, and Gaps in Information," *Journal of Political Economy* 70 (October 1962), pp. 124–28, with the permission of the author and the publisher. Copyright 1962 by the University of Chicago.

*According to Denison, who is now at the Brookings Institution, increases in capital inputs explain less of our recent economic growth than do labor inputs (adjusted for increased education). Several other factors that have affected the rate of growth in national product are analyzed, including advances in knowledge and scale economies.*

This brief paper concerns a rather speculative and wide-ranging document on economic growth. It is not a study of the economics of education, but in it I was forced to make a foray into this field. The entire study focuses—in quantitative terms—upon three questions. What have been the sources of past United States growth? What will be the probable future growth rate? How much could the future growth rate be altered by various actions that might be considered?

My interest in the sources of past growth arose partly because quantitative estimates were needed to approach the other two questions, but mainly because of the feeling that a systematic and simultaneous look at all the possible sources of growth should give rise to a more objective appraisal of each than the more usual examination of only one source in isolation.

Tables 1 and 2 show the estimates. One shows the sources of growth of total real national income, the other of real national income per person employed. The tables divide growth broadly between the contribution of increased inputs and that of increased output per unit of input.

The general approach to measurement of the contribution of increased inputs is simple (although there are some fairly complicated refinements that I shall not discuss here) and rather conventional. If all inputs increase 1 percent, output should increase 1 percent. (I actually assume output will increase more than 1 percent, but the excess is shown separately in the tables as the contribution of economies of scale.) If labor earnings represent 73 percent of the national income, then labor must represent 73 percent of total inputs, and a 1 percent increase in labor input alone will increase national income by 0.73 percent. There are considerable advantages

## Table 1 Allocation of Growth Rate of Total Real National Income among Sources of Growth

| | PERCENTAGE POINTS IN GROWTH RATE | | | PERCENT OF GROWTH RATE | | | |
|---|---|---|---|---|---|---|---|
| | 1909–29[a] (Commerce) | 1929–57 | 1960–80[b] | 1909–29[a] (Commerce) | 1909–29[a] (Kendrick-Kuznets) | 1929–57 | 1960–80[b] |
| Real national income | 2.82 | 2.93 | 3.33 | 100 | 100 | 100 | 100 |
| Increase in total inputs | 2.26 | 2.00 | 2.19 | 80 | 71 | 68 | 66 |
| Labor, adjusted for quality change | 1.53 | 1.57 | 1.70 | 54 | 48 | 54 | 51 |
| Employment and hours | 1.11 | .80 | .98 | 39 | 35 | 27 | 29 |
| Employment | 1.11 | 1.00 | 1.33 | 39 | 35 | 34 | 40 |
| Effect of shorter hours on quality of a man-year's work | .00 | –.20 | –.35 | 0 | 0 | –7 | –11 |
| Annual hours | –.23 | –.53 | –.42 | –8 | –7 | –18 | –13 |
| Effect of shorter hours on quality of a man-hour's work | .23 | .33 | .07 | 8 | 7 | 11 | 2 |
| Education | .35 | .67 | .64 | 12 | 11 | 23 | 19 |
| Increased experience and better utilization of women workers | .06 | .11 | .09 | 2 | 2 | 4 | 3 |
| Changes in age-sex composition of labor force | .01 | –.01 | –.01 | 0 | 0 | 0 | 0 |
| Land | .00 | .00 | .00 | 0 | 0 | 0 | 0 |

| | | | | | | | |
|---|---|---|---|---|---|---|---|
| Capital | .73 | .43 | .49 | 26 | 23 | 15 | 15 |
| Non-farm residential structures | .13 | .05 | — | 5 | 4 | 2 | — |
| Other structures and equipment | .41 | .28 | N.A. | 15 | 13 | 10 | N.A. |
| Inventories | .16 | .08 | N.A. | 6 | 5 | 3 | N.A. |
| United States owned assets abroad | .02 | .02 | N.A. | 1 | 1 | 1 | N.A. |
| Foreign assets in United States | .01 | .00 | N.A. | 0 | 0 | 0 | N.A. |
| Increase in output per unit of input | .56 | .93 | 1.14 | 20 | 29 | 32 | 34 |
| Restrictions against optimum use of resources | N.A. | −.07 | .00 | N.A. | N.A. | −2 | 0 |
| Reduced waste of labor in agriculture | N.A. | .02 | .02 | N.A. | N.A. | 1 | 1 |
| Industry shift from agriculture | N.A. | .05 | .01 | N.A. | N.A. | 2 | 0 |
| Advance of knowledge | N.A. | .58 | .75 | N.A. | N.A. | 20 | 23 |
| Change in lag in application of knowledge | N.A. | .01 | .03 | N.A. | N.A. | 0 | 1 |
| Economies of scale—independent growth of local markets | N.A. | .07 | .05 | N.A. | N.A. | 2 | 2 |
| Economies of scale—growth of national market | .28 | .27 | .28 | 10 | 10 | 9 | 8 |

[a]"Commerce" and "Kendrick-Kuznets" headings refer only to the growth rate of total product. Contributions in percentage points under the Kendrick-Kuznets heading would be identical with those shown under the Commerce heading except for "Real national income," 3.17; "Output per unit of input," 0.91; and "Economies of scale—growth of national markets," 0.32.

[b] Growth rate based on high-employment projection.

Note: Contributions in percentage points are adjusted so that the sum of appropriate detail equals totals. Percents of the growth rate have not been so adjusted.

## Table 2  Allocation of Growth Rate of Real National Income per Person Employed among Sources of Growth

| | PERCENTAGE POINTS IN GROWTH RATE | | | PERCENT OF GROWTH RATE | | | |
|---|---|---|---|---|---|---|---|
| | 1909–29[a] (Commerce) | 1929–57 | 1960–80[b] | 1909–29[a] (Commerce) | 1909–29[a] (Kendrick-Kuznets) | 1929–57 | 1960–80[b] |
| Real national income | 1.22 | 1.60 | 1.62 | 100 | 100 | 100 | 100 |
| Increase in total inputs per person employed | .66 | .67 | .48 | 54 | 42 | 42 | 30 |
| Labor, adjusted for quality change | .42 | .57 | .37 | 34 | 27 | 36 | 23 |
| Effect of shorter hours on quality of a man-year's work | .00 | −.20 | −.35 | 0 | 0 | −12 | −22 |
| Annual hours | −.23 | −.53 | −.42 | −19 | −15 | −33 | −26 |
| Effect of shorter hours on quality of a man-hour's work | .23 | .33 | .07 | 19 | 15 | 21 | 4 |
| Education | .35 | .67 | .64 | 29 | 23 | 42 | 40 |
| Increased experience and better utilization of women workers | .06 | .11 | .09 | 5 | 4 | 7 | 6 |
| Changes in age-sex composition of labor force | .01 | −.01 | −.01 | 1 | 1 | −1 | −1 |

| | | | | | | |
|---|---|---|---|---|---|---|
| Land | −.11 | −.05 | −.04 | −9 | −7 | −3 | −2 |
| Capital | .35 | .15 | .15 | 29 | 22 | 9 | 9 |
| Non-farm residential structures | .07 | .01 | N.A. | 6 | 4 | 1 | N.A. |
| Other structures and equipment | .17 | .10 | N.A. | 14 | 11 | 6 | N.A. |
| Inventories | .08 | .03 | N.A. | 6 | 5 | 2 | N.A. |
| United States owned assets abroad | .02 | .01 | N.A. | 2 | 1 | 1 | N.A. |
| Foreign assets in United States | .01 | .00 | N.A. | 1 | 1 | 0 | N.A. |
| Increase in output per unit of input | .56 | .93 | 1.14 | 46 | 58 | 58 | 70 |
| Restrictions against optimum use of resources | N.A. | −.07 | .00 | N.A. | N.A. | −4 | 0 |
| Reduced waste of labor in agriculture | N.A. | .02 | .02 | N.A. | N.A. | 1 | 1 |
| Industry shift from agriculture | N.A. | .05 | .01 | N.A. | N.A. | 3 | 1 |
| Advance of knowledge | N.A. | .58 | .75 | N.A. | N.A. | 36 | 46 |
| Change in lag in application of knowledge | N.A. | .01 | .03 | N.A. | N.A. | 1 | 2 |
| Economies of scale—independent growth of local markets | N.A. | .07 | .05 | N.A. | N.A. | 4 | 3 |
| Economies of scale—growth of national market | .28 | .27 | .28 | 23 | 20 | 17 | 17 |

a "Commerce" and "Kendrick-Kuznets" headings refer only to the growth rate of total product. Contributions percentage points under the Kendrick-Kuznets heading would be identical with those shown under the Commerce heading except for "Real national income," 1.57; "Output per unit of input," 0.91; and "Economies of scale—growth of national markets," 0.32.

b Growth rate based on high-employment projection.

Note: Contributions in percentage points are adjusted so that the sum of appropriate detail equals totals. Percents of the growth rate have not been so adjusted.

in using growth rates rather than percentage changes in the calculations, and this is what I have actually done. Thus, if labor input
increased at an average annual rate of 1 percent over some period
and labor earnings averaged 73 percent in this period, the assumption
is that the increase in labor inputs contributed 0.73 percentage
points to the growth rate of total real national income. (This result
is subject to several refinements, but it indicates the general approach.)

I treat a change in the average quality of labor in exactly the
same way as an increase in its quantity, and it is here that education
comes into the study. If, in the previous example, the average quality
of labor increased at an average annual rate of 1 percent because of
more education, 0.73 points in the growth rate would be ascribed to
this factor.

My study devotes a chapter to education, in which the
estimation of changes in the average quality of the labor force
resulting from education is described. In brief, earnings differences
between groups of males of similar age, classified by education, are
taken to represent differences in their contributions to production or
quality. Educational groups differ not only by the fact of education
but by natural ability, amount of experience, and other factors. Of
the total earnings differentials, three-fifths are assumed to *result* from
differences in education and associated offsetting differences in work
experience, as distinguished from natural ability, energy, and other
factors. This provides weights for combining groups with different
amounts of education. Distributions of the labor force by years and
days of schooling were then constructed. This permitted a series
representing the average quality of labor, as affected by education
(including its impact on experience) to be derived.

The results may be summarized as follows:

1. From 1929 to 1957 the amount of education the average
worker had received was increasing almost 2 percent a year, and
this was raising the average quality of labor by 0.97 percent a year,
and contributing 0.67 percentage points to the growth rate of real
national income. Thus, it was the source of 23 percent of the growth
of total real national income and 42 percent of the growth of real
national income per person employed. (Note, however, that the

contribution of all sources making a positive contribution exceeded 100 percent, since there were also adverse developments.)

2. Additional education contributed only a little more than half as much to growth between 1909 and 1929 as between 1929 and 1957.

3. From 1960 to 1980, education will contribute a little less to growth than it did in 1929–57. The contrast would be much sharper were it not for an expected shift in labor force composition toward the younger, better-educated age groups.

4. For the longer run, it seems quite impossible to maintain the *past rate of increase* in the quantity of education offered the young. A sharply accelerated improvement in the quality of education would be needed to prevent the contribution of education to growth from declining.

Clearly, there are a number of points at which additional information would permit the estimates to be improved. Much the same gaps plague those who have been studying a related subject, the return to education, and to close them would be of broad interest.

1. My attempt to adjust for changing quality of labor resulting from additional education is confined to formal schooling. On-the-job training and other relevant forms of adult education are wholly omitted for lack of information. I am not even sure whether this increased or decreased, per worker, during the periods with which I am concerned. Mincer's study of on-the-job learning is a welcome beginning of investigation of this subject.

2. My measure of the amount of education received by the labor force is strictly quantitative (years and days). I frankly despair of getting a measure that would adjust for changes in the quality of a day's schooling.

3. The Census data on years of schooling received suggest that respondents systematically overstate their education, the prevalence of overstatement increasing with age. If this is so, projections of educational achievement forward or backward by the cohort method are biased, and I have introduced an adjustment to my series in an attempt to eliminate this bias. The 1960 Census data provide one check on the validity of this adjustment. Aside from this,

the reasons that each age cohort reports itself so much better educated in 1950 than in 1940 is a subject that should yield to intensive research.

4. Another assumption is that increasing the number of days of school per year has raised the average quality of labor by the same amount as a similar percentage increase in the number of years of schooling. I see no way to check this assumption from economic statistics. Educators may have some judgments concerning it.

5. The assumption that three-fifths of observed income differentials for males at the same age result from more education (as offset by less experience) is the one I consider to be the most arbitrary and important. The question involved here is crucial for all studies of the economics of education. Given a large amount of resources, and given the assumption that the associated variables that concern us most are aptitude, application, and neighborhood environment and characteristics closely associated with neighborhood, it seems to me that this question might be fairly well resolved. We could get the school records of children in, say, the fourth grade in 1925 from a large number of schools, classify them by school grades, intelligence quotient, and school, and track them down to find out their current earnings and how far they went in school. To reverse the process and track a large sample of current adults back to get their early records might be easier. It would also be less satisfactory but possibly not so unsatisfactory as not to be worthwhile. The University of Pittsburgh's "Project Talent" plans to follow the careers of present students, for whom complete data are available, for twenty years. This should provide an ideal test but results are far in the future.

6. It was necessary for me to assume (to measure the contribution of education to growth) that the improvement in female labor (and labor of males under twenty-five) as a result of increased education paralleled that of males. Census cross-classifications of annual income, education, and weeks and hours worked would make it possible to eliminate this assumption.

7. More information on any changes in income differentials associated with amount of education would be useful (my estimates

assume no change), especially if the reasons for any change could be deduced.

The three following comments are less closely tied to the estimates presented.

First, one would like to see some elaborate tabulations made from the 1960 Census that would cross-classify the data for income by education by sex and age (at least for adult males) with a large number of other variables—geographical location, industry, occupation, perhaps place of birth, as a minimum. It is not evident what this would show, but I am enough of a pragmatic empiricist to be confident we would learn much that is of great interest. At the least, we would get some idea of the extent to which many of the income differentials we commonly observe when people are classified by residence, industry, etc., are merely reflections of differentials in education.

Second, it would be instructive to reproduce my national tabulations (or something better) on a regional basis. How much of the narrowing of regional income differentials is the result of the narrowing of differentials in the education of the labor force? Of this, how much is due to differential changes in educational systems and how much to migration? Unfortunately, I do not know where long-term data could be obtained; special tabulations from the 1940 and 1960 Census could cover this time span, at least for the first question.

Third, my study deals only with education in general, without distinction as to course of study. Income differentials for individuals classified by type of education would be illuminating and presumably helpful both to students selecting high-school and college programs and to attainment of a rational allocation of resources. My impression, which I hope is wrong, is that hardly any information exists except for that on graduates of professional schools (other than earnings of college graduates on their first jobs, which is not very helpful).

All reference to the relationship of costs and returns from education is omitted because others know a great deal more than I about the subject.

# MARY JEAN BOWMAN

# Converging
## Concerns of
## Economists and Educators

*T*he allocation of resources to education is a decision process
which can benefit from studying returns from educational
*investments in human capital. Mary Jean Bowman, Professor of*
*Economics at the University of Chicago, carefully distinguishes*
*between the private and social aspects of investment in education.*
*Other major concepts emphasized are opportunity costs, income-time*
*flows and time preferences, and partial compared to global analyses. A*
*sophisticated and yet nonmathematical treatment of crucial economic*

Reprinted from Mary Jean Bowman, "Converging Concerns of Economists and
Educators," *Comparative Education Review* 6 (October 1962), pp. 111–19, with
permission of the author and publisher.

Notes to this essay will be found on pages 276–278.

*concepts, this article carefully identifies limitations to the economic analysis of education. Opportunity cost relationships, the importance of education to growth and productivity, the question of skill obsolescence, and the impact of innovation on human capital investment needs are among the many subject areas reviewed by the author. The rate-of-return approach can be of crucial importance in developing a rational public policy toward investment in education, according to Professor Bowman.*

   The recent surge of interest in the economics of "investment in education" is less novel than is sometimes believed. This line of work is nonetheless a break with the past in its broader scope, in the sharpness with which problems are identified, and in methodological ramifications. Each new insight, as is to be expected, raises more questions than it settles. Characteristically, what spreads most widely is any whiff of results that conform to wishes. The progressively sharpened questions arouse less interest outside economic circles though their emergence may be the more important part of what is happening and may offer the greater challenge to allied disciplines.

    The first and main task of this paper is to clarify the conceptual nature of the rate-of-return, or allocative approach to the task of analyzing investment in education. This includes examination of the component concepts involved in the basic analytical construct, with some suggestions concerning the range of applicability of these concepts. We will then turn to a consideration of several sets of problems that cross the boundaries where "economics" and educational research tend to dead-end, often side by side but without effective linkage or interpenetration.

    Selection of the rate-of-return models as the central theme is dictated by two considerations.[1] First, this kind of model, which is central to analysis of all problems involving decisions with regard to the allocation of investments to one use or another, is far more fully developed than any other with which economists have approached problems in the economics of education. Second, it is the approach that most clearly illuminates the zones within which the concerns of economist and educator converge, and where better interdisciplinary communication and joint research efforts offer the greatest promise.

## THE CONCEPTUAL FRAMEWORK
## OF ALLOCATIVE ANALYSIS

Allocative analysis is basic to both private and public decision making. On the normative or policy side it asks such questions as these. How large a share of available resources should go into roads as against schools? Into secondary versus elementary schooling? Into technical schools versus on-the-job training? Into college versus adult education? Back of the normative analysis lies the theoretical framework as a positive discipline dealing with economic phenomena: What returns relative to costs may be expected from various alternative actions, and why have the present allocations of resources come to be what they are? Such questions are not neatly bounded within "economics" but flow into other disciplines, until finally interests and competence of the economist fade and others must take up the tasks of both measurement and interpretation.

The most embracing and refined theoretical construct applicable to economic analysis of investment in education is represented by the rate-of-return approach. Though its rigorous application is normally frustrated by inadequate data, the basic propositions and techniques are pervasive and indispensable for any rational analysis. When the returns relative to costs that would be realized from added investment in one direction exceed those anticipated from investment in another, most people would concur that the former is economically preferable. Arguments arise not over this broad statement but over interpretations of costs and returns, the reliability of the empirical rate-of-return calculations, and the uses to which they are put.[2] To cut through the confusion one must start with a simplified sketch of the underlying conceptual model. In doing so a distinction must be made between "private" and "social" decision models and within the latter between what are here christened "partial social" and "global social" models.

### The Private Decision-Making Framework

Human beings respond individually to rewards and penalties of many kinds, whether an economy is collectively organized or is essentially a private-enterprise system. Private rates of return to private investments in education characterize all societies with formal education. These returns are in principle measurable, though the economic measures will have little significance in an essentially coercive state. "Private" returns to schooling are as real in the Soviet Union today as in this country and at least as readily identified. However, the empirical referents used for expository purposes will be mainly from the United States. Translation of the analysis into a Russian context or the context of an economy with a large subsistence sector requires no theoretical modification, though the latter especially will require modifications of the methods of measurement.

The private rate of return to investment in college education, for example, is what this education adds to a man's personal lifetime income stream expressed as a ratio to what he (or his family) have given up to procure that education (its costs). Thus we look at what education adds to income, what it costs, and the way these are linked by "rate of return."

The implications of this framework for conceptualizing and measuring costs are commonly misunderstood. To repeat: Costs, conceptually, are what the individual gives up to obtain the added education, say four years of college. One part of these costs is the money laid out for tuition, books, etc. The other part is the income he goes without in not having a job (net of any part-time-job income he may receive while studying or any scholarship). This second category of cost usually is called private "opportunity cost."[3]

Educators attempting to apply these concepts sometimes make a basic error that can lead to gross exaggeration of opportunity costs. The error is to include "subsistence" as an additional cost beyond those named above. Since a most able economist was guilty of this error in an article in this REVIEW,[4] such a mistake by others is hardly surprising. The double-counting involved in adding in subsistence is easily seen: If he were not in school, the youth (or his family) would still have to pay subsistence, presumably out of earnings on a job. In attending school he foregoes the earned income but not that plus subsistence. Precisely the same logic applies when "social" as when "private" costs are under examination.

Economic return from the private point of view is the amount added to a man's lifetime income by virtue of his having received the increment of schooling under examination. How much (given: native ability, parental status, etc.) does the additional schooling add to private income, and over what time path? (Any added expense associated with the added income, such as income tax, would of course be deducted.) The time path of income flow is important because a given income twenty years hence is worth less than the same income today; leaving "time preference" aside, if it were received today it could be invested to yield a larger sum with interest compounded over the twenty years. The private rate of return on a given increment of schooling is the rate at which the education-induced increments to income over a lifetime would have to be discounted to equate their value with the costs of a given increment of schooling as of the date at which those costs are incurred.

### The Social Framework

Measurement of social rates of return parallels conceptually that of private rates.[5] The "social" rate of return is the rate of discount on the incremental stream of national income (attributable to a given increment in the population's education) that would equate the present value of that income stream with the presently incurred total costs of providing the education. Social costs are what the society gives up (in what it could otherwise produce) when it invests resources in the education under consideration. However, without further specification this is an ambiguous statement.

Social costs and returns include the private ones; they are the latter plus or minus the associated costs incurred by and incomes accruing to parties other than the individuals who receive the given education. "Partial-social" costs and returns include all those that can be subsumed within the grasp of marginal analysis, irrespective of what individuals or agencies may be involved.

Let us suppose that people receive incomes equal to what their services are "worth" to others and that the difference between the incomes of high school and college graduates is attributable solely to the added schooling. The increment to national income for each additional person trained beyond high school through college could then be measured accurately by his *pre-tax* income increment, whereas in private accounting it was measured by his *post-tax* income increment. Partial-social costs are analogously approximated by the following summation: public expenditures plus philanthropic expenditures on schools plus private money outlays plus private opportunity costs. Notice that expenditures by foundations or public agencies on scholarships are netted out in arriving at private opportunity costs since they are merely income transfers and involve no diversion of real resources into education.

The social accounting just outlined was "partial" in two potentially significant ways. First, unless the proposition that people are paid what their services are worth to others is stretched unreasonably, secondary and diffusive effects on national income are ignored. For example, the effect of educating women on the ultimate productivity of their sons is left out. Second, this accounting tacitly ignored some of the economic interaction associated with "lump" changes and the accompanying measurement problems.

The methodological implications of these two omissions are similar. The "global" view of social returns that includes these diffusive and "lump" changes raises problems of structural change that cannot be analyzed with concepts geared primarily to adjustments occurring in small and easy steps. In this broader context the "rate of return" concept loses its precision. Nevertheless, an allocation problem remains.

Faced with these dilemmas, some economists throw out the whole rate-of-return apparatus. But this would be to discard tools that can be extremely powerful when properly used. The scope for applying private and social rate-of-return and related concepts is broad, though often more refined data must be procured or the biases of available data known. In fact, the impetus to get the relevant data is one of the main justifications for the approach. In its absence, tacit estimates of rates of return by anonymous officials will often guide or *mis*guide decisions.[6]

It has occasionally been asserted that rate-of-return analysis is of no value for the guidance of either private decisions or public policy because what has happened in the past does not tell us what will emerge in the future.[7] But such an argument applies to every kind of evidence that might conceivably be collected; there are no tools by which the future can be measured directly. What it boils down to is what clues concerning the future are provided, and how we can best use evidence of various kinds in combination to arrive at decisions as sound as are humanly possible. Rate-of-return analysis is the major tool among several in this endeavor. It provides a more precise and refined guide to *direction* of adjustment than any other yet available to us. This does not mean that it is infallible or adequate when large, lump changes are under consideration; it cannot specify how big a jump would be warranted in one leap. In fact, such analysis tells us that it is quite possible to overshoot the mark; the rate of return can be reduced too far as interactive adjustment increases opportunity costs at the margin and reduces the marginal increments to income. This is not all we would like to know, but it is much more knowledge than would be available if we were to discard the theoretical apparatus and try to work by rule of thumb.

It should be noted also that allocative models can contribute to an understanding of growth processes even though they do not explicitly focus attention on such processes. The repetition of "static" studies of rate-of-return patterns in one after another setting begins to fill in a picture of the moving scene, just as multiplication of camera still shots creates a movie.

The battle lines among economists arguing these issues, it is important to notice, are not coincident with free-enterprise versus collectivist orientations. In fact, in their national accounting the Soviet economists are increasingly making use of precisely the rate-of-return approach set forth here—though they of course put different labels on some of the terms.[8] In the process they are helping to refine the concepts. Meanwhile, other self-styled Marxists have begun to develop labor-equivalent units of measurement that might ultimately prove helpful in assessing economic systems in which there are large subsistence sectors.


## INTERDISCIPLINARY LINKS AND RESEARCH OPPORTUNITIES

The remaining pages of this article suggest some of the areas of research in which interests and competencies of economist and educator may converge. Many of these suggestions involve progressive steps in the disaggregation of data to differentiate more fully among segments and kinds of education, a necessity if research on the economics of education is to become as operationally useful to the educator as it should be. Closely related, but somewhat different, are the problems of research that involve analysis of on-the-job training and its comparison with roles of the schools in economic productivity. Finally, we will look briefly at a topic that is more dynamically centered, edging into problems of growth and structural change that are otherwise of necessity omitted here.


### A Classification of Reasons for Rate-of-Return Differences

Most of the important research opportunities on the frontiers between economist and educator can be highlighted by examining the factors that may account for divergences between rates of return to various kinds or levels of education and between educational and other investments. Actually, the latter emerge indirectly when we look at the former. It is not necessary to begin with precise, let alone correct, estimates. To avoid confusion, most of what follows will refer at least tacitly to the American setting; to modify the empirical referents to fit the many and diverse societies in which the comparative educator is interested would extend the discussion indefinitely without adding anything substantial to the essential ideas.

Subject to minor modifications, the major discrepancies among observed rates of return in any given case may be classified as follows:

1. Distortions in measures of private incremental returns.
2. Distortions in measures of private costs.
3. Differences among *true* private rates (eliminating 1 and 2).
4. Observed differences between private and partial social rates.
5. Unobserved differences between private and partial social rates.
6. Differences among *true* partial social rates (observed differences corrected for 1, 2, and 5).
7. Differences between global and partial social rates.

Item 7, the differences between partial and global social rates of return, is extremely important for analyses that focus on the major changes in economic structure that accompany significant economic growth. However, to treat this subject within the space allotted for this paper would be quite impossible, aside from the fact that other analytical tools are needed to supplement rate-of-return analysis or even largely to displace it. A few such tools are available, but they are weak ones. Global social returns will therefore be disregarded here except as they come in incidentally on the periphery of the discussion.

Items 4 through 6 may be passed over briefly. Enough has been said about 4, which is attributable mainly to governmental and philanthropic action and reflects past public decisions. The potentially important element in 5 is created by administered pricing of human skills that is out of line with contributions to national product.[9] In a centralized bureaucracy where the elite control the supplies of their numbers and set their own salaries, collected through compulsory taxation, this can be a major distortion indeed. The presence of extremely high rates of private return is a signal to investigate this factor, a task for which the economist is well equipped.[10]

Differences among the *true* partial social rates (item 6) are, prima facie, the measures that would be most directly relevant to the public policy maker seeking guidance in public investments. They provide the initial normative guides insofar as the productivity criterion is applied—the only criterion dealt with here (though not the only one of interest to the writer). But sound policy necessitates knowing why and how things come to be as they are. Leaving explanations of items 4 and 5 to political scientists or sociologists, we now turn to the elements of 1, 2, and 3. We take these up in reverse order, moving progressively deeper into noneconomic territory; when we come to 2 and 1 we will look not only at distortions but at what may determine true values.

## Discrepancies among "True" Private Rates of Return

Empirical measurement of rates of return to investments in education has barely begun, and there are no comparisons among types of school or curriculum. There has been considerable work on two kinds of comparison: (1) among the professions (and between these and college graduates at large), and (2) among successive increments of schooling from primary school to college.[11] The latter is here designated "incremental level" comparisons. The former can be called "specialized-occupational" comparisons and could relate to comparisons of carpenters with electricians as well as of lawyers with physicians. The factors that are most likely, a priori, to explain differences among rates of return within these sets are partially overlapping. These factors are:

A. Relevant to both sets of comparisons
1. Lags in adjustment to changes in relative demands for the human skills involved. Studies of engineers relative to other occupations over a period of years illustrate these adjustments in both directions.
2. Restricted numbers of places in the type or segment of education that yields the higher return, thus blocking response to what would otherwise be favorable econo-

mic opportunities. Inadequate capital markets limiting
borrowing for education can have a similar effect.

B. Relevant primarily in comparisons among "specialized-
occupational" educations

   3. Scarcity of special abilities required for a given occupation.

   4. Nonmonetary occupational preferences. If men wish to
be professors even at a sacrifice in income, the rate of
return to their training is lowered; if some nonmonetary
aspects of a vocation are unpleasant, the rate of return
would tend, other things equal, to be high.

C. Relevant primarily in comparisons of "incremental levels"

   5. Persisting ignorance about personal economic advantages of schooling; e.g., the persistence of a large
income advantage of those finishing eighth grade over
those dropping out earlier may in large part reflect such
ignorance among parents and adolescents.

   6. Pervasively strong personal-income time preferences
that exceed even high observed rates of return. This
may be important among large sub-populations and is
closely related to factor 7.

   7. Pervasive preferences for leisure over income. This is
the obverse of "achievement motivation," but is a
simpler concept; it includes disinclination to work at
studying as well as at "work."

   8. Strong value placed on education as a good in itself (a
"consumer good").

Among these eight factors, the first two clearly fall within the
sphere of the economist and are of major concern to him, though
others may be interested in the factual information produced. They
involve study of economic structure and adjustment processes as
well as establishing parameters. The other six factors interest the
economist primarily as he desires evidence to establish parameters
for a research or policy problem, but several of these are more central
to the concern of other social scientists, including educators. Impor-

tant problems in these areas tend to be neglected because of lack of communication among disciplines, due in part to isolation but also to the difficulties of translation among the several academic languages.

## Opportunity Costs and School Drop-Outs

Opportunity cost is the value of the next-best choice. Study of these costs has only begun, but as it is pressed economists will be driven further into comparative studies of socioeconomic systems, including more intensive analysis of nonmarket segments of production. In addition to his own tools, the economist needs more sociological awareness and a fresh approach to measurement, but only he can clear away the difficulties in analyzing and measuring opportunity cost. What, then, is the interest of the educator in such assessment?

Measurement of opportunity costs is an essential element in any analysis that would attempt to explain rates of persistence in school. As a first approximation, it might be considered to be "the economist's" theory. According to this theory, school continuation rates will rise, other things equal, when opportunity costs fall; continuation rates will fall when opportunity costs rise. Lest some readers immediately challenge this by observing that income opportunities foregone are higher than they were, as are school continuation rates, two points should be noticed. First, opportunity costs are institutionally conditioned and for elementary and high school age groups they have almost certainly been reduced; important among the changes that have brought this about are child labor laws and the shift from labor-intensive to mechanized farming. Second, the main "other things equal" considerations for the economists are the incentives to attend school arising from the prospective effects upon one's income; income-earning capacity has clearly risen over time whatever may have happened to marginal rates of return.

The economist finds this deliberately simplified theory useful for his usual purposes, but his purposes rarely require the full-bodied study of factors in school drop-outs that must be of concern to educators. When this is the core of a problem rather than its boundary, it becomes necessary to focus more directly on what the economist builds into his models under the labels "ignorance" and "preference functions." Direct assessment and measurement of these types of variables require qualifications of a kind that are not within the economist's competence. Clearly, if the crude and unsophisticated discussions of drop-outs that have pervaded educational literature and research are to be replaced by something that is sounder and scientifically more respectable, a cooperative effort among economists and educational sociologists and psychologists is required.

## Identifying the Contribution of Education to Productivity

What part of the average earned-income differentials empirically associated with a given increment to schooling is attributable to that education, what part to personal traits explaining both schooling and later earnings? This question is basic for the economist, and it divides into parts of equally central interest to educators. What do schools of what kinds, with what methods and curricula, do to what kinds of pupils to prepare them for vocational life? Collaboration in research design and data collection is needed here also.

Two classificatory schemes would be important. One would be by types of schools and training—not merely the Ivy League versus other colleges sort of distinction, which has received so much attention, but kinds of preparation in schools and kinds of schools supposedly turning out subprofessional people, for example. There is a vast and important field for comparative study of these variations and their effects both within the United States and between countries. The other classification would differentiate students by traits such as intelligence, aptitudes, initial attitudes, parental background, etc. Educators start this task with a rich background of prior work, but the links with economic productivity effects are weak or lacking. Educators come up to one side of an academic wall, economists to the other, but the two rarely find the openings where they should meet. Little attention has been given to what men of given ability but differing types of education manage to accomplish as producers, or of the relations between academic achievement and later economic performance. Some projects designed to pursue such questions could start with samples of adults, tracking back from present jobs, incomes, and ability tests to analyze educational histories. Other long-term projects should start with samples of pupils now in school and follow them deep into their adult working lives.

### Training in Schools and on the Job

There is no sharp line between the differentiation by types of schooling and that between education within the schools and on the job. Societies differ greatly in the locus of many training functions (apart from confusion over labels on the schools). Until recently assessment of the importance of on-the-job training posed some of the most frustrating problems for economists dealing with education. These problems are by no means solved. However, starting with rate-of-return models, Gary Becker and Jacob Mincer have recently developed theoretical and empirical analyses, respectively, of the extent of such training in this country.[12] There are many imperfections in their work, but it is nevertheless an important beginning; indeed, it may prove to be a critical breakthrough in the development of tools for analysis of the roles of on-the-job training and ultimately also for broader comparisons among societies that differ substantially in their educational and training systems.

When all this is said, the fact remains, nevertheless, that the economist working alone is not likely to get into the intensive analysis of variations in the roles and efficiency of differing kinds of schooling and their relations to on-the-job training that are of vital interest to many educators.

Research along these lines would require methods and data of kinds similar to those specified in the preceding section, and could indeed be regarded as their extension into a particular problem area. One promising project, for example, would be study of work-performance differentials at intermediate and subprofessional levels within selected enterprises as those differentials may relate to prior schooling and work experience. A preliminary step would be development and pilot testing of measures for the delineation of several dimensions of capability.

## Innovation and Obsolescence

In turning attention to innovation and obsolescence, we depart from the comparatively static framework, within which most of the previous research could be fitted, to enter the field of growth dynamics. However, the entry is at the point at which we remain on firmest ground, and where the connections with topics already discussed is the closest. Within this topic, emphasis here is on the aspects of economic dynamics to which fundamental educational research can probably make the greatest contribution, an exceedingly important contribution.

The meaning of the word "innovation" is sometimes misunderstood; it is not the same thing as "invention." Innovation is action that puts invention to use, and organizational invention and innovation are quite as important as technological. Whether one subscribes to a Schumpeterian theory of growth and long cycles as arising out of waves of innovation or not, it is clear that both innovation and obsolescence are concomitants of economic change.

In a rapidly changing society the threat and appearance of obsolescence of human skills means two things. (1) Investment in specialized skills can be risky, and it is far more important than in a more sluggish economy that basic education should equip its graduates to adapt to change. There is probably a more general understanding of these points than of most of those mentioned in these pages. Yet these imperatives throw light on the reassessments now going on in many countries today. (2) Obsolescence has implications for the distribution of educational investment over the life span of the individual. This aspect of the question has received far less attention than is its due. Too seldom do we step back and ask whether we may be piling up too much education of youth at the expense of refresher courses and upgrading work among adults—the quite different matter of rising leisure and adult education as a consumer good aside. This is one of the critical dynamic issues to the assessment of which allocative models might lend a particularly valuable helping hand, but only if much preliminary work on research design is done.

Finally, if deviants and innovation play the vital part in economic progress that most economists would ascribe to them, educators face an especially serious challenge. Do their efforts encourage or throttle the willingness to take constructive chances and to engage in creative activities entailing such chances? For that matter, was America fortunate that the colleges of the late nineteenth century were so loosely knit, so diverse, in fact so lacking in standards? The initial work on "creativity" needs expanding to examine how schools condition their pupils not merely to pass tests or to conform to social norms, but to strike out in variant paths. As McClelland has suggested by his studies of "achievement motivation," such facets of education may be vital for many aspects of a society and not merely for economic growth.

# BURTON A. WEISBROD

# Investing in
## Human
### Capital

*T*his *selection, written by Burton A. Weisbrod, Professor of Economics at the University of Wisconsin, firmly establishes the basis for economic analysis of human capital. Investments in health and education are primary sources of human capital formation that play a welfare as well as an economic-growth role. Expenditures designed to ameliorate disease, supply quality medical care and adequate housing, and improve education appear to receive inadequate attention from society. Private* and *social benefits from human capital formation*

Reprinted from Burton A. Weisbrod, "Investing in Human Capital," *Journal of Human Resources* 1 (Summer 1966), pp. 5–21, with permission of the author and publisher. Copyright 1966 by the Regents of the University of Wisconsin.

Notes to this essay will be found on pages 278–279.

*and the public policy implications of investment in education are given*
*special attention in this article. The existence of spillover benefits*
*accruing to society in addition to the more readily measured income*
*benefits places major responsibility for human resource development in*
*the public sector—a responsibility which must be met in proportion to*
*existing needs.*

## I. INTRODUCTION

This paper is about people. It is also about productivity and
growth of an economy. And it is about the proper role of government
in a society devoted to using its limited physical and human resources
wisely for the economic and social well-being of its people.

A nation's output of goods and services, and thus its capacity
to raise living standards, is limited by its resources and by the state of
technological knowledge regarding how to utilize them. Of the
traditional triumvirate of resources—land, labor, and capital—only
capital has been thought of generally as subject to significant and
appropriate social control. Land is given by nature, while population
and hence the labor supply have been considered to be determined
by forces outside the economic system.

The state of technological knowledge, too, has been considered
to be determined largely outside the economic system, except to the
extent that resources were directed toward research and development.
Moreover, knowledge is significant largely to the extent that it
becomes embodied in resources—in the form of man-made capital.

With society's supply of land and labor and the state of the
technological arts being largely beyond its control, society's ability to
escape from mass poverty and to achieve wealth depends critically
upon its success in accumulating capital—machinery, equipment,
plant, and other man-made producers goods. If the stock of capital
can be increased sufficiently, output and living standards can rise
despite growing pressure of population on the fixed supply of land.

The trouble with this conventional if somewhat caricatured
explanation of the economic growth process is that it fails to explain
the growth in United States output in this century. Students of U.S.

economic development have consistently concluded that increases in the stock of reproducible physical capital account for only half or less of the growth of our per capita output during this century. What accounts for the remainder?

There are a number of possible answers. Economies of scale may have permitted output to rise proportionately more than the increases in resources. *Improvements in the quality of capital goods* may have occurred without being reflected in prices. *Improvements in techniques of organizing production*, which increased productive efficiency, may have taken place.

But an alternative and possibly the principal answer may be that the stock of total capital has grown much more rapidly than our conventional measures indicate. Capital may exist in intangible form, as well as in the tangible, traditional forms of factories and machines. Intangible capital may be embodied in people—in labor resources. This would constitute a hybrid class of productive resources—a combination of labor and capital which might be called "human capital." Studies of the sources of economic growth that have measured only changes in the stock of *physical* capital (plant and equipment) have been incomplete; they have neglected the growing investment in *human* capital.

The concept of human capital is actually an old one in which interest has been revived within the last decade. What may have been the first reference to the social value of a person as a special kind of capital asset was made by Sir William Petty in 1687. Concerned about the economic losses from the London plagues, Petty estimated the value of an Englishman's production, the extra probability of his death if he remained in London, and the cost of transportation from the city. He then concluded that an expenditure to move people—and thereby to save lives—would indeed be a financially wise investment. The return would be eighty-four-fold!

Neither Petty then nor any of us now—even if *no* payoff had been found—would have advocated public disregard of health hazards. Yet the knowledge that an expenditure on relocation would actually be a profitable investment in human resources may reinforce the social resolve to take appropriate action.

Human capital represents resources which man has utilized to augment his personal productivity. Expenditures on information, labor, mobility, health, education, and training all are capable of enhancing the productive capacity of a worker—his human capital. I would regard health and education as the two principal forms of expenditures on human capital, and I shall give attention to each. However, the discussion of health expenditures will be abbreviated, so that I can devote primary attention to education. For education is the area of human resource development in which we face today the most pressing issues of public policy, the greatest and most rapidly climbing demands upon the public purse, and the most challenging opportunities for farsighted social leadership.

In sections II and III, I will analyze private and social, monetary and non-monetary benefits from health and educational investments in human capital. Section IV will then draw some implications from the analysis—for over-all public policy with respect to investments in people, and particularly for investments in their education.

## II. HEALTH AS AN INVESTMENT

A healthier worker is a more productive worker—absent less from the job and more productive and creative while on it. Substantial resources have been devoted in Canada and in the United States to improvements in health and these have brought into being— among other benefits—a more effective labor force.

In the United States, total public and private expenditures on health and medical care have nearly doubled in the last eight years— soaring from less than $18 billion in 1955 to $34 billion in 1963. This represented an increase in the share of Gross National Product devoted to health from 4.7 percent to 6.0 percent.

The rate of increase in Canada has been even more rapid. Between 1955 and 1961, the latest year for which I have located Canadian data, expenditures on health and medical care rose 90 percent, while in the United States they rose 63 percent. In the short space of those six years, Canada increased spending on health from

3.2 percent to 4.5 percent of its growing gross national product.

Life expectancies continue to inch upward, responding in part to these health expenditures. In Canada, life expectancy at birth is nearly five years greater today than it was only twenty years ago.

Thus, whereas we have traditionally referred to *expenditures* on health, we now must recognize that a substantial fraction of those expenditures are truly *investments*—in increased longevity and lifetime labor productivity, as well as in increased human happiness and decreased suffering. Moreover, *preventive* health expenditures can be doubly valuable investments. Not only may they reduce the incidence and production-cutting effects of disease, but by liberating labor and capital resources that are now devoted to *caring* for the victims of disease, they may permit these resources to add to the production of other goods and services.

Let me illustrate in specific terms the investment character of health expenditures. A half-dozen years ago I estimated the dollar value of productivity losses resulting from polio in the United States; it ran to at least $46 million per year.[1] This included production lost from the victims of the disease, as well as the cost of resources devoted to treating and caring for them. More recently I have estimated the cost of preventing these economic losses by immunizing everyone in the United States under age 35, and then immunizing the newborn each year. This massive attack would cost only some $27 million per year—a small price to pay for an annual return of $46 million.

At the aggregate level, data from the United States National Health Survey permit us to make a crude estimate of the potential production being lost because of ill health, and this loss is the as-yet-unrealized payoff from additional public or private investment in medical research and disease prevention, cure, and treatment. In the year ended June 30, 1962, approximately 400 million workdays were lost by employed people because of illness or injury, or six days per worker. This is a loss of more than 2 percent of total manpower available to the economy. And it takes no account of either premature deaths or the debilitating effects of illness and accidents for those who remain on the job, but with impaired efficiency.

I do not suggest that public policy decisions on whether to embark on health programs should rest solely on their narrow economic "profitability" or contribution to economic growth. They should not. The point to be emphasized is that health programs may contribute handsomely to economic progress, *as well as* to the broader aspects of mankind's welfare. My research indicates that the United States has been paying a price of more than $700 million per year in economic costs of tuberculosis and over $2 billion per year in costs of cancer.[2] Better health often is very good business. The fact that national income accounts show essentially no health services under "investment" indicates the re-thinking of conventional practices that is needed.

While much of the benefit from improved health accrues directly to the persons affected, there are also important benefits to others in society. In the jargon of economists, there are "external" benefits. Such external effects are particularly clear when contagious diseases are involved, for then the health of one person affects the health of others. They also exist in the form of benefits to employers, for whom a healhtier labor force means less absenteeism and enhanced on-the-job productivity. And they exist in the form of benefits to taxpayers generally; for them a healthier population means, among other things, reduced needs for welfare payments to those whose illness has brought poverty. For all these reasons, there is a national stake in medical research too. New methods for disease prevention, and for treatment, cure, and rehabilitation of the ill, will often spread benefits throughout the society.

To some extent, the investment aspect of improved health is reflected through growing governmental support for medical and health-related research (see Table 1). There are, however, many and complex reasons for this support, only one of which is that better health "pays." Yet, when health program policies are being debated at high government levels, the economic aspects of improved health as an investment in human resources is playing an increasingly prominent role—a role which would be still greater, I would judge, if economists had contributed more to an understanding of the magnitudes of benefits from specific health programs. Nevertheless, the mere recognition of an investment component to health expenditures is itself a major step toward rational government decision-making.

### Table 1    Sources of U.S. Funds for Medical and Health-related Research

| Years | Total, in millions of dollars | SHARE OF FEDERAL GOVERNMENT | |
| | | In millions of dollars | Percentage |
|---|---|---|---|
| 1940 | 45 | 3 | 7 |
| 1947 | 88 | 28 | 32 |
| 1957 | 397 | 186 | 47 |
| 1960 | 715 | 380 | 53 |
| 1970 | 2,300 | 1,610 | 70 |

**Sources** 1940–60 are from U.S. Senate, Committee of Consultants on Medical Research to the Subcommittee on the Departments of Labor and Health, Education, and Welfare of the Committee on Appropriations, *Federal Support of Medical Research* (May 1960), p. 24; 1970 data are from unpublished projections developed for the Rockefeller Foundation Exploratory Study Report of the Ad Hoc Committee to Study Voluntary Health and Welfare Agencies. The federal government estimate of $1.6 billion is consistent with the Bureau of the Budget projections for 1970 expenditures by the National Institutes of Health: low estimate—$1.2 billion; medium—$1.3 billion; high—$2.0 billion. U.S. Bureau of the Budget, Special Study, *Ten-Year Projection of Federal Budget Expenditures* (1961), p. 48.

## III. EDUCATION AS AN INVESTMENT

Better health—resulting from expenditures on research, prevention, and care and from improved diets and more satisfactory housing—has surely contributed to economic growth by creating a more productive stock of human capital. But an even larger contributor has been education. Properly conceived, education produces a labor force that is more skilled, more adaptable to the needs of a changing economy, and more likely to develop the imaginative ideas, techniques, and products which are critical to the processes of economic expansion and social adaptation to change. By doing so—by contributing to worker productivity—the education process qualifies handsomely as a process of investment in human capital.

The increasing level of formal education among the U.S.

labor force has been continuous and sizeable. In 1940, the male labor force aged 18–64 averaged (a median of) 7.7 years of schooling. By 1952 it averaged 10.6 years, and by 1962, 12.1 years, somewhat more than a completed high school education.[3] In Canada, the educational investments embodied in the male labor force have also been rising, more modestly, from 7.6 to 7.8 years between 1941 and 1951,[4] but more rapidly, to around 8.5 years or more, between 1951 and 1961.[5]

The value of education, like the value of all forms of investments in people, is far more than financial. Education is a vital segment of the full life. Still, while we attach great significance to the cultural value of education, public policy toward higher education has apparently emphasized more pragmatic aspects of education, at least in the United States. In an excellent recent monograph, Alice M. Rivlin traces the history of Federal legislation affecting higher education in the United States.[6] She finds that, in case after case, beginning as long ago as 1785, federal legislation ostensibly designed to aid higher education actually had more practical objectives, such as aid to farmers (land grants for establishing agricultural universities) and reduction of unemployment (college-classroom construction in the 1930's). Citizens, or at least legislators, seem to have demanded consistently some evidence that the support of higher education is a profitable investment.

The National Defense Education Act—involving substantial loans, grants, and fellowships—may have signaled the beginning of a new era in which higher education *in general*—not merely those parts which have narrowly practical value—is receiving public attention and support. Yet efforts by economists to determine the financial returns from education in general and the contribution of education to economic growth may be interpreted as attempts to discover whether this new attitude toward higher education is justified on narrow financial grounds. The final verdict is not yet in.

But the growth of expenditures on education continues. Public education expenditures in the U.S. climbed above $24 billion in 1963, from $10 billion only a decade earlier.[7] Since 1900, total expenditures on education in the United States have increased four times as rapidly as total expenditures on physical plant and equipment; in 1900, education expenditures were only 9 percent of investment in plant and equipment, but by 1956, they were 34 percent,[8] and now they are 37 percent.

In analyzing the economic value of education, it is useful to view education as an industry—a user of resources and a producer of outputs. An economy has limited resources and cannot produce all the goods and services we would like to have. Therefore, efforts should be expanded to identify and to measure the values of the education industry's outputs, as well as the costs of all the resources it uses. It is not enough to exhort the virtues of education. While some urge that education merits added support, others press for more resources for health, while still others are urging the expansion of efforts to improve diets or housing, or construct more parks or wider and safer highways.

Unhappily, we must make choices. If they are made without recognition of the full benefits and costs of alternative uses of resources, we are not likely to choose wisely. Within this context, the following sections are devoted to what is known, and to what is not known, about the forms and magnitude of benefits from educational investments in human resources. Private and public benefits will be examined.

By "benefits" of education I mean any of three types of effects: those that increase production possibilities, such as increased labor skills; those that reduce costs and thereby make resources available for more productive uses, such as the reduced crime and law enforcement needs that education may bring by enhancing earnings; and those that increase welfare possibilities directly, such as development of public-spiritedness or social consciousness.

### Private Benefits from Education

Direct economic gains to individuals from education are sizeable. Two measures of these gains are the greater incomes and the smaller unemployment rates which added schooling seems to bring. Data for both the United States and Canada (Tables 2 and 3)

### Table 2   Income and Unemployment by Years of Schooling Completed in the United States

| YEARS OF SCHOOLING COMPLETED | MEDIAN INCOME Males, Age 25 and Over 1959 | UNEMPLOYMENT RATE March 1962 (percent) |
|---|---|---|
| Elementary: | | |
| 8 years | $3,892 | 7.2 |
| High School: | | |
| 1–3 years | 4,846 | 8.3 |
| 4 years | 5,441 | 5.1 |
| College: | | |
| 1–3 years | 5,978 | 3.7 |
| 4 years | 7,388 | 1.5 |

**Sources** *U.S. Census, 1960;* and U.S. Department of Labor.

present similar and impressive pictures of the favorable relationships between an individual's educational attainment, his subsequent income, and the prospects for his unemployment.

But let me digress with some words of caution. With reference to the income-education relationship, it is probably not true that the high school dropout in the United States, for example, could increase his annual income from around $4,800 to $5,400 (Table 2), if only he would complete high school. We frequently forget the selection

### Table 3   Income and Unemployment by Level of Education in Canada

| LEVEL OF EDUCATIONAL ATTAINMENT | INCOME DISTRIBUTION 1959 | | | | UNEMPLOYMENT RATE February 1960 (percent) |
|---|---|---|---|---|---|
| | Under $3,000 | $3,000– 5,000 | $5,000– 10,000 | $10,000 & over | |
| Did not finish primary school | 43 | 33 | 22 | 2 | 18.7 |
| Finished primary but not secondary school | 24 | 34 | 37 | 5 | 8.0 |
| Finished secondary school or better | 20 | 23 | 42 | 15 | 2.7 |

**Source** Dominion Bureau of Statistics.

process by which some young people complete more schooling than others. In general, those students who do not drop out are more able, more ambitious, more anxious to learn, and come from families with better job "connections"—all of which assist in lifting their incomes. We cannot be sure how much of the additional incomes associated with additional education is attributable to these factors, and how much is attributable to the schooling itself. The monetary returns from investment in education are doubtless noteworthy, but they are probably not as large as the data in Tables 2 and 3 suggest.

Caution is also required in interpreting the dramatic data on unemployment rates in Tables 2 and 3. It is not unusual to find young people being advised not to quit school partly on the ground that their chances of being unemployed would be reduced if they remained. This approach is too simple. If, by the wave of a magic wand, the entire U.S. labor force could have been endowed with a college education, would the over-all unemployment rate of 6.0 percent in March 1962 have been reduced to only 1.5 percent (Table 2)—the rate for college graduates? I think not.

Education alone does not create jobs. It can, however, help cut unemployment by enhancing the matchability of labor-force skills with employer needs. When the task is attaining and maintaining full employment, education is not an adequate substitute for effective government fiscal and monetary policies and high levels of consumer and business demand. However, it is a valuable complement. Let us not expect too much from education, particularly in the short run. Its economic value lies primarily in its contribution to individuals' productive *potential*, rather than in its contribution to the economy's success in achieving that potential.

Having digressed to point up the dangers of over-stating gross economic benefits from education, let me also note that there are important costs as well as benefits of education to students and their families. Costs include more than cash payments. They also include the earnings and production *foregone* because potentially productive people are in school (or in the hospital or physician's office in the case of investments in health), instead of on the job. In fact, a recent estimate for the United States indicates that the costs of high school and college education in the form of foregone income exceed by more than 50 percent the costs incurred directly by the schools.[9]

Still, when *all* costs are considered, and when an allowance is made for the non-educational factors affecting schooling, our best available evidence for the United States is that formal education does pay in the direct form of enhanced employment opportunities and, thus, of greater incomes. Education is an investment which produces at least as great a financial return as does investment in corporate enterprise—around 10 percent for college, and even more for high school and elementary school.[10]

But the profitability of education does not rest alone on its productivity-increasing or money-income-increasing effects. Some of the value of education accrues to the individual in other forms. The fruits of literacy—an output of elementary education—include the value of its non-market use. Thus, to cite an illustration which closely touches many of us, if a man prepares his own income tax return, he performs a service made possible by his literacy. Were this service provided through the market, it would be priced and included in national income. Assuming that 50 million of the 60 million personal income tax returns being filed each year in the United States are prepared by the taxpayer himself, at a value of $5 per return, a rough estimate of the annual market value of the tax return services performed by taxpayers for themselves is $250 million. Obviously, this is only one minor form of return from literacy. But it is in addition to the benefits from elementary education which accrue in money form.

## Social Benefits from Education

If students were the only beneficiaries of schooling, the broad public support for education would probably wither. But as valuable as education is privately, it is even more valuable publicly. Its benefits take diverse forms which extend well beyond the individuals who receive it.

For one thing, education has an important intergenerational

value.[11] When today's students reach adulthood, their children will gain by virtue of the informal education received at home. Much learning takes place at home, where the child's attitude toward school is also largely shaped. Better educated parents are more likely to raise children who recognize the value of education, in terms of job opportunities, as well as in terms of cultural opportunities.

This means that the social value of educating women is not zero, even if they never enter the labor force to utilize the skills developed in school. It is a mistake to say that education has value to society only when additional earnings and *marketable* production result. If we think of an "investment" as involving future as distinguished from current returns, then education has an investment component in the form of these intergeneration benefits.[12]

Another group of beneficiaries from education is employers, who have a financial interest in the education and training of their employees. An employer's job would be much more difficult and expensive if he had to work with an illiterate and untrained labor force or had to educate and train his own workers.

Education also affects taxpayers in general, who pay—directly or indirectly—for the consequences of the lack of education. For example, insofar as lack of education leads to employment difficulties and crime, the costs of crime prevention, law enforcement, and social unrest—with the related welfare costs—will tend to be high.

These costs, however, may not fall upon taxpayers in the community or area having responsibility for the child's education. The migration of poorly educated people whose behavior patterns and educational attainments differ greatly from those prevailing in the areas they migrate to may necessitate additional effort and expense to permit the migrants to adjust to the new school conditions,[13] if they are children, or to the new social and economic conditions, if they are adults. Thus, *residents of areas of in-migration have a stake in the education of children in the areas of out-migration.* People in the U.S. North have a stake in education in the South. People in Ontario and British Columbia have a stake in education in the maritime provinces. In general, people who are or may be in the same fiscal unit with an individual have a financial stake in the investment in his human capital.

The nation as a whole reaps a return from education through the process of economic growth. In an important study of *The Sources of Economic Growth in the United States*, Edward Denison estimated that 21 percent of the growth of real national income per person employed between 1929 and 1957 was attributable to the greater education of the labor force, while another 36 percent was attributable to the "advance of knowledge," much of which is associated with educational advance.

### Broad Social Benefits

We have seen that some of the social benefits from education are enjoyed by individuals and groups that are reasonably identifiable. But some of the benefits are distributed so broadly that the nature of specific beneficiaries is obscure. These general social benefits are not less important by virtue of their pervasiveness.

For example, literacy is of value not only to the individual possessing it and to employers, but to the entire society. Without widespread literacy, the significance of books, newspapers, and similar information media would dwindle; and it seems fair to say that the communication of information is of vital importance to the maintenance of competition and, indeed, to the existence of a market economy, as well as to the maintenance of political democracy.

Education is, after all, much more than a means of raising productivity or otherwise bringing financial returns. It is also a means of inculcating children with standards of socially desirable attitudes and behavior and of introducing children to new opportunities and challenges. In a free society, it helps to develop greater awareness of, and ability to participate effectively in, the democratic process.

No statistics can be marshalled to "prove" that education itself brings about a stronger democracy, but the relationships between people's educational attainments and their participation in activities that help make a democracy strong are striking. For one thing, education appears to develop in people a sense of citizen duty. Measuring attitudes toward the importance of voting on a five-level

## Table 4 Percentage of the Population Voting for President of the United States in the 1952 and 1956 Elections, by Age, Education, Sex and Region

| | Non-South | | | South | | |
|---|---|---|---|---|---|---|
| Age and Sex | Grade School | High School | College | Grade School | High School | College |
| **Less than 34** | | | | | | |
| Male | 60% (52) | 78% (175) | 88% (81) | 19% (32) | 55% (69) | 81% (32) |
| Female | 44 (55) | 73 (285) | 90 (90) | 13 (47) | 41 (111) | 74 (23) |
| **34–54** | | | | | | |
| Male | 80 (156) | 87 (222) | 96 (103) | 55 (87) | 80 (54) | 88 (33) |
| Female | 71 (170) | 85 (312) | 91 (85) | 22 (97) | 56 (86) | 82 (38) |
| **55 and over** | | | | | | |
| Male | 87 (179) | 93 (96) | 100 (31) | 63 (72) | 71 (21) | 82 (11) |
| Female | 71 (173) | 91 (126) | 93 (30) | 31 (75) | 58 (33) | 86 (22) |

**Note** Sample sizes are in parentheses.

**Source** A. Campbell, W. Miller, P. Converse, and D. Stokes, *The American Voter* (New York: John Wiley, 1960), Table 17–11, p. 495. See also Table 17–2, p. 478.

scale,[14] interviewers from the Survey Research Center of the University of Michigan found that only 25 percent of the grade school graduates were classified in the top level, while 50 percent of the high school graduates and 60 percent of the college graduates achieved it. None of the college graduates was in the bottom level, though 2 percent of the high school graduates and 12 percent of the grade school graduates were.[15] Similarly, favorable effects of education have been found in its relationship with the degree of political participation. Moreover, as Table 4 shows, the percentage of persons who actually do vote increases with educational attainment.

A positive relationship between voter participation and education was also found in my own analysis.[16] Data on voter participation in the 1952 presidential election for each of the 48 states were correlated with (1) the median years of education of the population 25 years of age and older, for 1950, and (2) the percentage of the state population which was urban. The latter variable was included to isolate the presumably greater difficulty of voting in rural areas. The results indicated that schooling explained 42 percent of the interstate variation in voter participation. And when the percentage of population urbanized was held constant, it was found that 61 percent of the interstate variance not explained by urbanization was explained by schooling.

The brevity of this discussion does an injustice to the important and sometimes subtle ways that education strengthens democratic institutions. No attempt has been made here to be thorough in an area where economists probably have little to contribute. Instead, the objective has been simply to recognize the fact that some—and possibly the most important—forms of social benefits from education may defy monetary valuation.

### Recapitulation

We have found that the social benefits from education take many forms and accrue widely through time and space. Some of the benefits from education—and much of what has been said about education also applies to health and other forms of human investments—are not realized by people in the area which financed the investment. Because the location of gains from some human-resource investments are determined by population movement, the process of migration is a process of spatial shifting of those gains. This produces not only an interstate or interprovincial stake in effective policies of human-resource development, but an international stake as well.

The diversity and complex diffusion of benefits from investments in human capital raise important issues as to how education should be financed and what role government should play generally in the development of human resources.

## IV. PUBLIC POLICY FOR EDUCATIONAL INVESTMENT IN HUMAN CAPITAL

The education system produces many forms of benefits. Some interesting issues arise, once we recognize that there are external benefits from education (and better health)—benefits to people other than the immediate recipients. For one principle of financing expenditures is that those who benefit from some expenditure should pay for it. Even a partial use of this taxation principle would call for attempts to identify various groups of direct and indirect beneficiaries from investments in human capital and to assess charges in recognition of the distribution of benefits. I do not mean to suggest that the benefit principle should necessarily prevail in financing investments in human capital. However, since many benefits from education are very broadly dispersed, the application of this principle would, in fact, require broad financial support for education and other such investments.

This paper has underscored the need for social recognition of the process of human-resource investment. The previous pages have developed the views that education and health are not merely consumer-type expenditures, but are investments in human-resource productivity; and that benefits from these investments do not merely accrue just to the persons in whom they are made, but extend to other persons as well. Now it is appropriate to focus attention on the responsibility of government in this area.

To begin with, there would be a significant role for government in the human resource field, even if there were no external benefits—even if all benefits accrued to the individual. One reason is that, with particular respect to education, important decisions are made by young people, who may be poor judges of their long-term interests. Dropping out of high school may seem wise to a youth impatient to increase his earnings, but the wisdom of the decision becomes less obvious with the passage of time.

Of course, additional schooling is of value only to those who have the requisite ability and attitude toward learning. There may be little that society can do about a student's ability, but it may be able to shape his attitude toward schooling. This is the goal of many contemporary programs to prevent high school dropouts, in which well-trained guidance counselors can play an especially vital role. And *government has a responsibility to see that, through counselors and otherwise, people are fully informed about the long-run benefits from education, health, and other forms of investments in people.*

A second reason for public concern about the adequacy of private investment in human resources involves the ability of individuals to finance these investments. In education, a proper student attitude and the necessary intellectual ability are not sufficient; financial ability is also required. The costs of obtaining adequate education and health rations their use among low-income families. With respect to schooling, this would be true even if education, from elementary school through university, were "free." As noted above, much of the real cost of schooling is not the out-of-pocket expense, but the income lost by the student. In a poor family, the immediate pressure upon the youngster to augment family income—foregoing investments in his own human capital, if need be—may be enormous.

To some extent, the financial hurdles to private investments in human capital by low-income persons can be overcome by borrowing. But one should not forget the real obstacles to obtaining a loan for educational purposes through the private market. The capital market conventionally provides loans for the purchases of tangible assets which, if necessary, can be taken over by the lender. Loans for education and for other forms of investment in human capital have a special characteristic. The fruits they produce are intangible—they are embodied in people. Therefore, the asset cannot be attached by an unsatisfied lender. This fact limits the availability of private loans for financing education or other human capital investments. *Government can help to overcome limitations in the private capital market through programs of direct aid, loans, and guarantees of private loans to facilitate investment in people.*

But government responsibility surpasses the need to improve capital markets and provide counseling. It must help the nation to recognize that the benefits to *society as a whole* which result from investment in human resources exceed the direct benefits to the *individual* in whom the investment is made. It must help the nation to recognize that a society bent on economic growth—on raising living standards and erasing poverty—is a society committed to change; and change requires a creative, adaptable, and efficient labor force capable of creating innovations and adjusting to new, often unforseen, skill requirements. A rigid labor supply is a formidable obstacle to change.

Education can contribute mightily to economic growth by meeting the needs for flexibility and adaptability. But this implies a greater emphasis on the teaching of *basic* techniques and concepts and on the postponement of a student's specialization until late in the educational process. It also implies that the distinction between "vocational" and "general" education may in reality be a great deal more fuzzy than conventional usage suggests. In a world of changing technology and skill requirements, the training that appears to be "general" today may be extremely and directly useful in the world of work tomorrow. Similarly, education that appears today to be of direct vocational value may not only be obsolete later, but its narrowness may intensify the difficulties of adjusting to future manpower demands.

In recognition of the broad social and economic interest in investment in human capital, particularly through education and health, *it is appropriate and desirable for government policy to encourage individuals to invest more in themselves than they otherwise would, and perhaps in somewhat different ways.* For example, a teen-ager may prefer not to continue in school or take certain health measures, but the rest of society may prefer that he does, since, as we have seen, it will suffer in many ways if his education, training, and health are not satisfactory.

Today, tax laws provide greater incentives for investment in physical assets than for investments in human capital, because the former are more generally depreciable as a business expense than are the latter. *Reconsideration of tax policy so as to redress the imbalance is warranted.* Similarly, the tradition that the cost of a school building or a hospital is a "capital" cost—which can "appropriately" be financed by borrowing—while the cost of salaries for the teachers or medical personnel in that structure is a non-capital expenditure, leads to an unfortunate emphasis on *con*struction relative to *in*struction in the school and elaborate equipment relative to additional personnel in hospitals. Education and health expenditures other than on buildings and equipment also represent investments—less tangible but no less real than the investments in classrooms. *Government should recognize by its words and deeds the breadth of the investment concept and should help lower-level governments and private decision-makers to recognize it also.*

## V. CONCLUSION

Some readers may feel that health and education policies are moral issues that should not be subjected to the cold scrutiny of an economist. But surely one need not choose between an economist's view and a philosopher's view of wise public health and education policies. Both are relevant. Indeed, the discussion above has pointed to a number of important though unquantifiable benefits from investing in people. Returns in the form of enhanced productivity are relevant for wise policy-making. But so are non-economic considerations.

Actions taken by society directly influence the creation and the maintenance of human-capital values. Expenditures for education, training, health, and migration may contribute to the value of our human resources. Expenditures on the detection, treatment, and the prevention of accidents and floods and on the provision of adequate housing and diets—all these preserve and enhance the values of our human resources, just as do maintenance and improvement expenditures on physical capital.

Investments in human resources are not alone sufficient to insure rapid economic growth, let alone an effective democracy or a problem-free society. But it now appears that, as a society, we are paying too little attention to our enormously valuable stock of human capital, while we focus great attention on conventional investment. Health and education programs are primary devices for raising productivity and speeding social progress. Government has a critical role to play in promoting an effective human-resource-development program. The challenge is there to be seized.

# TEH-WEI HU
# JACOB J. KAUFMAN
# MAW LIN LEE
# ERNST W. STROMSDORFER

# Theory of
# Public Expenditures
# for Education

*T*he selection which follows, a portion of a larger study completed
at Pennsylvania State University by the authors for the United
States Department of Labor, develops the case for economic analysis
of educational expenditures. Although especially appropriate to
vocational technical education, the cogent arguments presented for
economic evaluation constitute the basis for a general theory of public
expenditures for education. The major dimensions to educational

This extract is taken from Teh-wei Hu, Jacob J. Kaufman, Maw Lin Lee, and
Ernst W. Stromsdorfer, *A Cost Effectiveness Study of Vocational Education*,
The Pennsylvania State University Institute for Research on Human Resources
(1969), pp. 6–19, with permission of the authors.

Notes to this essay will be found on pages 279–281.

*benefits and costs are identified as are the theoretical criteria used for
identification of the best mix of alternative programs.*

## INTRODUCTION

Educational services in the United States, especially the
elementary and secondary schools, are supported primarily by public
funds. In the fiscal year 1945/46 total educational expenditures by
federal, state, and local governments were about $4.4 billion. They
increased to $32.3 billion by the fiscal year 1965/66.[1] Allowing for
changes in the price level during this period, the expenditures in
the fiscal year 1965/66 were more than four times higher than in the
fiscal year 1945/46. Allowing for both changes in the price level and
growth in population during this period, the per capita public
expenditures for education in the fiscal year 1965/66 were still three
times higher than in the fiscal year 1945/46 (*i.e.*, $48 in 1945/46 and
$148 in 1965/66, in 1957/59 dollars). This increasing trend of public
expenditures for education reflects the public expression of increasing
demand for education.

What are the rationales governmental bodies use to spend a
large share of .public revenue (about one-sixth in the fiscal year
1965/66) for education? Are there guidelines for determining
"optimum" levels of public expenditures for education? How do
public expenditures for vocational and academic education fit into
these guidelines? And, finally, are there any feasible means to evaluate
these different educational programs on which public funds are
expended? The discussion of this chapter will focus on these questions.

## THE NATURE OF EDUCATION

Needless to say, education has its cultural and social value.
However, from the viewpoint of economists, education also has its
economic value. That is, educational services produced by schools
are both a consumption good and an investment good. If one pursues

education because knowledge is desired for its own sake, or if one considers that education can enrich one's life through increasing the variety and depth of intellectual pursuits, then educational services can be treated as a consumption good. In this sense, education is an end in itself. However, if one obtains educational services solely because of their impact upon future occupational choices and earnings, then educational services can be treated as an investment good. In this case, education is a means toward an end. It is understood, of course, that while educational services are both a consumption good and an investment good, an end and a means, the consumption and investment aspects vary for different kinds of education and for different people.

During the past decade, economists have largely emphasized the investment aspect of education.[2] Investment in human resources, especially education, is considered an important factor affecting the amount of saving and capital formation and, in turn, the long-run economic growth of the economy.[3] Education also affects the structure of wages in the labor market and thereby the structure of relative earnings.[4] Indeed, the results of economic research on education testify to the importance of the investment nature of education.

## THE ROLE OF GOVERNMENT IN EDUCATION

Even though the economy of the United States is primarily market oriented, the activities of government have substantial effects on educational services. And though the role of government in education varies at different levels—federal, state, and local—it is possible to summarize the general rationale for governmental support of education. The following discussion focuses on the justification for government support of elementary and secondary education.

### Satisfaction of Public Needs

The desire of the family for a child's education is the private demand for education. But the desires of other members of the community for the benefits of a well-educated citizenry constitute the public demand for education. Important externalities of education are part of the justification for public support.[5] Therefore, the need for education is a public need. Public needs are those needs desired by members of the economy for which, once provided, there is no possibility to exclude nonpayers from obtaining benefit of the services. Accordingly, public education can be considered as a public good.

In the market economy the market principle of price rationing and allocation will fail to provide this kind of public good to society. One solution to this breakdown in the market economy is to provide this service to the public through the budget principle instead of the market principle. According to the budget principle, the quantities of particular services provided are based on consumers' demands for alternative uses of the economy's limited resources.

One can argue that free education to individuals can be achieved through government transfer payments to parents or through subsidies to private schools. However, public schools may be desired because the society would like to have a common set of values and a common cultural heritage.

## Redistribution of Income

In the market economy, the allocation of the share of the total product is based on the productivity of the resources (production factors), the quantity of resources provided, and the prices of these resources. The result of this system of distribution is an unequal distribution of income: those resources which have relatively high productivity and which are relatively scarce will have high incomes. On the other hand, those resources which are less productive or in relatively greater supply will obtain relatively small amounts of income.

Social justice and, in some cases, economic efficiency require moderation of the extent of income inequality in order to provide low income people with an adequate standard of living. The government has several instruments to achieve the goal of income redistribution, for instance, progressive income taxes or heavy inheritance taxes linked with income subsidies to the poor. However, education also plays an important role in achieving the goal of income redistribution. Public education can provide equal opportunity for those who wish to acquire knowledge and skills, regardless of their relative degrees of wealth. Through education one can improve his productivity, reduce his unemployment, and increase his income in the long-run. It is now generally agreed that more highly educated and skilled persons tend to earn more than others, holding other factors equal. It has been shown by Jacob Mincer that education is the most powerful means to achieve income redistribution.[6]

## Efficiency in Production

If a production process is under the decreasing-average-cost condition throughout the relevant range of output, it may be more efficient for government to operate this process. To prevent inadequate use of facilities, where decreasing costs are persistent, government should provide the product free or charge a price equal to marginal cost.[7] The use of a bridge is a classic example for marginal cost pricing.

The studies of Hanson[8] and Riew[9] concluded that public schools have economies of scale. Hanson based his conclusions on a sample of relatively large public school systems (*i.e.*, those over 1,500 in average daily attendance (ADA)) while Riew relied heavily on small size high schools (*i.e.*, those less than 1,000 ADA). In reality, public schools attended by the greatest majority of pupils in an area are more likely to attain a scale of operation which provides education at lower average cost than private schools. Unless it is subsidized, a private school has to charge tuition at least equal to its average cost if the school wishes to avoid losses. Thus, the private school may operate on the declining portion of its average cost function and have chronic excess capacity.

## Economic Stability and Growth

In the modern economy, the government is not only concerned about optimum resource allocation and income redistribution, but also with the full employment level of the economy and with long-run economic growth. The rapid improvement of technology in the economy may create structural and technological unemployment. It is believed that education can increase one's ability to adjust to changing job opportunities[10] and, therefore, large scale free educational services may provide more stability in an evolving labor market and reduce unemployment.

Capital formation and technology are the two important elements in economic growth. Education can improve these two elements. Schultz estimated that the educational capital in the United States labor force was $535 billion in 1957, or equivalent to 42 percent of reproducible tangible wealth.[11] Denison estimated that education has raised the average quality of labor by about 30 percent during the period 1929 to 1957.[12] He attributed about 23 percent of the 2.9 percentage point growth rate in national income over the 1929–57 period as a result of education. Based on these studies, it is quite clear that an optimal level of investment in education should be insured in order to maintain a stable economy and a high rate of economic growth. Given current institutional arrangements, government at all levels will have to contribute its effort toward achieving this optimum.

Up to this point the discussion has put forth the reasons for supporting the government provision of educational services. There are certain aspects that do not favor government involvement in education, however. For instance, public schools do not always provide freedom of choice with respect to varying consumer income and tastes and, therefore, interfere with consumer sovereignty in education.[13] As an example, some parents may prefer that the amount of resources available to education be used for improving the quality and quantity of teachers and texts rather than for athletic items. But in the public school system there is no way of expressing this preference unless it is done so by the approval of the majority of the parents. Furthermore, under a public school system, the ability of parents to spend extra money on their children's education within the system is limited. If parents want to spend more money, they can only transfer their children to a private school by paying tuition and other costs in addition to the financial burden they must continue to share for public school expenditures.

With regard to efficiency, the private operation of schools may be under the constraint of the profit motive and this thereby provides an incentive for cost minimization. Under the private school system, ill-managed and low quality schools cannot survive due to free competition among schools. Therefore, the private operation of schools may reduce costs and upgrade the quality of education.

## OPTIMUM ALLOCATION
## OF PUBLIC EXPENDITURES FOR EDUCATION
## —VOCATIONAL-TECHNICAL VS. ACADEMIC

A basic assumption in economics is that goods are scarce and that consumers prefer to have more goods rather than less. Therefore, it is generally desirable to employ resources in those uses where they have the highest productivity. Given the total amount of resources available for public education, it is relevant to determine the optimum allocation of expenditures on different programs such as vocational-technical and academic education.

### Theoretical Criterion

On the assumption that the goal of government programs is to maximize the social welfare, the social welfare function, with respect to different government programs, may be written in the form:

$$W = w (g_1, g_2, \ldots, g_n) \tag{1}$$

where $W$ is the social welfare (or it can be denoted as social benefits) and the $g$'s represent the output of different government programs.

The maximization of function (1) is subject to the constraint of the government budget, namely

$$B = \sum_{i=1}^{n} (a_i + c_i g_i) \qquad (2)$$

where $a_i$ is the fixed cost of the $i$th government program, $c_i$ is the marginal cost of the $i$th government program, and $B$ is the total government revenue.

The Lagrangian multiplier is used to solve the maximization problem, that is:

$$w(g_1, g_2, \ldots, g_n) - \lambda \left[ \sum_{i=1}^{n} (a_i + c_i g_i) - B \right] = 0 \qquad (3)$$

where $\lambda$ is the Lagrangian multiplier. Differentiating this expression with respect to $g_i$, then:

$$w_i - \lambda c_i = 0 \qquad (4)$$

where $w_i = \dfrac{\partial W}{\partial g_i}$ is the marginal benefit of the $i$th program. From this it follows that:

$$\frac{w_i}{w_j} = \frac{c_i}{c_j} \qquad (i, j = 1, 2, \ldots, n) \qquad (5)$$

and also that:

$$\frac{w_i}{c_i} = \lambda \qquad (6)$$

Thus, in equilibrium, as shown in equation (5), the maximization of social benefits is achieved if the ratio of marginal benefit in this example of two government programs is equal to the ratio of the marginal cost of these programs; that is, the marginal benefit is proportional to the marginal cost.

An application of this principle to the optimum allocation of public expenditures on vocational-technical versus academic secondary education is to spend resources on each program to the point where the marginal benefit–marginal cost ratio of vocational-technical education is equal to the marginal benefit–marginal cost ratio of academic education. In other words, other conditions equal, if the ratio of marginal benefits to marginal costs of vocational-technical education is higher than that of academic education, then the government should increase its expenditures on vocational-technical education up to the point where the two ratios are equal. This can be done within a fixed budget by shifting funds from academic to vocational-technical education or by expanding any extra public funds on vocational-technical education as additional funds become available. More explicitly, the optimum amount of public expenditures for vocational-technical and academic education is at the point where the additional benefits from an additional dollar spent on these two educational programs would be equal.[14]

### Measurement of the Theoretical Criterion

The theoretical criterion for the optimum allocation of government expenditures is clear cut. However, when the criterion is applied to government educational expenditures, two major difficulties are confronted. First, the existence of externalities of educational services can cause difficulties in deriving an accurate measurement of benefits or costs.[15] For example, while the financial returns to a student as a result of education can be measured, market forces fail to evaluate the non-financial returns of his education, such as the benefits to future generations or the benefits to his neighborhood. Such benefits as the increased productivity of his co-workers due to his existence as a better educated person are reflected in the market but are extremely difficult to identify and measure. Second, the application of the theoretical criterion to government educational expenditures is more complicated than that of government investment in such areas as highway construction or flood control because the benefits and costs, when involving human resources, are likely to be more general than those measured by simple economic indices such as earnings or employment. . . .

## PROGRAM EVALUATION
## FOR DECISION MAKING

Program evaluation is aimed at measuring the relative desirability of alternative programs in terms of economic criteria in order to provide decision makers with a rational choice among the alternative courses of action for achieving some stated objective. The program-planning-budget system (PPBS) is one of the most important instruments that has been applied in evaluating different programs both in the government and the private sector. PPBS is a combination of two operational techniques:[16] program-budgeting and systems analysis. These two techniques can be treated as either mutually related or independent.

### Program-Budgeting

Program-budgeting was introduced in the Department of Defense in 1961. Previously, defense expenditures were structured in the traditional budget form—by line item. Because the traditional budget form could not determine the feasibility of a weapon system or evaluate its efficiency, Charles J. Hitch introduced a system of program-budgeting.[17] The term "program" refers to the ultimate objective of many interdependent activities.

There are two essential characteristics of program-budgeting. First, the budget of government is organized by programs rather than by objects of expenditures, as traditional budgets are usually organized. In other words, program-budgeting is an objective-oriented program structure which presents data on all of the operations and activities of the program in categories which reflect the program's end purposes or objectives. Second, the program shows not only current needs but also future needs for resources, as well as the financial implications of the programmed outputs. The planning function is concerned with time, substance, and resources. In effect, program-budgeting contains two important pieces of information for decision makers: the ultimate objectives and the intermediate

objectives of the planned program and the information on financial
resource allocation needed to achieve the objectives.


## Systems Analysis

Systems analysis is a quantitative analysis. It is designed to
provide a criterion or standard for decision making so as to achieve
some rationality and optimality in the planning. Therefore, systems
analysis is a complementary tool for program-budgeting. There are
several alternative names for systems analysis, including cost-
effectiveness analysis, cost-benefit analysis, utility analysis, or operations research. These terms have the same meaning both from an
economic and methodological point of view.

The major concerns of systems analysis are with the assessment of costs (the welfare foregone) and benefits (the welfare gained).
System analysis will be referred to as cost-benefit analysis in the
subsequent presentation.

Cost-benefit analysis is a technique which concerns itself
with the optimum allocation of resources. It is a tool of analysis
which assesses the alternative courses of action in order to help
decision makers to maximize the net benefit to society. The essence
of this analysis lies in its ability to evaluate the total value of benefits
against the total costs.

Cost-benefit analysis normally comprises several steps. The
first and most important step is the identification of costs and
benefits of a given program. This procedure may appear to be
obvious, but in practice it raises a number of fundamental issues of
methodology and economic theory. For instance, should the tax
exemption to a public school system be considered as a cost or not?
If considered as a cost, to whom is it a cost? Or, should the reduction
of government transfer payments due to education be considered as a
benefit or not? If considered as a benefit, to whom is it a benefit? And,
especially, how far is one to go in attempting to enumerate and
evaluate external benefits and external costs of a program ? . . .
Table 1 illustrates some important elements of costs and benefits of

## Table 1   The Definitions and Elements
## of Costs and Benefits of Education

| SOCIAL | PRIVATE |
|---|---|
| *Costs* | *Costs* |
| Definition: Opportunity costs to the society at large (welfare foregone to the society as a result of expending resources on education rather than on other goods or services). | Definition: Opportunity costs to the individual (welfare foregone of the individual as a result of expending resources on education rather than on other goods or services). |
| Elements: | Elements: |
| 1. Schools' direct expenses incurred due to providing education services (e.g., operation expenses and capital expenses). | 1. Students' direct expenses incurred due to attending school (e.g., tuition, books, transportation). |
| 2. Opportunity costs of non-school system inputs (e.g., PTA donations to school, foregone earnings of students). | 2. Foregone earnings of students. |
| *Benefits* | *Benefits* |
| Definition: Welfare gained by the society at large as a result of education. | Definition: Welfare gained by the individual as a result of education. |
| Elements: | Elements: |
| 1. A greater rate of economic growth (e.g.. increased productivity of the associated workers). | 1. Students' additional earnings due to education. |
| 2. Good citizenship and reduction of crime. | 2. A broader appreciation of one's environment. |
| 3. Continuation and exploration of knowledge and culture. | 3. The acquisition of knowledge for its own sake. |

education. The elements of costs and benefits of both vocational-technical education and academic education of high schools are similar but vary in degree.

Second, it is often desirable that the list of benefits and costs, both private or social, be expressed as monetary values in order to arrive at an estimate of the current net benefits of a program. The benefits and costs are usually reflected via the price mechanism through the working of the market forces of supply and demand. In certain circumstances, however, market forces may fail to reflect all costs and benefits. This is the fundamental distinction between private and social costs and benefits. Therefore, the quantification of all costs and benefits of a program is difficult, if not at times virtually impossible. Assuming that these difficulties have been surmounted, the analyst is left with an estimate of net benefits of the project.

Finally, a comparison must be made of the stream of annual net benefits and the cost stream of the program. There are three basic alternative criteria in evaluating a program:[18] the benefit-cost ratio, the internal rate of return, or the present value of net benefits. Each criterion has its own advantages, but, given real world constraints, the results of each may not be consistent with the other two. In order to apply these criteria, cost-benefit analysis has to make assumptions as to the size of the rate of interest which is to reflect the social or private opportunity cost rate of investment funds. Unfortunately, there are many rates of interest observed in the market, each reflecting the yield on alternative types and mixes of investments. . . .

In spite of the evaluation difficulties in cost-benefit analysis, the analysis has been successfully applied in various fields. The pioneering empirical work was undertaken in the 1950's on water resources development.[19] Military defense is a public good of the most fundamental type. It would be stretching terminology to use a "rate of return" to investment in defense. Most of the work on this subject is, therefore, concerned with "cost-effectiveness analysis," dealing with such issues as the relative potency of different weapon systems in relation to given costs.[20] Lately, cost-benefit analysis has been applied to the fields of education, health, urban renewal, government research and development, and other areas.[21] The present study is concerned with the application of cost-benefit analysis in evaluating vocational-technical education and academic education in the senior high school.

## SUMMARY

Cost-benefit analysis is an economic methodology which concerns itself with the optimum allocation of resources. To evaluate the alternative courses of action in government educational programs, it is necessary to discuss the theory of public expenditures for education. This article has discussed the rationales for governmental agencies to spend a large share of revenue for education. Given the total amount of resources available for public education, it is relevant to determine the optimum allocation of expenditures among various educational programs, in this case, vocational-technical and academic secondary education. The optimum amount of public expenditures for vocational-technical and academic education is at the point where the additional benefits from an additional dollar spent on these two educational programs would be equal.

# part two

# Returns
## from
### Investment
# in Education

GARY S. BECKER

# Underinvestment in College Education?

*T**he possibility of underinvestment in college education haunts developed and less developed nations alike. Gary Becker, Arthur Lehman Professor of Economics at Columbia University, analyzes this issue by comparing internal rates of return on educational investments in human capital to other investment alternatives in nonhuman capital. Becker notes that his analysis is confined to direct returns only, indicating that the rates of return on college investments and physical capital are both in the eight to nine percent range after accounting for*

Reprinted from Gary S. Becker, "Underinvestment in College Education?" *American Economic Review Proceedings* 50 (May 1960), pp. 346–54, with permission of the author and publisher.

Notes to this essay will be found on pages 281–282.

*differences in human abilities. As a consequence, the argument for underinvestment in college education cannot be based upon direct monetary returns from such investments. Nonpecuniary benefits and external returns required to assess social costs and benefits must therefore carry the burden of justifying or refuting the claim that there is underinvestment in college education.*

# I

In the last few years the United States has become increasingly conscious of its educational program and policies. Not only have Congress, state legislatures, and local bodies paid greater attention to this issue, but large numbers of books, articles, talks, and academic studies have also been devoted to it. This concern has been stimulated by developments in the cold war which apparently have increased the power of the Soviet Union relative to the United States. These developments are primarily the rapid economic growth of the Soviet Union in the postwar period and their obvious success in missiles and space technology.

The near panic in the United States engendered by the more spectacular Soviet accomplishments has in turn spawned a re-examination of American policies and procedures relating to economic growth and military technology. Re-examinations begot by panic almost always overestimate and overstress weaknesses and underestimate points of strength. It is perhaps not surprising, therefore, that most recent studies of American education have found it seriously deficient at all levels and in most aspects, be it the effort required, the subjects pursued, or the amount given. It is widely believed that not enough is spent on education, especially at the college and postgraduate levels, that too few of the ablest high school graduates continue their studies, that school curricula at all levels are insufficiently challenging, and that more students should be majoring in the natural sciences and engineering.

For some time now I have been conducting a study for the National Bureau of Economic Research of investment in and returns to education in the United States, especially at the college level. This study is not directly concerned with educational policy but some of the results may have relevance to the issues currently being discussed. They seem to be especially relevant in determining whether too little is spent on college education and whether the quality of our college students could be improved. This paper discusses these questions in light of the contribution of college graduates to economic growth and military technology.

The concept of economic growth used here follows that used in calculations of national income and in comparisons of the economic performance of the Soviets and the United States, and excludes, among other things, nonmonetary income. In restricting this discussion to economic growth and military technology we thus exclude the effect of education on nonmonetary returns as well as on democratic government, equality of opportunity, culture, etc. The effects on growth and technology have been greatly emphasized recently; so it is especially important to discuss them. This limitation does mean, however, that we are not attempting a complete analysis or evaluation of the effects of college expenditures. A detailed derivation of the results used here will be found in the larger study to be published by the National Bureau.

## II

The economic effects of education can be divided into the effect on the incomes of persons receiving education and the effect on the incomes of others. This distinction largely corresponds to the distinction between private and social (*i.e.*, external) or direct and indirect effects. Data from the last two Censuses and from other surveys giving the incomes of persons with different amounts of education make it possible to form a judgment about the direct economic effects. The Census data giving the incomes of male college and high school graduates were used to estimate the direct return to college after being adjusted for other differences between high school and college graduates, such as in ability, race, unemployment, and mortality.

The average return from college so computed is related to the average cost of college, the latter including foregone earnings or opportunity costs as well as direct college costs. Returns are related to costs by an internal rate of return—the rate of discount which equates the present value of returns and costs. In other words, it is the rate of return earned by the average college graduate on his college education. If this rate of return was significantly higher than the rate earned on tangible capital, there would be evidence of under-investment in college education.

The rate of return relevant to a person deciding whether to go to college is a private rate, computed for private returns net of income taxes and for private costs. This was about $12\frac{1}{2}$ percent in 1940 and 10 percent in 1950 for urban white males. The difference between these rates resulted almost entirely from the growth in the personal income tax during the forties. The rate of return in 1940, and to a lesser extent in 1950, seems large and is probably larger than the average rate earned on tangible capital. (Some evidence on this is presented shortly.)

But this is not the relevant rate in determining if there is underinvestment in education. First of all, the rate of return should be computed on total college costs, not only on those paid by students. Since in 1940 and 1950 students paid only about two-thirds of these costs, there is a considerable difference between the rates earned on private and on total costs. Second, while returns collected by the state in the form of personal income tax payments are in principle an external return, it is convenient to adjust for them now, especially since this eliminates most of the difference between the rates of return in 1940 and 1950. If then the before-tax return to college is related to the total cost of college, a rate of return of about 9 percent is found for both 1940 and 1950. The adjustment for taxes raised the return in 1950 to about the same level as in 1940, but the adjustment for private and public subsidies to colleges reduced both rates about three percentage points. The rate of return no longer seems especially high in either year and it is an open question whether it is higher than the return on tangible capital.

Even 9 percent is probably too high an estimate of the return to all college graduates since it refers only to urban male whites. The rate of return to nonwhites seems to be about two percentage points lower than this.[1] I made no estimates of the return to women and rural graduates and know of none made by others, but since women participate in the labor force less than men, the direct money return to them is probably much less than to men.[2] The average return to rural graduates is probably also less than that to urban graduates. Thus the average return to all graduates would be lower than the 9 percent return to urban white males. That this difference might be substantial is evident, not only from the presumed large difference in returns to urban white males and others, but also from the fact that the former are only about 45 percent of all graduates.

The average return on college expenditures could be compared to the returns on almost an endless variety of tangible capital goods, ranging from consumers' durables to government capital. It is easiest—and perhaps for our purposes most relevant—to compare it to the average return on capital owned by business enterprises. George Stigler has been preparing estimates of the return to assets owned by manufacturing corporations. Preliminary results indicate that the rate of return on these assets, after payment of the corporate income tax, averaged about 7 percent, both from 1938 to 1947 and from 1948 to 1954. This does not seem, however, to be the relevant rate to compare with the less than 9 percent earned on college capital which was computed before the deduction of income taxes. The latter should be compared with the return before payment of the corporate income tax. During this period, the before-tax return of manufacturing corporations averaged more than 12 percent of their total assets. The data for nonmanufacturing corporations are less readily available and I do not have an estimate of the return to them. But since corporate income tax rates were so high during this period, it is extremely unlikely that all corporations averaged less than 10 percent or greater than 13 percent before taxes. Although even less is known about unincorporated enterprises, it is unlikely that their rate of return averaged much less than 5 percent or greater than 8 percent.

The average rate of return to business capital as a whole

depends on the rates of return to the corporate and unincorporated sectors and on the relative importance of each sector. It would appear that corporate capital is about 60 percent of all business capital. If this measures the relative importance of the corporate sector and if 10 and 5 percent measure the average returns to corporate and unincorporated capital, then the average return to all business capital would be 8 percent.

The substantial difference between these estimates and those of others results not from difference in the basic data but in the operations performed. Most studies use private college costs rather than total costs, make no adjustment for the differential ability of college graduates, deal only with urban white or all urban males, and use a long-term interest rate to measure the rate of return elsewhere. They estimate the return to college education at about 15 percent, and elsewhere at about 5 percent, clearly suggesting underinvestment in college education. Using total costs reduces the rate of return on college to about 11 percent; adjusting for differential ability reduces it further to about 9 percent, and including nonwhites, females, and rural persons reduces it still further. On the other hand, the before-tax rate of return to business is much higher than the long-term interest rate because of risk and liquidity premiums and the heavy corporate income tax. The average rates of return to business and to college education—adjusted for these factors—do not seem very far apart.

The evidence on direct returns is limited and these estimates of direct returns subject to considerable error, but it would appear that direct returns alone cannot justify a large increase in expenditures on college education relative to expenditures on business capital. To justify large increases it is necessary to show either that improved evidence would widen the difference between the estimated returns to college and business capital or that indirect (*i.e.*, external) returns are much larger for college than for business capital. The direct return to college was estimated from the incomes of persons differing in age and education; ideally one would like to have the lifetime incomes of persons known to differ only in education. Improvements in panel techniques and in our knowledge of the abilities of different persons may someday produce evidence close to the ideal. It remains to be seen, however, whether our conclusion about the relative returns to college and business capital is greatly changed.

External or indirect effects are very embarrassing to the economist, since his theories say little about them, he has few techniques for measuring them, and he usually does not even think that he knows much about them. In particular, little is known about the external effects from college education, although it is easy to give some examples. Thus college graduates did the pioneering work in molecular physics, and it may eventually benefit (or hurt) everyone. Einstein, Fermi, and the other pioneers received only a small fraction of the total increase (or decrease) in income resulting from their work. But it is much easier to give these examples than to assess their quantitative importance or, what is even more difficult, to compare them with external effects from business capital. Some maintain, quite persuasively, that college education had little to do with American economic growth throughout most of its history; others, equally persuasive, point to the importance of science in recent years and argue that future growth is closely related to scientific achievement; still others cite the laboratory and general increasing returns as examples of the sweeping external economies from investments in tangible capital.

Since direct returns alone do not seem to indicate underinvestment in education, those arguing this have to rely heavily on external returns. These may well be very important, but in light of our ignorance it is not surprising that no one has yet demonstrated that they are (or are not) sufficiently important to push the total return from college education much above the return elsewhere. It is this ignorance about external returns which prevents any firm judgment about the adequacy of expenditures on college education.

Even those maintaining that external economic and military effects are important would not maintain that they are equally important in all college specialties. But there would probably be little agreement on which specialties were likely to produce these effects, and with our present knowledge it would be impossible to prove that any specialty—no matter how removed it seems from economic and military questions—was unlikely to do so. Recent discussions of the role of college education in the cold war have, however, tended to emphasize scientific specialties to the exclusion of most others, and it is possible to determine whether important external economic and military returns[3] from science alone would imply large-scale under-investment in college education.

Science majors include persons majoring in natural science, mathematics, engineering, and applied biology, and in recent years they received about one-quarter of all bachelor's and first professional degrees.[4] This is probably a large overestimate of the number likely to produce external economies. Only science majors with advanced graduate training are likely to, but less than 5 percent of all science graduates go on for their doctorates, Scientists are more likely to produce these economies if they engage in research and development but just about 25 percent of all scientists are so engaged. Thus it would seem that well under half of all science majors or under 13 percent of all college graduates have a reasonable chance of produc-ing important external economies.

It was seen that the average direct return to college graduates is about the same as the average direct return to business capital. If the direct return to scientists was no lower than the direct return to other graduates[5] and if the external military and economic effects from scientists were important, the total return to scientists would be greater than the returns to business capital. There would be under-investment in scientists, and government assistance to the scientific field would be required to attain a more optimal allocation of capital. The number of scientists would be increased partly at the expense of business investment, partly at the expense of current consumption, and perhaps partly at the expense of other professions.

The important point to note, however, is that even a large underinvestment in scientists implies only a small underinvestment in college education as a whole. For example, the number of scientists with prospects of producing external effects could be increased by as much as 50 percent—a very sizable increase—and yet less than a 7 percent increase in the total number of college graduates would be required. The 7 percent figure is arrived at by assuming that none of the increase in scientists is at the expense of other college specialties and that a full 13 percent of all graduates fall into the relevant "scientist" category. Even 7 percent must, therefore, be considered a liberal upper estimate.[6] So the current demand for a large increase in scientists (or, more generally, expenditures on scientific training) to stimulate development could be met with a very modest increase in total expenditures on college education. This does not mean that underinvestment in scientists is unimportant, but only that it could be corrected with a relatively small expenditure.

## III

It is widely believed that the quality of the average college student could be substantially improved and that this would greatly aid our economic and military development. The available evidence does indicate that many who do not go to college rank higher in I.Q. or grades than many who do. For example, according to one study, 21 percent of high school graduates who do not go to college have I.Q.'s over 120, while 50 percent of college graduates have I.Q.'s less than 120. A similar picture emerges for grades.[7]

Such evidence alone does not demonstrate that an improvement in quality would aid progress, although it is almost universally accepted as sufficient evidence. If ability and education were substitutes rather than complements,[8] able persons would receive less than the average rate of return from college, and an improvement in quality would have an adverse effect on progress.[9] Some limited evidence on incomes obtained by the Commission on Human Resources and Advanced Training indicates, however, that able persons receive a greater than average direct return from college; so ability and education do seem to be complements. This evidence on incomes is supported by evidence from the supply side. If able persons really receive a higher return from college, they should have a greater incentive to go to college, and the fraction of able high school graduates going to college would be larger than the fraction of all graduates. This appears to be true, for the I.Q. and grades of entering college students is much higher than that of all high school graduates. There is probably an even greater difference in the indirect or external returns from college since persons of superior ability are usually required in the development of important ideas and inventions. Therefore, the total rate of return from college would seem to be positively correlated with I.Q.

There is considerable variation in the return to college and high school graduates of the same I.Q. or grades. It might be that most of the persons with high I.Q. or grades who do not go to college correctly anticipate a lower return from college than received by those who do go. If so, an increase in the number of high I.Q. or grade persons going to college might reduce the average return from college, even though there was a positive (but less than perfect) correlation between I.Q. or grades and returns. Both empirical and theoretical evidence indicate, however, that many of them do not go for reasons largely unrelated to the return that would be received. Most come from low-income and low-education families, and it is difficult to believe that their return from college would be so much lower than the return to equally "able" persons from wealthier and more educated families. Theoretical arguments support this conclusion. Economists have long stressed that imperfections in the capital market limit the amount invested in human beings through education and other kinds of training. These imperfections clearly would be most effective in low-income families and would help explain why a disproportionately large number of the able persons without a college education come from low-income families. Moreover, for economic and other reasons, college students are usually very young, in their late teens or early twenties, and young people tend to have relatively little knowledge of the economic opportunities available and of the returns to different investments. It is difficult to anticipate the return from college education because it has a large variance and accrues over a very long period; it is especially difficult for children from lower strata families since they are more ignorant of the returns to college education.[10]

It appears, therefore, that the average rate of return from a college education would be increased by an improvement in the quality of college students. How should this improvement be achieved? A full answer would take us way beyond the scope of this paper, but it is clear without much analysis that the appropriate policy would depend on why some able youngsters do not go to college. If imperfections in the capital market were primarily responsible, a policy designed to improve this market would be emphasized. If, on the other hand, ignorance about the returns from college were responsible, a policy designed to spread such information, especially among low-income families, would be emphasized.

## IV

Let me conclude by briefly summarizing the discussion. Several aspects of college education in the United States were examined in terms of their contribution to economic and military progress. The limited available evidence did not reveal any significant discrepancy between the direct returns to college education and business capital, and thus direct returns alone do not seem to justify increased college expenditures. This puts the burden on external or indirect returns since they would have to be important to justify increased expenditures. Unfortunately, very little is known about them; so a firm judgment about the extent of underinvestment in college education is not possible.

Many recent discussions have emphasized the external contributions of scientists to economic and military progress and have called for large increases in scientific personnel. Such an increase could be accomplished with a small increase in total college expenditures. A large increase in expenditures would be warranted only if external returns were produced by a much larger fraction of all college graduates.

A sizable fraction of all persons with high I.Q.'s or grades do not go to college after graduating from high school. It appears that an increase in the fraction of able persons going to college would raise the average return from college. An improvement in the quality of college students may well be an effective way to raise the contribution of college education to progress.

# Education
# and
# Income

*I*n this selection H. S. Houthakker of Harvard University, who has
also served as a member of the Council of Economic Advisers,
*presents one of the earlier analyses of the association of income and*
*educational attainment level by age group. After discussing some of the*
*arguments for and against discounting future income streams,*
*Houthakker shows the capital value of lifetime income at age 14 before*
*and after taxes using discount rates of 3, 6, and 8 percent. Some of*
*the common limitations of this approach are noted, including multi-*

Reprinted from H. S. Houthakker, "Education and Income," *Review of Economics and Statistics* 41 (February 1959), pp. 24–28, with permission of the author
and publisher.

Notes to this essay will be found on pages 282–284

*collinearity in independent variables. Although the observed income differentials do rise with additional education, Houthakker notes that we do not know the extent to which education as opposed to parental wealth or native ability, for example, is responsible for the positive association between education and income. In short, the additional income associated with increments of schooling may be subject to an upward bias of unknown magnitude for this reason.*

In the current debate on the financing of education, estimates of the money benefits which school attendance confers on ex-students are occasionally invoked. In an effort to shed some further light on this subject, this note presents some crude and limited calculations on the relation between education and income.

The approach to the estimation of life-time income chosen here is the so-called "cross-sectional" one, which involves the analysis of incomes received by people of different ages and educational histories during a single year. Relevant data are available from the 1950 Census of Population,[1] which tabulates total money incomes received in 1949 by a 3⅓ percent sample of the population aged 14 and over. Only males, irrespective of color, are considered in this paper.[1a]

The principal difficulty raised by this source of information[2] is that mean incomes are not stated; the table only gives the frequency distribution and the median for each education-age group. The median is clearly not the appropriate type of average for the present purpose; since the distributions are all positively skew, it is uniformly less than the (estimated) mean. Moreover the ratio of mean to median is larger at higher levels of education, indicating that the distribution is more unequal there than at lower levels. Hence a calculation based on medians would not even give the right *proportions* between life-time incomes for varying school attendance.

It was consequently necessary to estimate the mean incomes. For every income group (irrespective of age and education) a representative income was selected by inspection of the income distribution.[3] The figures used were as follows:

| INCOME RANGE | REPRESENTATIVE INCOME |
|---|---|
| $   1–  499 | $   400 |
| 500–  999 | 900 |
| 1,000–1,499 | 1,400 |
| 1,500–1,999 | 1,800 |
| 2,000–2,499 | 2,300 |
| 2,500–2,999 | 2,800 |
| 3,000–3,999 | 3,500 |
| 4,000–4,999 | 4,400 |
| 5,000–5,999 | 5,400 |
| 6,000–6,999 | 6,300 |
| 7,000–9,999 | 8,000 |
| 10,000–over | 22,000 |

The figure for the top group requires some explanation. It refers to an open-ended interval for which no information other than the *number* of incomes was collected. As is customary in these circumstances, it was assumed that the distribution of high incomes was of the Pareto type, an assumption for which the known points in the right-hand tail provided some support. The Pareto constant was estimated at about 1.9, from which the mean of $22,000 for incomes over $10,000 follows by a well-known formula.[4]

By applying these representative incomes to the number of persons in each income-age-education group the mean income before tax for all age-education groups was estimated.[5] The results are given in Table 1. Some of the figures, particularly those in the top right hand corner, are based on so few observations that they should not be taken too literally. There were, for instance, only 85 college graduates for whom income was reported in the 18–19 years age bracket, and only 107 high school graduates in the 14–15 years bracket.

In order to provide some insight into the variability of income within each cell, Table 1 also includes coefficients of variation (defined as the standard deviation divided by the estimated mean income). Actually the coefficient of variation is by no means an ideal measure for this purpose because the distribution within each cell has a rather unusual shape.[6] Thus in the younger and older age brackets the large number of zero incomes makes the distribution bimodal, resulting in a very large coefficient of variation. A better measure of variability is hard to find, however. It will be observed that the coefficient of variation for each education group falls off rather sharply with age, and then rises more slowly. The minimum appears to be reached at an earlier age in the lower education groups. Although the variability is relatively greater for high education groups at early ages, these groups show less variability in the highest age groups.

Table 2 shows income after tax. Only federal income taxes were taken into account. For each age-education-income group the representative income was multiplied by the tax rate, estimated as the ratio between "tax liability" and "adjusted gross income" in the appropriate bracket.[7] As in the case of income before tax, the figures were then weighted by the number of persons in each income group.

The after-tax incomes are plotted in Chart 1, from which it

### CHART 1
### Mean Income After Tax
### by Age and Years of School Completed

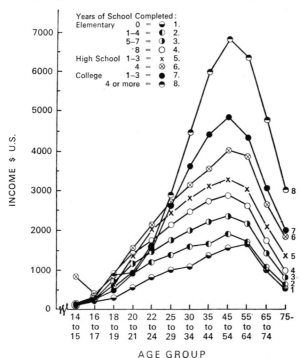

**Table 1  Mean Income Before Tax by Age and Years of School Completed[a]**
(Coefficients of variation in parentheses)

| Age | Elementary | | | | High School | | College | |
|---|---|---|---|---|---|---|---|---|
| | 0 | 1–4 | 5–7 | 8 | 1–3 | 4 | 1–3 | 4 or more |
| 14–15 | $112 (3.81) | $127 (2.65) | $ 90 (3.61) | $121 (3.74) | $129 (4.22) | $809 (1.65) | | |
| 16–17 | 251 (1.87) | 314 (1.70) | 280 (1.98) | 289 (1.95) | 231 (2.20) | 382 (2.08) | $361 (1.84) | |
| 18–19 | 377 (1.39) | 633 (1.07) | 760 (1.08) | 907 (1.12) | 701 (1.20) | 817 (1.02) | 540 (1.36) | $887 (1.07) |
| 20–21 | 638 (1.32) | 935 (1.01) | 1147 (.84) | 1512 (.67) | 1543 (.78) | 1639 (.74) | 900 (1.32) | 956 (1.72) |
| 22–24 | 809 (1.14) | 1192 (.81) | 1511 (.80) | 1868 (.69) | 2136 (.63) | 2285 (.64) | 1653 (.97) | 1763 (1.01) |
| 25–29 | 1042 (1.34) | 1474 (.92) | 1847 (.72) | 2292 (.65) | 2597 (.58) | 2934 (.64) | 2861 (.81) | 3135 (.90) |
| 30–34 | 1126 (.94) | 1667 (.87) | 2122 (.72) | 2646 (.69) | 2990 (.62) | 3465 (.58) | 4011 (.80) | 5042 (.88) |
| 35–44 | 1450 (1.14) | 1814 (.93) | 2405 (.82) | 2964 (.77) | 3385 (.77) | 3987 (.84) | 4972 (.92) | 7122 (.89) |
| 45–54 | 1671 (1.07) | 2007 (1.05) | 2534 (.95) | 3156 (.89) | 3640 (.96) | 4594 (.99) | 5609 (1.01) | 8225 (.89) |
| 55–64 | 1780 (1.12) | 1911 (1.10) | 2336 (1.03) | 2871 (1.02) | 3349 (1.07) | 4375 (1.11) | 5070 (1.12) | 7655 (.97) |
| 65–74 | 1095 (1.51) | 1205 (1.51) | 1555 (1.63) | 1891 (1.34) | 2348 (1.41) | 3029 (1.39) | 3514 (1.38) | 5660 (1.20) |
| 75– | 608 (2.08) | 712 (1.84) | 888 (1.99) | 1078 (1.96) | 1506 (1.91) | 2021 (1.96) | 2259 (1.81) | 3531 (1.64) |

[a] Based on 3½% sample from total U.S. male population, Income in 1949.

## Table 2  Mean Income After Tax by Age and Years of School Completed[a]

| Age | Elementary | | | | High School | | College | |
|---|---|---|---|---|---|---|---|---|
| | 0 | 1–4 | 5–7 | 8 | 1–3 | 4 | 1–3 | 4 or more |
| 14–15 | $107 | $125 | $89 | $119 | $125 | $769 | | |
| 16–17 | 247 | 309 | 275 | 283 | 227 | 371 | $352 | |
| 18–19 | 366 | 619 | 737 | 876 | 680 | 793 | 528 | $855 |
| 20–21 | 619 | 904 | 1106 | 1452 | 1474 | 1564 | 860 | 904 |
| 22–24 | 782 | 1149 | 1445 | 1776 | 2024 | 2158 | 1567 | 1663 |
| 25–29 | 904 | 1406 | 1756 | 2164 | 2443 | 2745 | 2655 | 2878 |
| 30–34 | 1082 | 1585 | 2005 | 2478 | 2790 | 3202 | 3642 | 4461 |
| 35–44 | 1374 | 1714 | 2191 | 2750 | 3115 | 3614 | 4390 | 6044 |
| 45–54 | 1575 | 1878 | 2351 | 2899 | 3296 | 4062 | 4842 | 6835 |
| 55–64 | 1670 | 1789 | 2170 | 2633 | 3027 | 3844 | 4374 | 6360 |
| 65–74 | 1037 | 1137 | 1455 | 1751 | 2132 | 2692 | 3080 | 4757 |
| 75– | 583 | 682 | 837 | 1004 | 1373 | 1784 | 1996 | 3001 |

[a] Based on $3\frac{1}{2}$% sample from total U.S. male population. Income and federal tax rate in 1949.

will be noticed that on the whole a longer school attendance is positively correlated with higher mean income, except for the age groups below 30. As discussed below, this cannot necessarily be interpreted as a causal relation. In all education groups annual income rises with age until a maximum is reached in the 45–54 age groups, though not until the 55–64 group for those who never attended school. After that the peak mean income falls off first slowly, then rather sharply.

These figures gain in interest when they are summed over all ages, starting at the lowest age for which incomes are reported (14 years).[8] In order to give proper weights to the different ages, the chance of survival according to the mortality experience of 1949–51[9] was taken into account. Thus the weights refer to a hypothetical population whose age-composition was determined by the mortality after age 14 in those three years, whereas the actual composition of the 1949 population was of course the result of natality, mortality, and international migration during the preceding century.

Capitalization of a stream of income inevitably raises the question of discounting. I have no final opinion on this matter, and will confine myself to a statement of the arguments *pro* and *contra*, and a calculation based on some of the alternatives.

In favor of discounting are the obvious considerations that expenditure on education is an investment not fundamentally different from other investments, and that from a private point of view the cost of borrowing, and from a social point of view the return in alternative uses, should be taken into account. These considerations are not too helpful, however, in determining what rate of interest to use. The cost of borrowing for educational expenses is probably either very low (for those with access to the more or less charitable funds established for that purpose) or very, even prohibitively, high (for those without such access and without suitable collateral). The rate of return in alternative uses is also far from uniform, depending as it does on the degree of riskiness and on imperfections of the capital market.

Arguments against using a discount rate are that some discounting is already implicit in the adjustment for survival, and that in a growing economy every individual may expect an upward trend in his own earnings superimposed on the cross-sectional pattern for a particular year. Perhaps neither of these two factors is sufficient in magnitude to make discounting unnecessary, but the reader who feels that they are has only to consult the first column of Table 3.

That table gives the capital value at age 14 of life-time income, both before and after tax, for four different rates of interest. As one would expect, the capital values are very sensitive to the discount rate used, so that the figures in every column are much smaller than the corresponding figures in the column to the left. Moreover the proportionate reduction is the more considerable, the higher the level of education, in accordance with the previously noted fact that the income advantage of the better-educated does not apply to their early years. Taxes are also more important, absolutely and relatively, at higher levels of education.

Even so the capital values increase uniformly with level of schooling for all discount rates considered. In other words, the increment in capital value associated with each successive level of education is nearly always positive. The only exception is in the "College, 1–3 years" group, which at eight percent discount (and also, after tax, at six percent) has a lower capital value than the "High School, 4 years" group. Hence it may not be true, in the case of higher learning, that it is better to have loved and lost than never to have loved at all.

Many other conclusions may be drawn from Table 3, but they need not be spelled out here. Instead some remarks about the limitations of this type of analysis are in order. That the results are subject to the validity of the data and methods used hardly needs saying, though it may be worth repeating that the calculations are based entirely on 1949 patterns of income, school attendance, and mortality. What is perhaps more important is that Table 3, in particular, does not justify any immediate inferences concerning the money benefits attributable specifically to education as such, as distinct from the other factors that influence a man's income.

This point (recognized also by Glick and Miller) may be

## Table 3 Capital Value at Age 14 of Life-Time Income by Years of School Completed

| Discount rate (percent) | Before Tax | | | | After Tax | | | |
|---|---|---|---|---|---|---|---|---|
| | 0 | 3 | 6 | 8 | 0 | 3 | 6 | 8 |
| **Years of school completed:** | | | | | | | | |
| **Elementary:** | | | | | | | | |
| 0 | $64,132 | $26,220 | $13,014 | $8,896 | $60,785 | $24,944 | $12,428 | $8,515 |
| 1–4 | 79,386 | 33,939 | 17,492 | 12,179 | 75,021 | 32,189 | 16,638 | 11,730 |
| 5–7 | 100,430 | 42,758 | 21,834 | 15,098 | 93,571 | 40,006 | 20,537 | 14,252 |
| 8 | 124,105 | 52,923 | 27,037 | 18,700 | 115,277 | 49,425 | 25,380 | 17,592 |
| **High School:** | | | | | | | | |
| 1–3 | 142,522 | 59,734 | 30,008 | 20,514 | 130,933 | 55,260 | 27,945 | 19,188 |
| 4 | 175,160 | 72,475 | 36,328 | 24,990 | 157,940 | 66,055 | 33,466 | 23,149 |
| **College:** | | | | | | | | |
| 1–3 | 198,268 | 78,138 | 36,547 | 23,793 | 175,206 | 69,651 | 32,912 | 22,400 |
| 4 or more | 280,989 | 106,269 | 47,546 | 30,085 | 238,761 | 91,335 | 41,432 | 26,454 |

illustrated from the figure of $100,000 often alleged to be the money value of a college education. This figure is presumably derived from Glick and Miller[10]...whose numerical results are similar to those in my Table 3, for zero discount rate, before tax. Granting even that interest and taxes may be ignored, it is still not true that an individual chosen at random could increase his life-time income by $100,000 by completing 4 years of college plus a small amount of graduate work,[11] rather than stopping at high school. The reason is that those who had completed four or more years of college probably differ in at least two other respects from the population mean: they are likely to have a greater native or acquired intelligence (acquired, that is, prior to entering college), and come from families with higher incomes. Both these factors increase the chance of entering and completing college; both also increase the expected lifetime income in the absence of a college education. This is particularly true for the second factor, if only because a prosperous family background will normally lead to the inheritance of property income.

The implication is that the differences between successive rows in Table 3 systematically *overstate* the specific effects of education on income: the bias is all one-way. Indeed we cannot even be sure that the apparent effect of education on income is not completely explicable in terms of intelligence and parents' income, so that the *specific* effect of education would be zero or even negative. The evidence which could settle this point is not available; off-hand I would hardly expect the extreme possibility just mentioned to be realized. On the other hand the popular figure of $100,000 for the average value of a college education can only be regarded as an upper bound, from which little or nothing can be inferred concerning such questions as the proper level of college tuition.

# W. LEE HANSEN

# Total and Private
## Rates of Return to
### Investment in Schooling

*A*  *mong studies of the rate of return to investment in schooling,*
*W. Lee Hansen's article represents a methodological classic on*
*estimation of internal rates of return. Professor Hansen of the Univer-*
*sity of Wisconsin computes returns to total and private resource costs*
*and also makes a distinction between before-tax and after-tax monetary*
*returns. The distortion effects of taxable returns and public subsidies to*
*education are recognized in this analysis which also derives marginal*

Reprinted from W. Lee Hansen, "Total and Private Rates of Return to Investment in Schooling," *Journal of Political Economy* 71 (April 1963), pp. 128–40,
with permission of the author and the publisher. Copyright 1963 by the University
of Chicago.

Notes to this essay will be found on pages 284–286.

*rates of return. In addition to revealing that the internal rate of return to investment in education tends to peak near the completion of high school, Hansen draws comparisons between the rate of return and competing analytical approaches. The implications of private rates of return exceeding public rates and variations in rates of return by increment of schooling are explored. Hansen concludes that further research is needed in many areas, including comparison of expenditures on formal schooling and other human capital investments.*

The costs of schooling and the money returns resulting from investment in schooling are currently receiving more and more attention by economists, not only because of their possible implications for economic growth, but also because they may help individuals to determine how much they should invest in the development of their own human capital. This note provides some further evidence on these two topics; it presents estimates of internal rates of return based on both total and private resource costs for various amounts of schooling, from elementary school through college.

The fragmentary treatment of both the costs of schooling and the money returns to schooling found in much of the recent literature provided the stimulus for preparing these internal rate-of-return estimates. For example, Miller calculates life-time income values by level of schooling,[1] Houthakker estimates, on the basis of alternative discount rates, the present value of income streams associated with different levels of schooling,[2] Schultz provides estimates of total resource costs of education by broad level of schooling,[3] and Becker and Schultz calculate for several levels of education the expected rates of return, sometimes on a total resource cost basis and at other times on a private resource cost basis.[4] Given this diversity of treatment, it is difficult to obtain an over-all picture of the relationship among rates of return to different amounts of schooling or to see the nature of the differences between the rates of return as viewed by society and those viewed by individuals. Moreover, the relationship among the various methods of contrasting the economic gains from education—the lifetime income, the present value, and the rate of return comparisons—has been obscured.

It becomes important to understand what some of these relationships are when society and individuals allocate such a large portion of their resources to schooling. At the societal level, for example, we might be interested in determining whether to allocate more funds to reduce the number of dropouts from high school or to stimulate an increased flow of college graduates. As individuals, we would more likely be concerned with deciding whether to continue or to terminate our schooling, on the basis of the relative costs that will be incurred and the benefits that will accrue. To this end, the comprehensive sets of internal rates of return developed here should be useful as a first approximation in seeking answers to questions of this kind.

At the outset, it should be made clear that the measured rates of return are money rates of return; any other costs and benefits associated with schooling are excluded from consideration. In addition, there are problems of measurement, many of which have not been resolved, that make the estimation of even direct money rates of return difficult. Some of these difficulties are discussed in Part I, which outlines the methods and data employed. Part II presents evidence on rates of return to total and to private resource investment in schooling. Part III contrasts three different methods of measuring the economic gains to schooling, while Part IV offers some concluding comments.

## I. ESTIMATION PROCEDURES

To estimate internal rates of return to investments in schooling, we require data on costs—total resource costs and private resource costs—for various levels of schooling as well as data on age-income patterns by each level of schooling. From these, life-cycle cost-income streams can be established that show for each level of schooling the flows of costs incurred during schooling and the subsequent flows of additional income that can be attributed to that schooling. The internal rate of return is then estimated by finding that rate of discount that equates the present value of the cost outlays with the present value of the additional income flows.

The basic source of income data is the *1950 Census of Population*,[5] which provides distributions of income for males by age and level of schooling in 1949. From these, average income figures can be calculated for each age-schooling category, as shown in Table 1. Although Houthakker had previously presented such figures, his method of estimation produces a rather peculiar bias.[6] In addition, Houthakker's data show mean incomes of all males over age fourteen, whether they were receiving income or not. But to the extent that only income recipients are represented in the data shown here in Table 1, most of the males outside the labor force, either because of school attendance (younger males) or retirement (older males), are probably excluded. Exclusion of these groups seems likely to provide better estimates of the age-income profiles, particularly at their extremities.

In order to make the task of estimating the rates of return more manageable, the age-income profiles were assumed to commence at the "average" age of completion of each level of schooling.[7] For those with one to four years of schooling, the average amount of school completed was taken as two years; hence the age-income profile for this group was assumed to begin at age eight. For the next group, those with five to seven years of school, six years of schooling were assumed, so that its age-income profile begins at age twelve. The other level of education groups and the ages at which their age-income profiles were assumed to begin are as follows: eight years, age fourteen; one to three years of high school, age sixteen; four years of high school, age eighteen; one to three years of college, age twenty; and four years of college, age twenty-two. In fact, however, for age groups under fourteen the age-income profiles take values of zero, because no income data are collected for these groups.[8]

Two major cost variants are used in the calculations—one for total resource costs and the other for private resource costs. The rationale and procedures for estimating total resource costs have been set forth by Schultz.[9] Total resource costs include (1) school costs

## Table 1  Average Income by Age and Years of School Completed, Males, United States, 1949

| Age | Elementary | | | | | High School | | | College | |
|---|---|---|---|---|---|---|---|---|---|---|
| | 0 | 1–4 | 5–7 | 8 | | 1–3 | 4 | | 1–3 | 4 or more |
| 14–15 | $610 | $350 | $365 | $406 | | | | | | |
| 16–17 | 526 | 472 | 514 | 534 | | | | | | |
| 18–19 | 684 | 713 | 885 | 1,069 | | $429 | | | | |
| 20–21 | 944 | 1,009 | 1,216 | 1,535 | | 941 | $955 | | | |
| 22–24 | 1,093 | 1,227 | 1,562 | 1,931 | | 1,652 | 1,744 | | $1,066 | $1,926 |
| 25–34 | 1,337 | 1,603 | 2,027 | 2,540 | | 2,191 | 2,363 | | 1,784 | 4,122 |
| 35–44 | 1,605 | 1,842 | 2,457 | 3,029 | | 2,837 | 3,246 | | 3,444 | 7,085 |
| 45–54 | 1,812 | 2,073 | 2,650 | 3,247 | | 3,449 | 4,055 | | 5,014 | 8,116 |
| 55–64 | 2,000 | 2,045 | 2,478 | 3,010 | | 3,725 | 4,689 | | 5,639 | 7,655 |
| 65 or more | 1,140 | 1,189 | 1,560 | 1,898 | | 3,496 | 4,548 | | 5,162 | 5,421 |
| | | | | | | 2,379 | 3,155 | | 3,435 | |

**Source** See nn. 5 and 6.

incurred by society, that is, teachers' salaries, supplies, interest and depreciation on capital, (2) opportunity costs incurred by individuals, namely, income foregone during school attendance, and (3) incidental school-related costs incurred by individuals, for example, books and travel. Private resource costs include the same three components except that in (1) above, tuition and fees paid by individuals are substituted for society's costs which are normally defrayed through taxation.

In developing the cost figures used in these estimates, whether on a total or a private resource basis, the opportunity costs were taken directly from the age-income profiles of the alternative level of schooling being used in the calculations. For example, at age eighteen the opportunity cost for the person undertaking four years of college is the income that the high-school graduate would obtain from ages eighteen to twenty-one. This procedure made it unnecessary to rely upon indirectly estimated opportunity cost figures and yielded at the same time a more detailed set of opportunity costs by age and level of schooling.[10] In completing the estimates of per student total resource cost, school costs paid by society and school-related expenditures incurred by individuals were derived from Schultz's results.[11] In completing the estimates of private resource costs, the amount of tuition and fees paid per student was obtained from already available estimates.[12] Again, the school-related costs from Schultz's work were used. While the latter costs have an arbitrary quality to them, they seem to be reasonable.[13] The cost figures, exclusive of opportunity costs, by age and grade are summarized in Table 2.

Lifetime cost-income streams were then constructed for each level of schooling with the help of the appropriate age-income profiles and the age-cost estimates. This was done by taking the difference between the cost-income profile for a given level of schooling and the income profile for the particular base level of schooling used in the comparison. For example, in the case of investment in four years of college, the income profile for the base group, high-school graduates, begins at age eighteen. The cost-income profile for the person who completes four years of college also begins at age eighteen; during the four years to age twenty-one it reflects both school and school-

## Table 2 Average Annual Per Student Costs, Exclusive of Opportunity Costs, by Age and Grade, United States, 1949[a]

| Age | School Level (1) | Total Resource Costs | | | Private Resource Costs | | |
|-----|------------------|---------------------|---|---|------------------------|---|---|
| | | School Costs (2) | Other Costs (3) | Total (4) | Tuition and Fees (5) | Other Costs (6) | Total (7) |
| 6–13 | Elementary | $201 | | $201 | | | |
| 14–17 | High School | 354 | 31 | 385 | | 31 | 31 |
| 18–21 | College | 801 | 142 | 943 | 245 | 142 | 387 |

[a] Though these cost data are indicated as being for 1950 in Schultz, "Capital Formation by Education," *op. cit.*, they actually apply to the 1949–50 school year. Thus these data may overstate somewhat the costs of schooling relative to the income derived from that schooling.

**Source** col. (2), *elementary school:* Schultz, "Capital Formation by Education," *op. cit.*, Table 3, col. (11). 1950 figure divided by number of elementary-school students in 1950, from *Statistical Abstract*, 1955, Table 152; *high school:* Schultz, "Capital Formation by Education," *op. cit.*, Table 5, 1950, col. (4) divided by col. (1); *college: ibid.*, Table 6, 1950, col. (4) divided by col. (1).

Col. (3), *elementary school:* assumed to be zero; *high school: ibid.*, Table 5, 1950, col. (5) divided by col. (1); *college: ibid.*, Table 6, 1950, col. (4) divided by col. (1).

Col. (4), sum of cols. (2) and (3).

Col. (5), *elementary school and high school:* assumed to be zero; *college:* based on average tuition and fee charges, derived from *Biennial Survey of Education, 1955–56*, chaps. i and iv, after adjusting veteran charges for non-tuition items (see n. 12).

Col. (6), same as col. (3).

Col. (7), sum of cols. (5) and (6).

related costs and thereafter the somewhat higher income profile of the college graduate. The cost-income stream, the *difference* between these two profiles, reflects at ages eighteen to twenty-one both school and school-related costs as well as opportunity costs; at ages beyond twenty-one the difference reflects the net income stream resulting from four years of college. An additional adjustment is required to reflect the incidence of mortality; this involves adjusting the net cost-income stream downward to reflect the probabilities that at each age the costs or returns will not be incurred or received, respectively.[14] Finally, the internal rates of return must be estimated by finding that rate of discount which sets the present value of the cost stream equal to the present value of the net return stream.

When considering private rates of return, it is important to show them on both a before- and after-tax basis. Not only will all rates of return be lower after tax, but also the relative declines in the rates will differ, given the progressivity of tax rates and the positive association between income and educational levels. The differences among the before-tax and after-tax rates could be of considerable importance to individuals in the determination of their own investment planning.

To estimate the after-tax incomes and rates of return, the original income data in Table 1 were adjusted for federal income tax payments; while it probably would have been desirable to adjust for all types of taxes, this could not be done in view of the paucity of data. Subsequently, the rates of return were calculated in the same way as described for the before-tax data. The actual after-tax income figures were obtained by multiplying each income figure by the appropriate ratio of after- to before-tax income, derived from Houthakker.[15] These ratios prove to be almost identical to those that would have resulted had the marginal tax rates been applied to the distributions of income recipients in calculating after-tax income.[16]

As in most empirical studies the available data prove to be somewhat unlike those that we require, and so the rate of return estimates do not provide a full picture of the profitability of schooling.[17] Therefore, several features of the data and the nature of their effects on age-income profiles, and hence on rates of return, deserve mention before the results are discussed. First, since only income rather than earnings data are available, the income profiles used reflect in part receipts from other assets. On the assumption that the relative income from other assets is a positive function of the level of earnings itself, the impact of this would presumably be to raise the age-income profiles of the higher level of schooling groups. Second, certain problems of "mix" exist within the data. For example, among those with little schooling there may be heavy concentrations of certain minority groups, such as Negroes and Puerto Ricans. If they are effectively discriminated against, then the age-income profiles of the lower level of schooling groups would be depressed below their expected level. On the other hand, at higher levels of schooling the age-income profiles may be raised somewhat by reverse discrimination that favors sons, relatives, and others of higher social-economic status. Third, since those people who complete more schooling ordinarily possess greater intelligence, as measured by intelligence scores, some part of the differential income received might have accrued to them anyway. Although our present knowledge makes it difficult to separate the impact of intelligence and schooling, the observed income differences among the lower and higher levels of schooling undoubtedly overstate, and by increasing amounts, the differentials attributable to schooling.[18] Fourth, all cost elements were considered as investment even though some portions might better be regarded as consumption. To the extent that any of the cost is considered as consumption, the investment costs are overstated.[19] Fifth, all estimates rest on cross-section cost-income relationships and thereby ignore future shifts in the relationships of the cost-income streams. And, finally, any number of other factors may impinge on the observed income differentials, in the form of education at home, on-the-job-training, and so forth.

While some would suggest that the presence of such problems seriously limits any conclusions concerning the empirical relationships between income and schooling, it nevertheless seems worthwhile to set forth the rate of return estimates in their crude form.[20] From them some preliminary conclusions about resource allocation can be drawn.

## II. INTERNAL RATE OF RETURN ESTIMATES

### The Return to Total Resource Investment

Internal rates of return to total resource investment in schooling appear in Table 3. The boxed figures in the diagonal to the right show the rates of return to each successive increment of schooling and can be interpreted as "marginal" rates of return. For example, the rate of return to the first two years of elementary school is 8.9 percent, to the next four years of elementary school 14.5 percent, and so on to the last two years of college 15.6 percent. Although the marginals provide all of the necessary information, average rates of return to successively more years of schooling can be derived from the marginals; since the average rates are of some interest, they are also shown in the columns. For example, in column (1) we see that at age six the expected rate of return to investment in two years of elementary schooling is 8.9 percent; the rate of return to investment in six years of elementary schooling (the weighted average of the two marginals) is 12.0 percent, and so on to the investment in sixteen years of schooling, which yields a 21.1 percent rate of return.

Several features of the configuration of rates of return deserve comment. First, the marginal rates rise over the first few years of schooling, reaching a peak with the completion of elementary schooling. This clearly suggests that rapidly increasing returns to schooling prevail over the early years and that a small initial amount of schooling, the first two years, has relatively little impact on earning power. Second, the trend in the rates is downward thereafter, though it is not smooth by any means. While the rate of return to the first two years of high school drops dramatically, it rises somewhat with the completion of high school. The rate drops once again for the first two years of college, and it then displays a significant rise with the completion of four years of college. At this point one can only speculate as to the reasons underlying these declines.

Evidence such as this on the marginal or incremental rates of return is ordinarily used in discussing resource allocation. If on the basis of these rates of return a given amount of resources were to be

## Table 3 Internal Rates of Return to Total Resource Investment in Schooling, United States, Males, 1949[a]

| To: | | From: (1) | (2) | (3) | (4) | (5) | (6) | (7) |
|---|---|---|---|---|---|---|---|---|
| | Age → | 6 | 8 | 12 | 14 | 16 | 18 | 20 |
| | Grade → | 1 | 3 | 7 | 9 | 11 | 13 | 15 |
| | Age / Grade | | | | | | | |
| (1) | 7 / 2 | 8.9 | | | | | | |
| (2) | 11 / 6 | 12.0 | 14.5 | | | | | |
| (3) | 13 / 8 | 15.0 | 18.5 | 29.2 | | | | |
| (4) | 15 / 10 | 13.7 | 15.9 | 16.3 | 9.5 | | | |
| (5) | 17 / 12 | 13.6 | 15.4 | 15.3 | 11.4 | 13.7 | | |
| (6) | 19 / 14 | 11.3 | 12.1 | 11.1 | 8.2 | 8.2 | 5.4 | |
| (7) | 21 / 16 | 12.1 | 12.7 | 12.1 | 10.5 | 10.9 | 10.2 | 15.6 |

[a] All rate-of-return figures are subject to some error, since the estimation to one decimal place was made by interpolation between whole percentage figures.

spent on schooling, the ranking of the marginals from high to low is as shown in Table 3. Grades 7–8, 15–16, 3–6, 11–12, 9–10, 0–2, and 13–14.[21] At an alternative rate of return to society of, say, 10 percent, investment in all grade levels except the last three would be justified. Were the alternative rate, say, 7 percent, only the last level would be excluded.

Viewing the matter in this fashion would be quite satisfactory if the rates of return declined steadily as we moved to successively higher increments of schooling, but because the marginal rates fluctuate some averaging is required. If we look at marginal rates for broader increments of schooling, for example, eight years of elementary school, four years of high school, and four years of college, then the rates of return to additional investment quite clearly decline, as shown by the respective figures: 15.0 percent (col. [1], row [3]), 11.4 percent (col. [4], row [5]), and 10 .2 percent (col. [6], row [7]). At an alternative rate of return of 10 percent, investment in all levels of schooling becomes profitable. But were the original rates considered independently of each other and an alternative rate of return of 10 percent prevailed, it would not pay to permit any new enrollments, the schooling of those people in elementary school would be terminated at Grade 8, and of those people already in high school and college, only students in their last two years of each would be allowed to graduate. To allocate investment in schooling this way would obviously reflect a very short-run view of the implied economic opportunities.

However, it might be desirable to consider some longer time horizon instead, particularly if the alternative rate of return were expected to remain reasonably constant over time. Given an alternative rate of return of, say, 10 percent, investment through the completion of college could easily be justified for each age group currently enrolled, since every rate of return figure in the bottom row (row [7]) of Table 3 exceeds 10 percent. Understandably, this result is no different than that obtained earlier.

On the basis of even longer-run considerations only the rate of return to investment in the schooling of new school entrants may be relevant, especially if schooling is thought of as a good to be purchased in large, indivisible quantities, for example, schooling from

Grade 1 through college, or schooling from Grade 1 through high school. In this case the rates of return shown in column (1) indicate yields of 13.6 and 12.1 percent, respectively, and suggest the obvious advantages of seeing to it that everyone completes college or high school, as the case may be. In fact, this averaging of the marginal rates makes such investment attractive at an alternative rate as high as 12 percent.

## The Return to Private Resource Investment

Internal rates of return to total resource costs of schooling are of undeniable importance in assessing the efficiency with which an economy's resources are allocated, but for individuals and/or their parents the relevant rates of return are those based upon private resource costs. These private rates of return both before and after tax are shown in Tables 4 and 5, respectively; the tables are to be read in the same fashion as Table 3.

For all levels of schooling under eight years, private rates of return have no real meaning (they are infinitely large) since opportunity costs are assumed to be zero, school-related costs are negligible, and tuition and fees are not charged. Above Grade 8, however, all private rates of return before tax are higher than the total rates of return shown in Table 3, with the greatest disparities appearing at the younger ages and lower levels of schooling, where individuals pay smaller proportions of total resource costs; private rates of return after tax are also higher than total rates of return with but two exceptions. Otherwise, the general configuration in both the columns and the diagonals appears to be about the same for both total and private rates, whether before or after tax, though the levels do differ.

When individuals and/or their parents plan an investment program in schooling, the private rates of return justify securing more schooling than do the rates of return on total resource investment. For example, the marginal rates of return to elementary, high-school, and college schooling are infinite (col. [1], row [3]), 15.3 percent (col. [4], row [5]), and 11.6 percent (col. [6], row [7]), respectively. Thus, investment in schooling through college is still profitable even if the private alternative rate is as high as 11.5 percent. But, on an after-tax basis, the alternative rate of 10 percent just permits private investment at the college level (Table 5, col. [6], row [7]).

When schooling is viewed in large blocks, a somewhat different picture emerges. If the decision-making age is fourteen and the objective is to complete schooling through college, the alternative rate of return would have to exceed 12.9 percent (col. [4], row [7]) on a before-tax basis and 11.5 percent on an after-tax basis for the investment to be unprofitable. If the decision-making age is six and the objective is to complete schooling through college, the alternative rate would have to exceed 18.2 percent (col. [1], row [7]) on a before-tax basis and 17.2 percent on an after-tax basis, for the investment to be unprofitable.

A comparison of the total rates of return with the private rates of return after tax is of interest in suggesting the extent to which distortions in the private rates caused by federal income taxes are offset by the counter-distortion of subsidized schooling. An examination of the results in Tables 3 and 5 indicates that even though income taxes do substantially reduce the levels of private rates of return, public subsidization of schooling makes the private rates of return net of tax considerably more attractive than the rate of return earned on total resource investment. Only two exceptions appear (col. [6]); these suggest that the student pays more than his own way in securing schooling at the college level. This might indicate the need for a re-study of the assessment of the costs of college against the individual, unless the possible underinvestment in college training that would be produced is regarded as acceptable in some broader sense. But these exceptions aside, the fact that private rates of return after taxes exceed the total rates of return would, in the absence of restraints on sources of private financing, probably give rise to overinvestment in schooling by individuals. However, a fuller treatment of the effects of other forms of taxation and methods of financing schooling would be required before any definitive judgment could be reached.

## Table 4  Internal Rates of Return to Private Resource Investment in Schooling, before Tax, United States, Males, 1949[a]

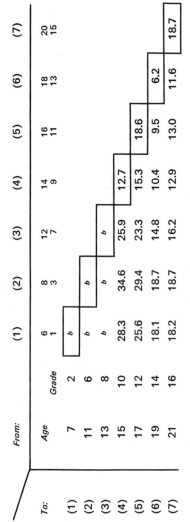

| From: | | | (1) | (2) | (3) | (4) | (5) | (6) | (7) |
|---|---|---|---|---|---|---|---|---|---|
| | Age | | 6 | 8 | 12 | 14 | 16 | 18 | 20 |
| | | Grade | 1 | 3 | 7 | 9 | 11 | 13 | 15 |
| To: | Age | Grade | | | | | | | |
| (1) | 7 | 2 | b | | | | | | |
| (2) | 11 | 6 | b | b | | | | | |
| (3) | 13 | 8 | b | b | b | | | | |
| (4) | 15 | 10 | 28.3 | 34.6 | 25.9 | 12.7 | | | |
| (5) | 17 | 12 | 25.6 | 29.4 | 23.3 | 15.3 | 18.6 | | |
| (6) | 19 | 14 | 18.1 | 18.7 | 14.8 | 10.4 | 9.5 | 6.2 | |
| (7) | 21 | 16 | 18.2 | 18.7 | 16.2 | 12.9 | 13.0 | 11.6 | 18.7 |

[a] All rate-of-return figures are subject to some error, since the estimation to one decimal place had to be made by interpolation between whole percentage figures.

[b] This indicates an infinite rate-of-return, given the assumption that education is costless to the individual to the completion of eighth grade.

## Table 5 Internal Rates of Return to Private Resource Investment in Schooling after Tax, United States, Males, 1949[a]

| To: | From: | | (1) | (2) | (3) | (4) | (5) | (6) | (7) |
|---|---|---|---|---|---|---|---|---|---|
| | Age | | 6 | 8 | 12 | 14 | 16 | 18 | 20 |
| | | Grade | 1 | 3 | 7 | 9 | 11 | 13 | 15 |
| (1) | 7 | 2 | b | | | | | | |
| (2) | 11 | 6 | b | b | | | | | |
| (3) | 13 | 8 | b | b | b | | | | |
| (4) | 15 | 10 | 27.9 | 33.0 | 24.8 | 12.3 | | | |
| (5) | 17 | 12 | 25.2 | 28.2 | 22.2 | 14.5 | 17.5 | | |
| (6) | 19 | 14 | 17.2 | 17.5 | 13.7 | 9.4 | 8.5 | 5.1 | |
| (7) | 21 | 16 | 17.2 | 17.3 | 14.4 | 11.5 | 11.4 | 10.1 | 16.7 |

[a] All rate-of-return figures are subject to some error, since the estimation to one decimal place had to be made by interpolation between whole percentage figures.

[b] This indicates an infinite rate of return, given the assumption of costless education to the individual through the completion of eighth grade.

## III. ALTERNATIVE MEASURES OF PRIVATE
## ECONOMIC RETURNS FROM SCHOOLING

The economic returns to individuals from schooling can be observed from three different points of view: (1) the value of lifetime income as set forth by Miller,[22] (2) the present value of lifetime income as set forth by Houthakker,[23] and (3) the rate of return on investment in schooling as set forth here. While the lifetime income and present value of lifetime income methods, particularly the former, are rather widely used, they are not relevant to ranking the direct economic returns to schooling when schooling is treated as a type of investment expenditure. Both of these methods completely ignore the costs of schooling, while the lifetime income approach suffers from the further defect of ignoring the time shape of the returns. Because the rankings of the economic returns differ so substantially, it seems desirable to present all three measures of the returns and to discuss them briefly. To make the comparisons more manageable, we shall deal only with the additional returns to different amounts of schooling as seen at age fourteen. The before- and after-tax results appear in the upper and lower halves, respectively, of Table 6.

The value of additional lifetime income associated with higher levels of schooling is frequently cited as a justification for investment in schooling by the individual. Clearly, the values of additional lifetime income resulting from successively greater amounts of schooling (col. [1]) indicate that more schooling pays substantially larger dollar returns than less schooling.[24] But, since a portion of the costs of schooling is excluded from consideration,[25] the full extent to which these returns offset the costs of schooling is not at all clear. Even more important, the fact that the time flows of these returns also differ remains hidden in the calculation of the lifetime income values. By virtue of these omissions, the impression emerges that any and all amounts of schooling are worth obtaining.

Another method of measuring the economic returns to schooling involves comparing the present values of additional lifetime income, at various discount rates, to successively greater amounts of schooling. The values, at discount rates of 3, 6, 8, and 10 percent

## Table 6   Alternative Methods of Comparing Value of Private Economic Returns to Investment in Schooling, as Viewed at Age Fourteen, United States, Males, 1949

| Schooling from Completion of Grade 8 to Completion of: | Additional Lifetime Income (1) | Present Value of Additional Income at: | | | | Internal Rate of Return (Percent) (6) |
|---|---|---|---|---|---|---|
| | | 3 Percent (2) | 6 Percent (3) | 8 Percent (4) | 10 Percent (5) | |
| | | *Before Tax* | | | | |
| 2 years high school | $16,802 | $7,756 | $2,301 | $1,190 | $545 | 12.7 |
| 4 years high school | 46,038 | 18,156 | 6,488 | 3,601 | 1,949 | 15.3 |
| 2 years college | 66,763 | 23,800 | 7,352 | 3,215 | 996 | 10.4 |
| 4 years college | 141,468 | 49,429 | 17,252 | 8,722 | 4,135 | 12.9 |
| | | *After Tax* | | | | |
| 2 years high school | $14,143 | $5,081 | $1,956 | $996 | $436 | 12.3 |
| 4 years high school | 38,287 | 13,580 | 5,362 | 2,929 | 1,547 | 14.5 |
| 2 years college | 52,485 | 17,000 | 5,364 | 2,084 | 336 | 9.4 |
| 4 years college | 109,993 | 36,575 | 12,824 | 6,170 | 2,611 | 11.5 |

appear in columns (2), (3), (4), and (5), respectively.[26] Again, schooling pays at any or all of the discount rates used, though the rankings do shift about as the discount rate is varied. For example, at 3 and 6 percent the rankings coincide with those shown by the value of additional lifetime income, but at an 8 percent discount rate schooling to the first two years of college becomes absolutely less attractive financially than schooling to high school, whether before or after tax. And at 10 percent discount rate the after-tax return to schooling to the first two years of college falls below that to the first two years of high school. Even though the present-value figures are quite sensitive to the discount rate used, once again all schooling pays. But the basic flaw in this method of calculation is the omission of some of the costs of education from the calculation; specifically the method fails to subtract the present value of the non-opportunity costs from the present value of the additional income. Doing so would undoubtedly cause some additional changes in the rankings, particularly at the higher discount rates.

Finally, the rate-of-return approach remedies the defects inherent in the other two methods. The relevant data on internal rates of return from Tables 4 and 5 (see Table 6, col. [6]), reveal a much different ranking of the returns to schooling. On a before-tax basis, investment in schooling to completion of high school, with a 15.3 rate of return, yields by far the most attractive return, followed by schooling to college with 12.9 percent, and schooling to the first two years of high school with 12.7 percent; schooling to the first two years of college, with a 10.4 percent return, lags far behind.

When we shift to rates of return on an after-tax basis, the rankings of the return on schooling to the completion of college and to the completion of the first two years of high school change. Since the marginal tax rates are a function of the amount of the income differential, the effect of the tax on the college rate of return is decidedly greater than its effect on the rate of return to the first two years of high school, for example. Given the fact that the original rates of return were almost identical, the after-tax return to completion of college now drops considerably below that to completion of two years of high school.

In conclusion, it appears that ranking of the returns to investment in schooling by the rate-of-return method is clearly superior to the methods employed in the work of both Miller and Houthakker. Whether the more general rate-of-return rule is in fact superior to the present-value rule (when properly used) still remains an unsettled issue that will not be discussed here.[27]

## IV. CONCLUSION

Estimates of the internal money rates of return to both total and private resource investment in schooling have been presented to provide a more complete picture of the costs of and returns to schooling. While the rates of return to private resource investment obviously exceed those to total resource investment, we find that the rates of return to the various increments of schooling also differ and have somewhat different implications for resource allocation at both the societal and individual level. Basically, the marginal rates of return rise with more schooling up to the completion of Grade 8 and then gradually fall off to the completion of college. We also find that private rates of return after tax almost invariably exceed the total rates of return, a situation that could presumably induce private overinvestment in schooling. Finally, the rate of return provides a superior method of ranking the economic returns to investment in schooling than do the more conventional additional lifetime income or present value of additional lifetime income methods currently used.

Thus, one might conclude that the high rates of return to investment in schooling go a long way toward explaining, or justifying, this society's traditional faith in education, as well as the desire of individuals to take advantage of as much schooling as they can. But clearly we need to know much more about the relationship between income and ability, the importance of on-the-job training, the significance of education in the home, and so forth. My own suspicion is that full adjustment for these factors would have the effect of reducing the relative rates of return, especially at the higher levels of schooling.

In addition, we have barely begun to consider the possible disparity between the rate of return to total resource investment and the "social" rate of return to investment in schooling that takes additional account of those returns that are produced indirectly. Intuition as well as the little evidence available suggests that these returns may be considerable, but a full accounting of the economic value of schooling will have to await further work.[28]

# WERNER Z. HIRSCH
# MORTON J. MARCUS

# Some Benefit-Cost Considerations of Universal Junior College Education

*P**rofessor Werner Z. Hirsch and Morton J. Marcus are, respectively, Professor of Economics and Director and Research Fellow, Institute of Government and Public Affairs of the University of California. Their concern is with the economics of universal education beyond the high-school level, an issue which may be decided in the 1970s. In addition to using economic measures of direct benefits and costs, external factors such as teen-age underemployment need to be considered in evaluating the policy implications of this question. The*

Reprinted from Werner Z. Hirsch and Morton J. Marcus, "Some Benefit-Cost Considerations of Universal Junior College Education," *National Tax Journal* 19 (March 1966), pp. 48–57, with permission of the authors and publisher.

Notes to this essay will be found on pages 286–289.

*framework of analysis used by Hirsch and Marcus allows derivation of
benefit-cost ratios—a method competitive with, but analogous to,
estimated internal rates of return. By varying their benefit-cost
assumptions, Hirsch and Marcus derive upper and lower limits to
benefit-cost ratios for investments in universal junior college training.
They carefully explain many of the unknowns that relate to the probing
question of the economics of investment in universal junior college
training.*

## INTRODUCTION

For two decades Presidential reports have urged the inclusion
of the thirteenth and fourteenth years of schooling in the nation's
education program. In 1964 the Educational Policies Commission
of the National Education Association of the United States and the
American Association of School Administrators proclaimed:

> *The nation's goal of universal educational opportunity must be ex-
> panded to include at least two further years of education, open to any
> high school graduate, and designed to move each student toward
> intellectual freedom.*[1]

The report recommended two additional years of tuition-free
liberal education, on the basis that "it is in the interest of the nation
that the abilities of each person be developed through education up
to this level."[2]

What are the gains and sacrifices of extending the schooling
period to cover the thirteenth and fourteenth years? This paper
attempts to elucidate this question and to offer some tentative
estimates of economic benefits and costs for such a program and its
alternatives.

## FRAMEWORK FOR ANALYSIS

Policy alternatives are best evaluated when a consistent
analytical method is applied. One such method is benefit-cost
analysis. In this paper we will evaluate mainly a universal junior

college program's anticipated consequences for society as a whole rather than its various groups, and compare it with alternatives. In the tradition of systems analysis we will not only compare proposed alternatives, but also attempt to develop new ones and evaluate them. Such an examination, when a long-term horizon is contemplated, involves uncertainties which should be treated explicitly and kept in mind when reading the results of this analysis.

In this paper, monetary benefit and cost dimensions will be presented in attempting a comparison between different proposals; however, some qualitative evaluation of certain aspects will be offered The nonquantifiable aspects often carry more weight than the monetary ones in decision-making. The quantitative part of the benefit-cost analysis may play a modest but hopefully significant role in determining the desirability of universal junior college education. It can at best be looked upon as a first approximation to be modified as better data and methods of analysis become available.

## Costs

The costs of public education are the resources of society drawn away from alternative uses. These costs can relate to operating or capital resources. In our analysis only the following items will be quantified:[3]

1. Direct operating costs, i.e., salaries and wages, and purchases of nondurable commodities and current services.
2. Capital resource costs, i.e., the value of the capital stock employed.
3. Imputed operating costs, i.e., foregone earnings and miscellaneous costs to students and their parents.

Salaries, wages and supplies, as well as annual capital costs require little elaboration. Less often considered are the major private sector costs of universal public junior college education: (1) earnings foregone by students, and (2) miscellaneous incidental costs to the students and their parents, necessitated by the former's college attendance. In the first case, students 18 to 20 years old could work full-time for an income that would exceed whatever they could earn part-time while in college. Whether or not they could find employment would depend upon their skills, the supply of such skills already on the market, and their demand in the economy. Clearly the overall employment picture of the economy has a strong bearing upon this cost element of universal junior college education.

Furthermore, students require particular goods and services because they are in college, e.g., books, assorted supplies, some clothing, and transportation. To the extent that these needs are not met by public expenditures, either the students themselves (through part-time employment) or their parents bear the resultant costs.

### Benefits

The benefits of education can be looked upon as the increased resources available to society, i.e., both those which contribute to society's economic well-being and those which are embodied in the educated person and permit him to participate in society more fully.

Foremost among education's tangible benefits is the students' incremental output. In a competitive economy the individual's incremental earnings represent the added social value generated by investment in his education. Education can alter the skill composition of the labor force and can speed up response to the economy's changing requirements. Thus, the incremental earnings will reflect not only the general employment picture of the economy, but also the sensitivity of the schools (and the students themselves) to both short- and long-term labor market conditions.

A second tangible benefit is the decline in demands for public services, resulting from a decrease in social and personal disorders which can be associated with inadequate schooling. The demand for police services arising from youthful delinquency may well decline if additional educational expenditures permit these youths to further their education and find jobs. But if school attendance merely diminishes the current delinquency threat, education expenditures are being substituted for protective services through disguised incarceration.

A third benefit area is that of education-induced increments in the social product of second parties. Children growing up in a home environment that encourages intellectual growth and expression may contribute more to society than those whose early training rejects such values. Co-workers of the educated students can be considered second-party beneficiaries when informal education (through association, emulation, imitation and encouragement) increases output.

Then there are long-run community and personal benefits. These are mainly intangible because their manifestations are complex, circuitous and hard to isolate. They include improvements in the operations of a democratic government, an advanced technologically-oriented economy, and an aesthetically enriched culture—all of which benefit all members of society. These benefits are major, but at present cannot be expressed in quantitative terms.

Finally, mention should be made of the employment effect of universal junior college education, that is, the job opportunities for others which arise when members of the labor force enter junior college on a full-time basis.

## SOME BENEFIT-COST ESTIMATES

An effort will be made next to quantify some benefits and costs of the universal junior college proposal and of several possible alternatives. We will assume that students are eighteen years old when they enter college on a full-time basis, in the semester following graduation from high school, and that they remain in college for two years.

### Two Years of Higher Education

As a first approximation consider the costs and benefits of two years of college for male and female students attending any of the nation's institutions of higher education in 1960 (Column 1,

## Table 1 Benefits and Costs of Two Years Higher Education for Males and Females, 1960

*(Present values at 5% discount rate)*

| | (1) | (2) Junior Colleges | (3) Junior Colleges | (4) | (5) |
|---|---|---|---|---|---|
| | All Institutions | Today's Students | Potential Students | Liberal Arts Colleges | Technical Institutes |
| **Male** | | | | | |
| Operating costs | $3,058 | $1,269 | $1,396 | $1,771 | $1,615 |
| Capital costs | 733 | 371 | 408 | 614 | 585 |
| Foregone earnings | 349 | 349 | 349 | 1,038 | 1,098 |
| Miscellaneous private costs | 234 | 234 | 234 | 234 | 234 |
| Total costs | $4,374 | $2,223 | $2,387 | $3,657 | $3,532 |
| Incremental income | 4,330 | 4,330 | 2,165 | 4,522 | 3,126 |
| Net benefits (costs) | (44) | 2,107 | (222) | 865 | (406) |
| Benefit-cost ratio | .99 | 1.95 | .91 | 1.24 | .89 |
| **Female** | | | | | |
| Operating costs | $3,058 | $1,269 | $1,396 | $1,771 | $1,615 |
| Capital costs | 733 | 371 | 408 | 614 | 585 |
| Foregone earnings | 488 | 488 | 488 | 1,076 | 419 |
| Miscellaneous private costs | 234 | 234 | 234 | 234 | 234 |
| Total costs | $4,513 | $2,362 | $2,526 | $3,695 | $2,853 |
| Incremental income | 2,108 | 2,108 | 1,054 | 1,745 | 2,585 |
| Net benefits (costs) | (2,405) | (254) | (1,472) | (1,950) | (268) |
| Benefit-cost ratio | .47 | .89 | .42 | .47 | .91 |

**Sources** U.S. Bureau of the Census, *U.S. Census of Population: 1960 Educational Attainment;* U.S. Office of Education, *Costs of Attending College* (Bulletin 1957, #9); U.S. Office of Education, *Digest of Education Statistics: 1963 Edition;* U.S. Office of Education, *Statistics of Higher Education, 1957–58;* Wm. P. McLure, et al., *Vocational and Technical Education in Illinois.*

Table 1). Operating costs are assumed to equal the average costs per full-time equivalent degree-credit student. Capital costs use the same student base and are computed at 8 percent of the value of physical plant as the equivalent of capital consumption and interest charges.[4] Foregone earnings are based on the difference between the median income of persons eighteen and nineteen years old with one to three years of college and the median income of those with four years of high school only. Miscellaneous costs include only fees, books and school supplies. Students are assumed to live at home. All costs are for two years of schooling with the second year values discounted at a rate of 5 percent.

Benefit estimates are restricted to the incremental income a student can expect as a result of a two-year college education. They are based on cross-section data of the 1960 Census which provides income information for persons with high school and one to three years of college education. Adjustments are made for labor force participation rates, and the stream of future returns is discounted at a rate of 5 percent.

Findings presented in Column 1 indicate total costs of two years of higher education for males and females amount to $4,374 and $4,513, respectively; corresponding total benefits are $4,330 and $2,108. Thus a male student's attendance in college for two years yields a net cost of $44, or a return of 99¢ for every dollar invested. The return for a female's education is less than half that of the male, 47¢ on each dollar invested and a net cost of $2,405.

Before we dissuade potential college entrants, we should remember that we estimated only a single benefit element. Also we should look more closely at the assumptions underlying these figures. First, we should note that these estimates consider only a narrow range of factors germane to both personal and public decisions. The intangible factors have been omitted entirely. This is of great significance, for example, in the case of a female's education. We do not know how to estimate the increased value to society that comes about because children are reared by an educated woman. Beyond the income benefits, the educated woman transmits values and attitudes of lasting importance.[5]

Second, we observe in these data a phenomenon of our society that may not accurately reflect productive contributions. Education is a continuous process, but the reward structure is more nearly a step function. A premium is paid for completing a program with a terminal degree. The absence of a widely accepted certificate for two years of college may depress the earnings of those who do not continue for the full four years.

Third, the results presented in Table 1 have a downward bias on the cost side. Full-time students earn less through their part-time employment during the school year and full-time employment during summers, than workers who have full-time employment.

Further, in our estimates the student is credited with the median earnings for a group to which he does not belong—those with one to three years of college—until after completing his first year of college training. There is a tendency to overstate student earnings which, on the cost side, has the effect of understating the foregone earnings while incremental income, on the benefit side, is over-stated.[6]

## Junior College

Next we will use our benefit and cost estimates for two years of college training and modify them to focus upon junior college education. These estimates will attempt to relate to representative high school graduates who do not enter college. Initially we will not assume any differences in the ability, background, motivation, or aspirations of these students compared with high school graduates who currently continue in college. Further, we will assume that the employment conditions faced by these students, while in school and after completion of their junior college program, are the same as those experienced by persons with one to three years of higher education.

Column 2 of Table 1 presents benefits and costs of junior college education. Assumptions made earlier hold here too. The operating and capital cost figures presented in Column 2 are average costs of junior colleges. If these institutions are in the area of increasing costs, and we would expect this to be the case if only because of a relative inelastic supply of instructors, marginal costs would be higher than those indicated here.

Other than the lower operating and capital costs of the junior college, our estimates of Column 2, Table 1 are the same as those for all institutions of higher learning. On this basis, junior college education of a male student will yield a net benefit of $2,107, or a $1.95 return for each dollar of cost. As expected, female students do not fare as well; their attendance produces a net cost of $254 or a return of only 89¢ for each dollar of cost.

Let us reexamine the benefit assumptions made so far. Is it likely that under universal junior college education, training will yield the same benefits as those presently obtained by students spending two years in college? Is the prospective junior college student ready for and capable of pursuing a program comparable to that offered in our four-year or even our two-year institutions? In 1960 approximately four-fifths of those high school graduates who did not attend college were not in college preparatory courses in high school; less than half of those students graduating from high school were in college preparatory programs.[7] In short, under a universal junior college program, many youngsters would attend a two-year institution when their training, achievement level and commitment is below that of those who presently attend college. Therefore, we might find, for example, that the operating and capital costs for junior colleges educating these less prepared students would be 10 percent higher than the costs now reported, and on the other side of the ledger, that their incremental earnings would be only half of the increment currently accruing to those with two years of college. As shown by Column 3 of Table 1, there would be net costs of $222 and $1,472 for these potential male and female students, respectively. The corresponding benefit-cost ratios would be .92 and .42 for the potential students as compared with 1.95 and .89 for today's junior college students. While the latter figures might be looked upon as constituting an upper limit, the first set could be the lower limit.

## Other Programs

Let us now look at some other possibilities for two years of schooling beyond high school. Column 4 of Table 1 indicates the benefits and costs associated with the student attending one of the nation's liberal arts colleges in 1960. Here we assume that the student enters a particular set of occupations: a white-collar managerial position, or a clerical or sales-worker position. The assumption is made that the student would have entered the same occupations with four years of high school and that he undertakes the college training without a change in his employment aspirations. Compared with junior colleges (Column 2, Table 1) the higher liberal arts college costs are not offset by higher differential earnings; the ratio of benefits to costs, for both males and females, falls. Whereas the male student entering a job from junior college would realize a return of $1.95 for each dollar of costs, the liberal arts college student entering a white-collar occupation would realize a return of $1.24 for each dollar of costs. The female student benefit-cost ratio falls from .89 to .47, making liberal arts education and white-collar employment for the female about equal (in terms of percentage return) to the return on education in all institutions and to employment in the full range of occupations. In this latter case, however, the magnitude of the net cost falls by $455.

Next, we might want to consider the fact that many who are not in college are less likely to benefit from a liberal than from a technical or vocational education. Therefore we will examine two years of technical education beyond high school (Column 5, Table 1). Here the operating and capital costs are about half the level of costs for all institutions of higher learning and one-third again higher than the level of junior college costs.[8] It is assumed that the male student attending such institutions earns the differential income associated with educational requirements for designers, draftsmen, technical engineers, and technicians; the female employment opportunities considered are professional and technical positions, excluding teachers below college level. For both males and females the benefits equal about 90 per cent of the costs.[9]

To this point the discussion has been in terms of the universal junior college proposal in its limited institutional setting. A basic tenet of the Educational Policies Commission is that universal junior college education should be encouraged because "every student should have the job of discovery in many fields and should learn to think in many fields."[10] This rationale does not limit us to considering junior college alone as the place of expanding the experience and enhancing the intellectual capabilities of students.

Unless there are factors of emotional or intellectual maturity precluding an enrichment of our current educational program, we could devote the same amount of resources earlier in the student's education through a five-summer program following grades seven through eleven.[11] Five summer sessions of eight weeks each could provide the equivalent of an additional year of schooling. Table 2 presents this case. Here we are evaluating the program at its beginning. We assume that: (1) the operating and capital costs for one year of junior college are spent over the course of five summers; (2) students forego summer employment; (3) their annual miscellaneous costs are $15 per year; (4) as a result of the summer program they

#### Table 2  Benefits and Costs of a Five-Summer Program During High School Equivalent to One Year of Higher Education, 1960
*(Present values at 5% discount)*

|  | MALE STUDENT | FEMALE STUDENT |
|---|---|---|
| Operating costs | $651 | $651 |
| Capital costs | 190 | 190 |
| Foregone earnings | 683 | 442 |
| Miscellaneous private costs | 68 | 68 |
| Total costs | $1,592 | $1,351 |
| Incremental income | 5,150 | 1,989 |
| Net benefits (costs) | 3,558 | 638 |
| Benefit-cost ratio | 3.23 | 1.47 |

**Sources** See Table 1.

enter the labor force at age eighteen, earning the median income for high school graduates, plus one-half the differential income of the person with one to three years of college.[12] In this case, the monetized benefits for the male student exceed costs by over $3,500 and the benefit-cost ratio is 3.23; net benefits for the female are $638, with a ratio of 1.47. Even if the operating and capital costs of this program were twenty percent higher than shown in Table 2, and if the benefits were but half of those indicated for the male student, there would still be a net benefit of $815 and a return of $1.46 for each dollar invested. Simply put, it would be possible for the nation to provide the equivalent of a year of junior college, in a high school enrichment program, during the summer months, with larger returns on investment than result from two full years of junior college.

## SOME ADDITIONAL CONSIDERATIONS

### Program Costs

The foregoing analysis has been made in terms of the individual student. It fails to reveal the magnitude of costs and benefits to the nation if we had instituted this program in 1960. How many students would enter college? Table 3 shows some of the factors involved. Of the 1.8 million high school graduates of 1960, 42 percent entered college the following fall. All other considerations aside, the maximum number of additional students for whom we would have to provide teachers, classrooms, equipment, and parking spaces would be over one million. But unless we propose to interfere with existing preferences for post high school activities or believe that a universal junior college program would alter these preferences, there would be slightly fewer than 700,000 additional students for junior college enrollment. This is no small number.

Under the assumption that these 690,000 to 1,045,000 students are similar to today's students (Column 2, Table 1), the costs of sending them to junior college would range from $1.6 billion to $2.4 billion; benefits would be one-third again as great as costs,

### Table 3   Activities of June 1960 High School Graduates
*(in thousands)*

|  | MALES | FEMALES | TOTAL |
|---|---|---|---|
| 1960 high school graduates | 873 | 930 | 1,803 |
| Enrolled in college | 408 | 350 | 758 |
| Maximum additional junior college students | 465 | 580 | 1,045 |
| Armed forces, misc. | 117 | 7 | 124 |
| Special training (vocational education) | 45 | 125 | 170 |
| Full-time housewives |  | 61 | 61 |
| Potential additional junior college students | 303 | 387 | 690 |

**Sources** Sophia Cooper, "Employment of June 1960 High School Graduates," *Special Labor Force Report* #15; *Factors Relating to College Attendance, op. cit.; U.S. Census of the Population: 1960, Detailed Characteristics, U.S. Summary.*

ranging from $2.1 billion to $3.2 billion. But a less optimistic view (as in Column 3, Table 1) of these potential students would find costs ranging from $1.7 billion to $2.6 billion while benefits range from $1 billion to $1.6 billion. How would the direct costs for operations and capital facilities be financed? Are local governments, which finance junior colleges at present, expected to collect $1 – $2 additional billions from their already-pressed taxpayers for this, in preference to other activities, or are the states prepared to meet this cost? Or is the federal government prepared to increase its education budget by a third or more and finance this program in preference to others?

### Unemployment and Education

In addition to the considerations above with respect to the education of high school graduates, attention needs to be given to the effect of universal junior college education on national unemployment, especially in the short-run. Secretary of Labor, W. Willard Wirtz has stated that ". . . the single largest possibility of immediate attack upon the unemployment situation would come from getting 2 million teenagers out of the work force. There are $3\frac{1}{2}$ million of

them in the work force today who are out of school and in the work
force between the ages of 14 and 19 . . . those 2 million . . . should be
in school getting the kind of preparation they need for the employment which lies ahead."[13]

While the Educational Policies Commission report does not
mention the salutary effect universal junior college education is
likely to have on our unemployment problem, it should be included in
the examination as a truly significant issue. Perhaps it is so dominant,
particularly in the political area, that this proposal could be enacted
even in the absence of sizable returns on investment in junior college
education. At the same time we might only be postponing serious
unemployment problems by working so hard to have most 16–19 year
olds out of the labor force and in schools.

Studies of unemployment at present tend to confirm the
widely held view that the incidence of unemployment declines as
educational attainment rises. Robert A. Gordon's studies indicate
that from 1957 to 1962 relative unemployment rates increased somewhat for those with 12 years of schooling while hardly changing over
the period for those with 13 to 15 years of schooling.[14] But where
there would appear to be a trend in the relative unemployment
picture for the high school graduate, there is less certainty with
respect to those with some college education. Although employment
projections[15] indicate greatest growth in the next decade for the
occupation held by those with some college education, the broad
nature of these projections should not delude us into seeing the future
in terms of higher education alone. More intensive training in the
secondary schools for future employment opportunities could bring
a shift in the occupation profile of high school graduates that today
only seems possible through more extensive education.


## CONCLUSION

Our benefit-cost analysis underemphasizes some key considerations and conceals many others. It has not been possible here to
note all of the major considerations. We cannot profitably discuss a

universal junior college program unless we are graduating students from our high schools who are prepared for college curricula, or unless we expect to debase our existing program of higher education or perhaps shift the responsibilities of college preparation from the high school to the junior colleges through extensive remedial courses.[16] Would adding two junior college years further weaken the incentive of high schools to foster more intensive and effective education? In the extreme, youngsters might end up learning about the same, only over a longer period of time.[17]

On the other hand, our assumption should be recalled that the high school senior enters junior college immediately following graduation. American society does not shut the door on those who, either upon graduation from high school or later in life, wish to continue their education. "In increasing numbers, because of the maturity gained in military service, because of the example of their peers, because of rebuffs in the labor market, able, but previously unmotivated young people, are joining the ranks of the "late bloomers'."[18] Part of the broader issue to be considered is where in the jigsaw puzzle of American education these students can fit and who should bear the costs of their divergence from the typical or expected behavior patterns.

In effect, junior colleges are part of the nation's program of continuing education.[19] Also there exists the possibility of still further education for those who do attend junior college. Of junior college freshmen, one study revealed, about one-third transfer to senior college and of these, 40 per cent graduate with a bachelor's degree within four years of entering the junior college.[20] Thus, junior college need not be terminal education for all, although it is for most. We would expect that a still smaller portion of those not currently attending college after high school would later continue through to a full four-year program, but universal junior college training has further education potentialities that deserve attention.

There can be little doubt that as the demands of technology increase and as society gets more complex, the nation will require more education. However a key question remains: how far will the demand curve for education shift outward and how can we best meet

the increased demands? While the universal requirements are past
the high school level, they do not appear to be up to the junior college
level. Because of this consideration and since our analysis does not
point to a clear-cut advantage for a universal junior college program,
we need a good flexible transitional approach. A large-scale summer
school program which integrates work during as many as five summers with the regular high school program appears to offer many
advantages.

# A. J. CORAZZINI

# When Should
## Vocational
## Education Begin?

*P*ublic policy makers in education are nowhere faced with more
crucial resource allocation questions than in vocational education.
*In what magnitude and when should investments be made in industrial
trades, vocational agriculture, business and office education, or any one
of several other forms of specific training? Returns to investment in
education in the aggregate may be quite different from human resource
investment in alternative time periods and programs. A. J. Corazzini,*

Reprinted from A. J. Corazzini, "When Should Vocational Education Begin?"
*Journal of Human Resources* 2 (Winter 1967), pp. 41–50, with permission of the
author and publisher. Copyright 1967 by the Regents of the University of
Wisconsin.

Notes to this essay will be found on pages 289–290.

*now at Dartmouth College, evaluates the economics of two vocational
programs at the high school level compared to training subsequent to
high school. Although this study tentatively concludes that post-high
school training may not be the better investment alternative, the character of externalities and numerous intervening factors deserve further
consideration, as Corazzini observes. Special notice should be taken of
the use of the investment payback concept, differential opportunity costs
by program, and income-time streams—all of which are discussed in
Corazzini's analysis.*

In recent years, a large number of studies have pointed out
the profitability of public and private investment in education.
The rate of return on total high school costs has been estimated at
14 percent,[1] and the return on college costs has been estimated at
9 percent. The casual observer might suggest, upon inspection of
these data, that public decision-makers should allocate larger
quantities of limited community resources to the support of expanded
investment in public education. Unfortunately, such a recommenda-
tion overlooks a multitude of problems.

On the positive side, one might argue that these estimates
*understate* the return to the investment in education. As has been
pointed out elsewhere, the value of additional education has at least
two income components.[2] The first is the amount of additional earnings which result from completion of a given level of education. The
second is "the value of the 'option' to obtain still further education
and the rewards accompanying it."[3] In addition, the external benefits
resulting from the investment in education would increase its
over-all profitability.

On the negative side, it is obvious that most empirical work
deals with an average rather than a marginal return to the investment
in education.[4] It is the marginal rate of return to further investment
which is the relevant consideration for decision-makers, not the
average rate of return on past investment. Nonetheless, because in
practice average rates are the only measure of profitability available
to decision-makers, such data are used with the hope that they will
lead to more optimal investment decisions.[5]

When decision-makers approach the problem of vocational education, their task is made all the more difficult. In addition to determining whether there should be more education for all children, they must resolve the mix of that education. Given a decision to provide high school education, should they offer general or vocational education? Given a decision to provide an additional year or two beyond the high school level, should that additional year be junior college education or vocational-technical education? Given a decision to provide vocational-technical education, should that education be at the high school level or post-high school level? To make such choices, the costs of the alternative investments must be compared with the benefits of the alternative programs. To decide between vocational high school and vocational post-high school education, we would have to compare their relative costs and benefits.

There are, of course, both private and public costs to consider. Private costs are incurred by the individual. The largest immediate one is the opportunity cost of remaining in school rather than working. There are also direct school expenses which must be paid by the individual. Public costs consist of all the normal school expenses, both direct and indirect, incurred by the public authorities in the running of the school. Adding the public and private costs gives us the total resource costs of the program. In the first approximations, the benefits would be measured by the gains in lifetime income attributable to the education received by the individuals completing the respective programs.

When the choice is between vocational education at the post-high school level and the same education at the high school level, some interesting questions arise. Vocational education should be considered a partial substitute for on-the-job training. The question is whether to invest in that formal training during the first twelve years of schooling, or to add two additional years to the public education system. Formal training undertaken at the high school level must be accompanied by the basic general education provided all high school students,[6] but trainees entering a post-high school program already possess high school diplomas. In any event, there are those who have argued that the number of school years ought to

be decreased; for example, we have the "Machlup plan," which would
compress all the material now taught in twelve years into ten years.[7]
The provision of post-high school vocational-technical education
would extend what could be a twelve-year into a fourteen-year
program.

Graduates of post-high school programs would have to earn
more than those of high school vocational programs, if the investment in post-high school training is to appear rational. If high school
vocational graduates earned as much as post-high school graduates,
then the marginal return to the extra investment in education would
be zero. The individual would forego two years of earnings and incur
direct costs, but would receive no increase in lifetime income for his
investment.

The individual could receive a non-pecuniary benefit from the
knowledge that he had completed some sort of higher education
program. Also, he might obtain an indirect pecuniary benefit in the
form of an "option" to continue his education. In other words, if
completing post-high school vocational educational courses resulted
in a greater probability of going on for a four-year degree than
graduation from vocational high school, the "option" to obtain this
four-year degree might make the investment somewhat more attractive.

The requirement that post-high school vocational training
result in higher earnings holds only if the two competing programs
are identical. That is to say, if certain kinds of vocational education
require an educational background equivalent to a high school degree,
then obviously high school vocational training and post-high school
vocational training are not alternatives. It would be irrational for the
private decision-maker to forego earnings for two years beyond high
school without gaining added income. However, the added income
would not result from the formal training received, since he could have
gotten the same formal training at the high school level. Presumably,
those that graduated and then trained would have had more time to
spend in general education courses[8] which would prepare them for future on-the-job training programs. It is also possible that the quality of
the academic instruction given those at regular high schools is superior
to that given at vocational schools. Thus, these students could be con-

sidered better candidates for formal training and, having graduated from the training program, for further on-the-job training. Hence, the added income would simply be a premium paid by entrepreneurs to those individuals who demonstrated extra ability and potential expertise in graduating from high school and then undertaking formal training.

In a sense, then, either post-high school vocational training does not increase lifetime earning, and individuals would be irrational to invest in it; or it does bring increased earning because entrepreneurs pay a higher wage, not for the amount of formal training received by the graduate, but for the number of school years completed. Having outlined the framework in which a decision between high school and post-high school vocational training would have to be made, we turn now to an empirical investigation.

Educators in Worcester, Massachusetts, have chosen to set up both high school and post-high school vocational education programs. The high school program begins at the ninth grade level and continues for four full years; it offers the student his choice of eleven different training courses in the skilled trades. The post-high school program, covering two years, makes available the same eleven skilled trade courses and four additional technical training courses.

In September 1960, 176 boys entered the ninth grade vocational school.[9] Of the group that entered, 123 eventually graduated, although not always within four years of entrance. Out of the 123 graduates, 101 were placed in occupations directly related to their training, 76 of them graduating and being placed on jobs in June 1964. The placement records of these 76 were readily available to investigators.

In September of 1962, 121 students enrolled in the post-high school vocational program, and 90 graduated two years later. Forty-two graduates had taken the same training courses as had the high school vocational graduates, and 34 of these 42 were placed in occupations directly related to their training. Of the other 48 graduates, who had taken one of four technical training courses open only to post-high school students, 37 were placed in occupations directly related to their training. We begin our evaluation by comparing the placement

records of the 34 graduates who took the same training course as the
high school students with the placement record of the 76 vocational
high school graduates. The two groups are assumed to have received
the same help in finding jobs. If one group did receive more placement
guidance per pupil, the extra costs and benefits of this effort would
have to be accounted for in any over-all evaluation.[10]


## THE BENEFITS

With regard to starting salaries, we find that in two of the
eleven trade areas, the post-high school graduates received less than,
in three other trade areas the same as, and in the remaining six areas,
a higher starting salary than the vocational high school graduates.
The amount of the premium paid to post-high school graduates
varied from 5¢ to 35¢ per hour, with an average premium of 20¢ per
hour. For a 40-hour week, this would amount to $8 a week, or $400 a
year for a 50-week work year. The annual figure assumes that the
wage differential remains the same, in absolute terms, throughout
the working year. Taking each of the six trade areas separately, we
find that two paid a premium of 5¢ per hour, which is $2 a week or
$100 per year. Three other trades paid 25¢ per hour, amounting to
$10 per week or $500 per year. Finally, in one trade area, the premium
paid was 35¢ per hour—$14 per week or $700 per year.

The average starting wage for post-high school graduates who
took one of the eleven trade courses offered high school students was
$1.84 per hour; the average starting wage for the vocational high
school graduates was $1.76 per hour. Hence, over-all, the average
premium paid post-high school graduates was a mere 8¢ per hour—
$3.20 per week or $160 annually.

The picture is somewhat improved if we look at the 37 post-
high school students who took training open only to high school
graduates and were then placed in jobs related to their training. For
this group the average starting wage was $1.95 per hour, or 19¢ per
hour above the vocational high school graduates' starting salary and
11¢ per hour above the wage paid post-high school graduates of the

eleven trade course. The individual who graduated from one of these four technical training programs began his career by making about $8 per week or $400 a year more than if he had taken a trade course at the high school level.

## THE COSTS

The cost of vocational-technical education is always assumed to be greater than the cost of general education, but the exact relationship between the two is a matter for empirical investigation. Using data provided by the city of Worcester and the Worcester school authorities, we arrive at a measure of vocational education costs for that community (see Table 1). The exact figures, of course, may vary widely from community to community.

If we look only at public costs, we see that vocational high

### Table 1 Total Resource Costs, Worcester Public High School, Worcester Boys' Vocational School, Worcester 13th and 14th Grade Vocational-Technical School, 1963–64

| | $ PER PUPIL | | |
|---|---|---|---|
| | Public high schools | Vocational high schools | Post-high school vocational-technical |
| Total Public Costs | 532 | 1,210 | 1,230 |
| 1. Current cost | 452 | 964 | 984 |
| 2. Implicit rent[a] | 59 | 165 | 165 |
| 3. Property tax loss | 21 | 81 | 81 |
| Total Private Costs[a] | 1,176 | 1,176 | 2,544 |
| 1. School-related costs | 56 | 56 | 121 |
| 2. Foregone earnings | 1,120 | 1,120 | 2,423 |
| Total Resource Costs | 1,708 | 2,386 | 3,774 |

[a] Estimated using techniques in T. W. Schultz, "Capital Formation by Education," *Journal of Political Economy*, LXVIII (1960), p. 575; and in Machlup, *op. cit.*, p. 100.

**Sources** Worcester Public Schools, Office of the Superintendent; Worcester Boys' Vocational High School and Worcester Industrial Technical Institute; Office of the Assessor of the City of Worcester; and Massachusetts State Department of Education, Department of School Building Assistance.

school education in Worcester is about 2.3 times as expensive as regular high school education. Post-high school education costs about as much as vocational high school education. Hence, from a public cost point of view, there is little difference between buying two extra years of vocational-technical education and buying four years of vocational high school education. To illustrate this point, let us assume that all those now taking vocational high school education will be put in post-high school programs. Before they can enter, they would still have to graduate from regular high school. Since regular high school costs are one-half those of the vocational school, the four-year savings gained by keeping these people at the regular school would buy two years of post-high school vocational-technical training. Of course, if expanding post-high school enrollments caused marginal costs to rise, this might not be the case. Hence, for the conclusion to hold, we must assume that marginal costs are equal to average costs.

If we consider private costs, the picture is somewhat altered. The individual who foregoes two years of employment incurs real costs in the form of lost earnings. When direct school costs are added to these foregone earnings, we estimate a total yearly cost per pupil of $2,544. Thus, the total resource cost of adding two years of vocational training beyond the high school level is $3,774 per pupil per year. This compares with total resource costs of $2,388 per pupil for vocational high school and $1,708 per pupil for regular high school.

## AN EVALUATION

The graduate of post-high school training seems to have made a poor investment if he chose one of the eleven training programs open to vocational high school students. He has foregone two years of earnings and has incurred direct school costs for a total of $2,544 per year. In return, he received in the first year an average salary $160 greater than the vocational school graduate. Unless he can look forward to a much more lucrative career than his vocational school counterpart, it certainly appears that he should have chosen to train at an earlier age.

The graduate of the post-high school program who enrolled in training courses open only to high school graduates found himself in a somewhat different position. Again, his two-year costs were considerably higher than the immediate premium he received relative to the vocational school graduate: his costs were $2,544 per year, and his salary averaged $400 per year more than the vocational school graduate. However, his job was in the technician rather than the skilled trade category. In no way could it be argued that he would earn the same approximate lifetime income as the vocational school graduate.

The slightly higher starting salary paid to graduates of the post-high school training course who train in the same areas as vocational students appears to be a premium for having graduated from high school. It could be argued that whatever chance the post-high school graduate has of earning more in the same skilled trade than his vocational counterpart results from the greater ability he demonstrates by completing regular high school. Similarly, the potentially more lucrative technical careers began with training which required high school graduation as proof of ability.

We need not draw the conclusion that training really ought to occur at the post-high school level. Since private costs are much greater than the immediate wage premium paid to post-high school graduates, there is an obvious pay-back period involved. That is to say, there is some definite length of time during which all of the higher wages paid to these graduates relative to vocational high school graduates must be charged off against the initial deficit; the initial premium must be maintained and enlarged for some time, or the extra costs will never be recovered. Here we assumed that the average premium paid post-high school graduates relative to vocational school graduates in the same trades amounted to $160 per year, providing that the absolute difference in starting wages was maintained for the entire year. The difference between this figure and the private costs of $2,544 is $2,384. Unless the absolute difference in wages received by the two groups of graduates widens, it would take 15 years to pay back the costs incurred during one year of post-high school training. If the individual were to consider a discounted stream of extra returns and attempt to equate these extra returns with the present value of his extra costs, a longer pay-back period would be required. Indeed, this average differential of $160, if discounted at a 5 percent interest rate, would not equal the two-year discounted extra costs of $4,965 within the working life of the employee. The largest differentials of $500 and $700 per year, if discounted, would equal the extra costs within 15½ years and 10 years, respectively (Table 2).

### Table 2   Number of Years Differentials Would Have to Remain, in Order for the Present Value of Extra Costs to be Equal to Present Value of Extra Returns

| Wage Differential | Rate of 5% of Discount |
|---|---|
| $100 per year | Never equated[a] |
| $160 per year | Never equated |
| $400 per year | 21¾ years |
| $500 per year | 15½ years |
| $700 per year | 10 years |

[a] The two-year discounted extra private costs were $4,965.

**Source** Official records of the respective schools.

Given the highly uncertain nature of an individual's labor market experience, it seems that a fruitful technique would be to minimize the pay-back period. This could be accomplished by offering an accelerated training program during the last two years of high school. Those vocational students not able to proceed at the faster academic pace would take the ordinary four-year program. Those students who would ordinarily graduate from high school and then take vocational training could undertake a two-year program at the eleventh grade. Completion of training would also mean completion of high school. No added private costs would be incurred by these students. If their present higher starting salary is due to their higher ability, it should still be easy for entrepreneurs to distinguish between those that took a four-year program and those that took the training in two years.

Much the same sort of argument can be made for those who took technical training. If high school education is actually a necessary condition for this type of training, little change can be made. On the other hand, the average premium paid these graduates in the first year relative to vocational high school students was $400. This would mean a pay-back period of 5.3 years for one year of training beyond the high school level.[11] Again, if the stream of extra returns were discounted, it would take $21\frac{3}{4}$ years to equate these returns with the discounted extra costs (Table 2). Obviously, if technical training could be given at the high school level, it would be expedient to do so.

Finally, we have said that providing post-high school training could be a worthwhile undertaking, if the individual thereby bettered his chances of going on to four-year college. Looking at the actual numbers of Worcester vocational high school graduates and post-high school graduates who continued their education, we find that, from an entering vocational high school class of 176, only six (or 3.4 percent) continued their schooling beyond high school. Out of an entering post-high school class of 121, only three (or 2.5 percent) continued their schooling beyond the two-year training program. At least in this particular case, both programs seem to be terminal occupation training.

Several additional factors might modify the findings presented in this paper. We have discussed only starting wages here. Certainly, the vocational and technical school graduates should be followed over several years of their working life. Further, direct benefits in the form of lifetime income are actually only the most immediate return to educational investment. There may be several categories of external benefits which accrue to one or another of the training groups studied, which might alter considerably the tentative conclusion reached here. Moreover, to reach a final decision on whether to invest in high school vocational training, we would have to compare the vocational high school graduates with the graduates of ordinary high school.

# part three

Selected Issues
in the
Economics
of Education

JAMES MORGAN

MARTIN DAVID

# Education
## and
### Income

*M*ultivariate analysis is used in this paper to derive estimates of the net effect of education on earnings after attempting to adjust for other factors that also contribute to higher earnings. Three classes of dummy variables are used in the regression analysis. These include variables that have a prior affect on education, variables that may be partly determined by education, and other variables that do not

Reprinted from James Morgan and Martin David, "Education and Income," *Quarterly Journal of Economics* 77 (August 1963), pp. 423–37, and James Morgan and Charles Lininger, "Education and Income: A Comment," *Quarterly Journal of Economics* 78 (May 1964), pp. 346–47, with permission of the authors and publisher. Copyright 1963 and 1964 by the President and Fellows of Harvard College.

Notes to this essay will be found on pages 290–291.

*have a clear prior or subsequent effect on education. Generally, Morgan, David and Lininger feel that the impact of net education earnings is understated after making statistical adjustments for the 13 explanatory variables they use. They conclude that although the relationships are important, the quantitative effect of spurious correlation among explanatory factors is not excessively significant. In an appended comment, James Morgan and Charles Lininger report on changes in the value of education with the passage of time, suggesting that technological change may be increasing the investment value of education. Professors James Morgan and Martin David are on the faculty of the University of Michigan and Charles Lininger is currently with the Population Council in New York.*

Increased investment in education, whether public or private, has certain economic benefits, and can be thought of as yielding a social rate of return on the investment. This social value of return includes benefits such as greater flexibility of the labor force, the value of an informed electorate, the greater enjoyment of life and culture, as well as the most obvious benefit of the greater productivity of educated workers. Only the last of these benefits can be measured and evaluated easily. Therefore we restrict our analysis of the value of education to benefits that can be measured by increased earning potential, on the assumption that people's contribution to the economy is measured by what they earn. Productivity is best measured by hourly earnings. Annual money earnings indicate not only productivity but also reflect the unwanted unemployment of the less educated, and the desired extra leisure that can be afforded by those with more education. We should not attribute to education differences which result from the failure to preserve full employment, nor should we undervalue extra education because some of its benefit is taken in longer vacations or shorter hours. Hence, hourly earnings provide a better measure of the value of education than annual earnings.

Some of the difference in hourly earnings between education groups may result from parental influences and other factors correlated with education. If the effect of education on hourly earnings is adjusted to account for other correlated factors, data from a 1960 cross section of the United States indicate that investment in education pays a modest 4–6 percent return.[1] The implication is that much of the value of education to the individual lies in the security and stability of his income, and the kinds of occupations it makes possible rather than in higher hourly earnings.

Many qualifications must be made to these interpretations of the data, however. The flexibility and adaptability of the labor force, not measured here, may well represent an economic return to investment in education. The multivariate analysis may well have overadjusted. The measure of education is years completed, without any indication of quality.

## THE PROBLEM OF METHOD

Recent attempts to discuss the value of college education to the individual, or the social return to investment in education, have forced attention on the difficult empirical problem of isolating the effect of one variable (education) on another (lifetime earnings).[2].

The empirical problem arises even in using education to explain current earning rates because (a) there are many intercorrelated factors affecting a man's earnings, and (b) these factors are not all at the same stage in a causal chain. The isolation of the effect of education from that of other factors is possible by using multiple correlation if the intercorrelations are not too high and there are no serious interaction effects.

But the added difficulty is that the intercorrelations among the explanatory factors are not symmetrical. Some of these factors are logically prior, that is they can effect others but cannot be affected by those others. Completed education appears in the middle of a causal chain, with some factors, like the father's education, logically prior, and others, like a man's geographic mobility after he enters the labor force, logically subsequent to his formal education.

If the causal chain were sufficiently simple, we might suggest first removing the effects of all prior factors, like race, sex, parental education, and then correlating the individual's education with the unexplained residuals of his hourly earnings, forgetting any factors which are logically subsequent to education and could not have affected it. But things are not that simple. First, some of the same factors which seem logically prior may also have had their effect *through* influencing education itself, or may alter the impact of education on earnings. Secondly, while education may affect some logically subsequent things such as the individual's occupation and his geographic mobility, it does not determine them entirely. To omit them altogether from the analysis precludes the elimination of their independent influences. We have a choice between allowing them to take credit for some of what is really due to education, on the one hand, or failing to allow for differences in what people do with their education, on the other.

## PROPOSED PROCEDURES

There is, then, no easy or correct single solution of the problem of how to isolate the effect of education on earnings from the effects of other factors. It is a useful first step, however, to try to deal with the intercorrelation problem and to ask just how much net influence education seems to have in simultaneous multivariate analysis which includes such other factors as race, sex, parental education, mobility, and broad occupational choice.

In such an analysis, prior factors like the father's education will take credit for some of what would otherwise have been attributed to the individual's education. To the extent that the father's education has a direct effect on earnings, or operates through the son's occupation rather than through his education, this is proper. On the other hand, to the extent that it operates through its effect on the son's education, the multivariate analysis understates the effects of the son's education on his earnings.

Education will also lose credit to some subsequent factors like occupation, even though education may have been a prerequisite for the best occupations. To the extent that such variables reflect the way education has its effect, rather than independent influences, again the effects of education will be somewhat understated in the multivariate analysis. The truth, probably lies somewhere between the unadjusted gross differences in earnings for those with different levels of education, on the one hand, and the net estimates from the multivariate analysis. Hence, both sets of data will be presented.

Finally, since the data will be used later for estimates of life-time earnings and because the effect of education on earnings is different at different ages, age and education are used jointly. That is, separate education coefficients are derived for each age group in a single cross-section sample.

## STATISTICAL METHOD AND SOURCE OF DATA

The statistical technique used is multiple regression, using a separate dummy variable that takes the value one or zero, for each class of each explanatory factor. By incorporating one set of variables which represents a joint classification by age and education, we can estimate the net effects of belonging to any one age-education group after allowing for the effects of other influences.[3] The basic assumption of multiple regression is that the effects of the various other factors do not interact with one another, or with age-education.

The analysis takes account of the intercorrelations among the explanatory factors, but not of interaction effects beyond that between age and education. An investigation of possible interactions between education and race, sex, or being a farmer, by a separate analysis of white, nonfarmer males, indicates that such interactions exist but have a negligible effect on estimates of the effects of education and age on hourly earnings.

The data used here come from a national probability sample of approximately 3,000 heads of spending units, mostly men. The Survey Research Center's national sample was used, and the Center staff was responsible for all steps through the data processing. Even units living with relatives are counted separately if they keep separate finances and have some income. Wives, dependent adults, and the population in institutions and quasi-households, Y.M.C.A.'s, etc., are excluded. More than eight-tenths of the eligible respondents were interviewed, so nonresponse bias is small. Many questions and a substantial part of the interviewing time were given over to securing information on income and hours of work. For farmers and owners of unincorporated businesses, whose incomes are a mixture of return on invested capital and labor earnings, 6 percent of their investment in the farm or business was first subtracted from the farm or business income as a return on capital: the rest was considered labor earnings. Reported weeks of work and average hours per week provided an estimate of annual hours of work by which the earnings were divided to provide estimated hourly earnings.

Interview responses are, of course, subject to errors, and perhaps particularly estimates of hours worked. However, the data used here represent the best available techniques, and there is evidence that income reports are among the more accurate financial data derivable from interviews.[4]


## EXPLANATORY FACTORS
## IN ADDITION TO EDUCATION

The explanatory variables in the regression consisted of enough dummy variables to represent the following:

*Group 1*
    age and education (21 groups)
    race (2 groups)
    sex (2 groups)
    interviewer's assessment of ability to communicate (4 groups)
    level of grades in school and whether the individual was behind
        the usual grade when he left school (7 groups)
    a personality measure (need-achievement) and an attitude
        toward hard work (7 groups)

*Group 2*

> physical condition, whether disabled (4 groups)
> population of city where the individual now lives (6 groups)
> ratio of insured unemployment to covered employment in the
> state where the individual lives (5 groups)
> number of states lived in since first full-time regular job
> (6 groups)
> whether migrated out of the Deep South (6 groups)
> rural-urban migration since growing up (6 groups)

*Group 3*

> supervisory responsibility in job (3 groups)
> occupation (5 groups)

Those in the first group other than age-education may have been prior to education and thus have affected completed education. Those in the last group may be partly determined by education, but not entirely. The others are not clearly either prior to or the result of education. Since the focus of this paper is on the effect of age-education on earnings, detailed coefficients for all the other factors will not be présented.[5]

The analysis accounted for 35 percent of the variance, and each of the sets of variables made a significant contribution to the explanation according to a crude F-test, except the fifth: level of grades in school and whether the individual was behind the usual grade when he left school. The twenty-one age-education groups accounted for the largest part of the explanation, the set having a beta coefficient of .234.[6] Table 1 presents the average hourly earnings for each education group (column 1), the deviations of these from the over-all average of \$2.29 (column 2), and the dummy-variable regression coefficients (column 3). The deviations of the mean for each group from the over-all mean can be thought of as the gross effects of belonging to that age-education group. The regression coefficients can be thought of as the net effects of belonging to that age-education group, taking account of the other thirteen sets of variables. They reflect differences which would remain even if every

### Table 1   Hourly Earnings, Actual and Standardized, by Age and Education

(*for spending unit heads who worked in 1959*)

| Age and education | Average hourly earnings | | Net effect of belonging to an age-edu-cation group[a] | Number of cases |
|---|---|---|---|---|
| | Actual | As deviations from mean of $2.29 | | |
| **0–11 grades** | | | | |
| Under 25 | $1.51 | —.78 | —.52 | 76 |
| 25–34 | 1.95 | —.34 | —.22 | 251 |
| 35–44 | 2.02 | —.27 | —.09 | 297 |
| 45–54 | 1.92 | —.37 | —.09 | 332 |
| 55–64 | 2.00 | —.29 | —.04 | 269 |
| 65 and older | 1.52 | —.77 | —.37 | 104 |
| **12 grades** | | | | |
| Under 25 | 1.70 | —.59 | —.42 | 72 |
| 25–34 | 2.21 | —.08 | —.16 | 97 |
| 35–44 | 2.68 | .39 | .33 | 129 |
| 45–54 | 2.60 | .31 | .27 | 78 |
| 55–64 | 2.53 | .24 | .09 | 32 |
| 65 and older | 1.25[b] | —1.04[b] | —.83[b] | 5 |
| **12 grades and some college or nonacademic training** | | | | |
| Under 25 | 1.75 | —.54 | —.51 | 84 |
| 25–34 | 2.56 | .27 | —.04 | 142 |
| 35–44 | 2.62 | .33 | .19 | 139 |
| 45–54 | 2.83 | .54 | .36 | 99 |
| 55 and older | 2.57 | .28 | .10 | 77 |
| **College graduates** | | | | |
| 18–34 | 2.87 | .58 | —.07 | 98 |
| 35–44 | 3.77 | 1.48 | .85 | 82 |
| 45–54 | 4.13 | 1.84 | 1.27 | 53 |
| 55 and older | 3.25 | .96 | .43 | 53 |

**Source** Survey Research Center national sample.

Except where the mean wage rate is exceptionally small, the standard deviation of the rate within a group is roughly proportional to the mean so that the coefficient of variation remains about the same for all groups. The average coefficient of variation is .64.

[a] Adjusted for the simultaneous effects of other factors.
[b] Unreliable, too few cases.

age-education group were like the others in its distribution on the other thirteen factors.

The differences between the average deviations from the mean and the net effects represent the adjustments for intercorrelations among the various explanatory factors. They indicate the extent to which any one gross effect could be considered a spurious correlation attributable to some other factor. For instance, college graduates aged forty-five to fifty-four earn $4.13 per hour, or $1.84 more than the national average, but our analysis attributes only $1.27 of this difference to their age and education. One way to summarize the effect of taking account of the other factors is to compare the beta coefficients. Where only one factor (age-education) is used, the beta coefficient is identical with the simple correlation coefficient. For age and education the beta coefficient for the unadjusted deviations from the mean was .391 compared with .234 for the adjusted deviations.

Even though taking account of occupation, for instance, over-does the adjustments, and current earnings understate the differences that may exist in future years, education remains a powerful determinant of earnings. The effect of education on earnings is not a fictitious result of spurious correlations involving other factors like parental influences. Two factors were used which attempted to represent native intelligence, (1) the interviewer's assessment of the individual's ability to understand and answer questions, and (2) the respondent's report as to his grades in school combined with a determination of whether he had fallen behind his regular grade at the time he quit school. Both of them lose most of their punch when used simultaneously with age-education; the second of them becomes nonsignificant. Their beta coefficients were .061 and .027. Perhaps a better measure of intelligence used as one of the factors would have produced more effect, but most measures of intelligence are themselves to some extent the results of the educational process. Only a preschool measure of intelligence would really do the job.[7]

The data refer only to those who worked during 1959, so that any effects of education on labor force participation are omitted. Other data, not presented here, indicate that those with more education are less subject to unemployment, so that the effects of higher

wages are compounded by fewer hours of undesired idleness. However, if we blame unemployment not on the individual and his lack
of education, but on society, the data in Table 1 can be used to
estimate discounted present value of earnings for individuals with
different levels of education.

## SEARCH FOR INTERACTION EFFECTS
## AND MORE DETAIL ON EDUCATION

The sample includes some for whom we have reason to
believe education is a less powerful determinant of earnings—
Negroes, women, and farmers. The analysis was rerun without these
three groups but with the same explanatory factors (except sex and
race, of course). The adjusted coefficients for age-education were unaffected—the correlation between the new set and the third column
of Table 1 being .98. The subsample used had a higher mean ($2.60)
and the same variance, and the analysis explained 23 percent of the
variance. The beta coefficient for age-education, however, increased
from .234 to .279. The implication is that education does matter
more for white, nonfarm males, more of whom have advanced
education, but that the excluded groups are not large enough or
different enough to bias the estimates in Table 1.

Two problems remain. The education groups are rather broad,
the necessary result of using age and education jointly; and there
might be differential effects of some of the other factors like occupation as between the young and the old. The only way to deal with
these problems appeared to be to analyze separately those under
thirty-five and those thirty-five and older, still omitting the farmers,
females, and nonwhites, as well as omitting those not currently in
the labor force. A somewhat different set of explanatory factors was
used, dropping some, and adding two new ones:

*education (7 groups)*

*age (2 groups for those under thirty-five, 5 groups for those thirty-five
and older)*

*religious preference and church attendance (7 groups)*

*a personality measure (need-achievement) and attitude toward hard work (7 groups)*

*difference in education between the individual and his father (4 groups)*

*local labor market conditions (B.L.S. classification, 6 groups)*

*migration out of the Deep South (6 groups)*

*rural-urban migration since growing up (6 groups)*

*number of states lived in since first full-time regular job (6 groups)*

*supervisory responsibility (3 groups)*

The effects of the last items in this list might be considered merely the way in which education has its influence, thus leading to an underestimate of the importance of education. On the other hand, the analysis uses better measures of parental influences—religion, and the difference in education between the individual and his father. Table 2 gives a summary of the results.

The last analyses omitted occupation, the factor most likely to take credit for what is really the result of education. On the other hand, religion and achievement motivation may have helped determine the amount of education the individual completed as well as his earnings, yet education would take some of the credit in the statistical results. Again, however, education remained the most important single factor for both age groups.

The coefficients for education do not lead directly to the necessary age-education data for estimating lifetime earnings for different educational levels, but such data can be derived by taking the coefficients for education and for age and adding them. Since these coefficients represent deviations from two different means, for the two broad age groups, it is simpler to add the mean also. This provides an adjusted hourly earning estimate for each age and education group representing what the average earnings of that group would be if it were completely representative of the white, male nonfarmer working population in all other respects. These "adjusted" earnings are given, together with the actual hourly earnings for each age-education group in Table 3.

### Table 2  Summary of Four Multivariate Analyses

| | All spending unit heads who worked in 1959 (14 factors) | All white, male nonfarm spending unit heads who worked in 1959 (12 factors) | All white, male nonfarm spending unit heads who worked in 1959 (9 factors) | |
|---|---|---|---|---|
| | | | 18–34 | 35 and older |
| Mean hourly earnings | $2.29 | $2.60 | $2.41 | $2.82 |
| Proportion of variance explained by the multivariate analysis adjusted for degrees of freedom) | .34 | .23 | .24 | .23 |
| Beta coefficient[a] of the unadjusted deviations for: | | | | |
| age and education | .391 | .401 | | |
| education | | | .313 | .387 |
| Beta coefficients of the deviations adjusted for effects of other factors in the analysis | | | | |
| for: | | | | |
| age and education | .234 | .279 | | |
| education | | | .193 | .263 |

[a] The "beta coefficient" used is analogous to the beta coefficient in multiple regression using ordinary numerical variables. If we treated the adjusted coefficients for each factor or characterisitic as a new variable, and recomputed a regression with these 14, or 12, or 9 new "variables", the beta coefficients derived from this analysis would be identical with those given above.

## ESTIMATED LIFETIME EARNINGS

The earnings estimates in Table 3, multiplied by an assumed number of hours per year and discounted for any assumed expected working life at any desired interest rate, will provide lifetime earnings estimates net of the intercorrelations of education with the other factors used. A comparison of these estimates with a set derived from the actual hourly earnings will provide some measure of the extent to which previous estimates of the value of education may have been exaggerated because of the correlations between education and other things.

For example, if one discounts future earnings at 4 per cent back to age fifteen, assuming no earnings while in school and 2000 hours of work each year, the estimates for white, male, nonfarmers

### Table 3 Hourly Earnings, Actual and Adjusted by Age and Education[a]

*(for all white, male, nonfarmer heads of spending units in the labor force who worked in 1959)*

| Education | | Age | | | | | |
|---|---|---|---|---|---|---|---|
| | | 18–24 | 25–34 | 35–44 | 45–54 | 55–64 | 65–74 |
| 1–8 grades | actual | $1.70 | $2.12 | $2.23 | $2.26 | $2.21 | $1.74 |
| | adjusted | 1.85 | 2.26 | 2.58 | 2.59 | 2.61 | 2.04 |
| 9–11 grades | actual | 1.96 | 2.38 | 2.55 | 2.58 | 2.53 | 2.06 |
| | adjusted | 2.10 | 2.51 | 2.71 | 2.72 | 2.74 | 2.17 |
| 12 grades | actual | 1.92 | 2.34 | 3.04 | 3.07 | 3.02 | 2.55 |
| | adjusted | 1.99 | 2.40 | 2.90 | 2.91 | 2.93 | 2.36 |
| 12 grades and nonacademic training | actual | 2.19 | 2.61 | 3.00 | 3.03 | 2.98 | 2.51 |
| | adjusted | 2.02 | 2.43 | 2.85 | 2.86 | 2.88 | 2.31 |
| College, no degree | actual | 2.30 | 2.72 | 3.12 | 3.15 | 3.10 | 2.64 |
| | adjusted | 2.32 | 2.73 | 2.99 | 3.00 | 3.02 | 2.45 |
| College, bachelor's degree | actual | 2.71 | 3.13 | 3.90 | 3.93 | 3.88 | 3.41 |
| | adjusted | 2.46 | 2.87 | 3.66 | 3.67 | 3.69 | 3.12 |
| College, advanced degree | actual | 3.20[b] | 3.62[b] | 4.47 | 4.50 | 4.45 | 3.98 |
| | adjusted | 2.71[b] | 3.12[b] | 4.23 | 4.24 | 4.26 | 3.69 |

**Source** Survey Research Center.

Since the age effects within the two main age groups (eighteen to thirty-four and thirty-five to seventy-four) were estimated as part of the multivariate analysis, it is difficult to specify numbers of cases. There were only 15 cases of eighteen to thirty-four year olds with advanced degrees, so that the four numbers in the lower left corner are not reliable. No other group has less than 40 cases.

[a] Adjusted rates allow for the net effects of age and education "holding constant" all the other factors.

[b] Unreliable, too few cases.

who become heads of spending units are given in Table 4, both gross and adjusted for effects of other factors. It can be seen that finishing more school short of getting a college degree appears to be of small advantage, and adjusted for other factors, even a disadvantage if alternative investments yield 4 per cent. If education benefits a person at this level it is apparently in the form of steadier jobs rather than in differences in rates of pay sufficient to repay the lost earnings at a relatively high discount rate.[8]

The advantage of extending one's goal from a high school diploma to a college degree is, from Table 4, $17,050 gross, or $10,150 after adjusting, perhaps overadjusting, for other factors that can affect earnings, and beyond the 4 per cent return built into the estimates.

These findings are very much affected by the earnings foregone by continuing in school, as well as by the rate of discount. At age fifteen waiting seven years (through college) to start earnings can be thought of as eliminating seven years of immediate earnings

### Table 4   Value at Age Fifteen of Expected Future Earnings, Discounted at 4 Per Cent Assuming 2000 Hours of Work Per Year to Age Sixty-Five
(for all white, male, nonfarmer heads of spending units)

| | At age fifteen | |
| --- | --- | --- |
| Amount of education completed | Using unadjusted earning rates | Earning rates adjusted for other factors[a] |
| 0–8 grades | $86,600 | $96,000 |
| 9–11 grades | 91,100 | 96,500 |
| 12 grades | 91,100 | 90,300 |
| 12 grades and nonacademic training | 92,400 | 86,900 |
| College, no degree | 92,850 | 91,100 |
| College, bachelor's degree | 108,150 | 100,450 |
| College, advanced degree | 111,000 | 101,700 |

[a] Earning rate if the group were average in every other respect, that is, as to religion, personality, father's education, local labor market conditions, past mobility, and supervisory responsibility.

which are not discounted very heavily, more than twenty thousand dollars' worth.

If we ignore the period from fifteen to twenty-five years of age, the differences between a high school education and a college degree jump from $17,050 to $33,300 unadjusted, and from $10,150 to $25,500 adjusted. It is, of course, illegitimate to ignore the ten years from age fifteen to twenty-five, and the differences in earnings during that period. The *undiscounted* differences between high school degree and college degree are over $60,620 for the unadjusted earnings estimates, and $54,680 using the earnings estimates adjusted for the effects of other factors.

One could argue for a lower rate of discount in estimating value to the individual on the grounds that safe investments for the average man do not yield well. One could argue for a higher rate on the grounds that alternative social or private investments yield more, though such yield estimates are frequently tenuous. The computations are intended to be illustrative, not exclusive.


## QUALIFICATIONS

There are a number of important qualifications to be kept in mind in interpreting these results. First, data on earnings at a point in time are only rough indicators of future lifetime incomes. Increasing levels of real income and even more of money income, mean that current levels and differentials in income among today's older people underestimate the levels and differences which may exist some years hence when today's young people reach those ages. The average earnings in a cross-section sample may drop between the forty-five to fifty-four age group and those fifty-five to sixty-four, but those now fifty will almost certainly have higher average earnings in five years. Similarly, those who are not thirty-five will probably have higher incomes at age fifty-five than are suggested by present cross-section estimates for incomes of persons now aged fifty-five. One of the reasons for using 4 percent as a discount rate is to offset the underestimates of future levels and differentials in current data.

It is even possible that the whole pattern of differences in earnings will change as we turn out more college graduates. However,
Herman Miller has produced some evidence to indicate that no such
effect had appeared between 1939 and 1959.[9] Apparently the
increased supply of highly educated people has not yet reduced their
differential earnings rewards.

Secondly, as has been pointed out, the multivariate analysis
removes too much, and understates the effects of education. The
truth probably lies somewhere between the adjusted and unadjusted
estimates.

Thirdly, the quality of education differs between schools, and
over time. Had our measure of education been a more precise
measure of the quantity of education absorbed rather than years
completed, the estimated effects would almost certainly have been
larger. People of different ages received different kinds of education.
Whether the differences between levels now represent greater
differences in real education or smaller differences than a generation
ago is difficult to say.

Fourthly, education affects not only a man's productive value,
but also the extent to which he is subject to unemployment, or can
find second jobs. In looking at the value of education to the individual
both are relevant, but then one should also have to deduct estimated
taxes too. In looking at the value of education to society, we have
argued that unemployment should be blamed elsewhere than on low
education. Some unemployment, however, might be directly attributable to the lack of flexibility and foresight associated with less
formal education, so that again our results underestimate the value
of education to society. The much larger estimates of the economic
value of education in the article by Houthakker cited earlier, even at
higher discount rates, after taxes, and with mortality adjustments,
can be accounted for partly by the differences between hourly and
annual earnings. However, the Census data used by Houthakker and
others include property income, and the sample includes individuals
who had zero income because they were not in the labor force.
Similar problems of comparability arise with Herman Miller's data
cited earlier. One might argue that somewhat higher hourly earnings

are paid to the uneducated to compensate for the instability of their jobs, in which case hourly earnings differences would understate true differences in rewards.


## SUMMARY

Multivariate analysis has been used to derive estimates of the effects of education on hourly earnings relatively free from the effects of other factors correlated both with education and with earnings. Many problems remain, but as a first approximation the results would indicate that the objections to the use of simple average earnings of different age and education groups on the grounds of spurious correlation are correct but quantitatively not terribly important.[10]

The elimination of property and transfer income from the dependent variable, as well as the income of other earners and the effect of part-time work or unemployment, reduces the extent to which it could be claimed that in this analysis education is taking credit for things not truly the result of education.

The conjecture that the income differential related to differences in education is higher for whites than for Negroes is not directly tested, but its impact on the estimated effects of education on earnings is shown to be negligible when the analysis is rerun without Negroes, females, and farmers.[11]

Finally, the data presented here, when combined with estimates of the costs of education, and of possible future national gains in real income and in income differentials can provide the base for better estimates of the value of an education. If differences between education groups in the extent of unemployment are also to be attributed to education, the estimated value of education will be still greater.

It is not true that annual hours of work increase systematically with the level of formal education. Unemployment decreases, but longer vacations, less frequent holding of two jobs, and other voluntary substituting of leisure for income offset some of the unemployment differences. In this situation the use of annual earnings hides some of the benefits of education taken as leisure while blaming unemployment on differences in education.

## Education and Income: A Comment

JAMES MORGAN AND CHARLES LININGER

The recent article by Morgan and David, "Education and Income"[1] was based primarily on data for a single year, 1959, although it was noted therein that studies by Herman Miller indicated no tendency for the increased supply of highly educated people to depress their relative advantage in the labor market.

We recently tabulated data from four *Surveys of Consumer Finances* (1957, 1958, 1962 and 1963) to check further into the relation of education to income. The recent data show a larger differential than appeared five years earlier in the annual earnings of spending unit heads with more education as compared with those with less education.

Some of this increased differential may result from increased unemployment and shorter work weeks among the uneducated, but the change is so dramatic as to indicate that hourly earnings are also affected.

Table 1 shows the increased differential for employee heads of spending units 35–64 years of age, that is, excluding the young and the old, the self-employed and the farmers, and others not in the civilian labor force. Farmers and the self-employed were omitted since their income often includes a return to land or tangible capital. The continued emphasis in the economy on research and development, and the elimination of many unskilled jobs by automation are thus reflected in an increasing payoff to higher education. The detailed data by age groups seem to show that the increase is greatest

among college graduates between 45 and 54 years of age.[2] The
figures presented are subject to both sampling and reporting errors.
But the two pairs of years which were averaged in each case showed
the same patterns despite the sampling variability.

### Table 1  Mean Annual Earnings of Employee Heads of Spending Units Aged 35–64 Years by Educational Groups[a]

| Education of Head of Spending Unit | 1956–1957 Average | | 1961–1962 Average | | $(b-a)$ | $\left(\dfrac{b}{a} \cdot 100\right)$ |
|---|---|---|---|---|---|---|
| | Mean Earnings (a) | $n^b$ | Mean Earnings (b) | $n^b$ | | |
| 0–8 grades | $3,420 | 807 | $3,660 | 502 | $  240 | 107 |
| 9–11 grades | 4,530 | 509 | 5,650 | 387 | 1,120 | 122 |
| 12 grades | 5,060 | 646 | 5,740 | 421 | 680 | 113 |
| College, no degree | 6,330 | 307 | 8,340 | 204 | 2,010 | 132 |
| College, degree | 8,500 | 364 | 11,070 | 255 | 2,570 | 130 |

**Source** Survey Research Center, *Surveys of Consumer Finances.*

[a] For all spending unit heads excluding self-employed businessmen and farmers, house-wives, students, members of the armed services and retired persons.

[b] $n$ = number of cases.

The implication is clear, that the private and social value of
investment in education is *greater* than previously implied; the
value of investment in education will continue to remain great as long
as unskilled jobs are eliminated faster than the number of unskilled
workers decline, and the demands for technically trained people
increase faster than the supply.

# STEPHEN MERRETT

# *The Rate of*
## *Return to Education:*
### *A Critique*

*H*ow valid are economic analyses of human capital formation through education? Many limitations exist as the authors of previous selections have shown. Stephen Merrett's article identifies the problems encountered in measuring costs and benefits. If social benefits and costs are not measured, estimates of the rate of return from educational investments in human capital may be meaningless. After discussing some of the empirical problems and conceptual differences in the social and private benefit context, Merrett identifies the nature of

Reprinted from Stephen Merrett, "The Rate of Return to Education: A Critique," *Oxford Economic Papers* 18 (November 1966), pp. 289–303, with permission of the author and the Clarendon Press, Oxford.

Notes to this essay are on pages 292–293; References are on 267–268.

*the econometric problems involved in sorting out the effects of education on income. The author, Economic Adviser to the Ministry of Technology, United Kingdom, concludes that the human capital concept is incapable of dealing with many relevant benefits and costs of investments in education. For this reason he suggests that future research on the rate of return to educational investments in human capital should be abandoned.*

During the past decade economists in Europe and the United States have intervened in educational research, hitherto the province of sociologists and psychologists, by developing the concept of human capital. "Investment in education" is a stylization of the relation between formal learning and economic activity first introduced by Smith and later taken up again, only to be rejected, by Marshall. It can be expressed in the following way: education is a process of economic production which integrates a set of factors of production including the services of the "primary labor unit," the student. The product, the "machine," is a bundle of physical and mental skills indissolubly associated with the primary labor unit, and employed by him throughout his working life.

The rate of return on the "machine" can be calculated by discovering the cost and benefit streams associated with a given level of schooling. The social cost stream will be made up of:

1. Depreciation and interest on capital equipment, such as buildings and teaching machines.
2. Salaries of teachers and auxiliary staff.
3. Rent of land on which the institution is sited.
4. Materials such as textbooks and stationery.
5. Incidental costs to students such as transportation.
6. The opportunity cost of the time and effort of the student.
7. The value of net leisure forgone by the student which equals the value of the excess of the number of hours of leisure enjoyed by a full-time worker, over the leisure enjoyed by the student.

The benefit stream is calculated in a more indirect manner. A matrix is drawn up of the income of the population classified by age and education: for any given age the difference in the incomes of two education groups is taken as the benefit derived from the difference in their education, whether in the number of years received or the type of specialization. The variation of these residuals between age-groups is taken as an estimate of the time shape of the benefits.[1] Once the estimates of the cost and benefit streams have been made they can be summarized by calculating the internal rate of return.

The definition used of costs and benefits will not be the same for the social return as it is for private returns. The private cost stream will not include the full value of expenditures 1 to 4 above when these are provided free or at a subsidized rate by the State or private endowment funds. Similarly scholarships will be subtracted from the value of net income forgone. Private returns will be based on post-tax incomes. Social returns must make an allowance for the emigration of graduates and estimates should be adjusted for mortality and unemployment rates.

Having introduced the estimating procedure, the major difficulties involved in calculating costs will now be examined. Undoubtedly the most complex difficulty will be with student opportunity costs, which Schultz calculates as about 50 percent of total costs [16]. Vaizey, and Balogh and Streeten, have even suggested that this element of the cost stream should not be counted at all [17, pp. 42–43; 1, pp. 101–102]. But it seems clear that if the sector in question is regarded as "machine"-creating then it follows that the primary labor unit should be credited with a shadow wage, and that those labor costs should be included in the cost stream. The problem is that the wage is rarely paid in full and therefore has to be estimated.

The usual procedure is to take the excess of a high-school graduate's income over that of an undergraduate (in the case of university education). Unfortunately students differ systematically from non-students, characteristically having richer, better connected, more highly educated parents, being of above average intelligence and more highly motivated. If serious under-estimation of opportunity costs is to be avoided, some attempt must be made to control the measurement of income forgone for these factors [4]. Even were the two groups comparable, it may be mistaken to base the opportunity cost calculation on the average wages of the working group. The hypothetical wage income of the students is the measure of the long-run equilibrium loss to the community resulting from that part of the labor force studying and not working. However, were they working, the wage rates of their age-education cohort would be lower, unless the demand for its services were perfectly elastic. In that case an average-wage based estimate should be employed only for marginal changes in the student body.

Let the assumption be made that only marginal changes are being considered or that the demand curve is perfectly elastic. I now wish to demonstrate that the universally accepted rule for calculating opportunity-costs, "Sum up year-by-year student incomes forgone" is mistaken. Imagine a would-be student considering choosing between two careers. In both cases the gestation period of the "machine" is the same, and money outlays per annum on teaching staff, laboratory equipment, etc., are equivalent; in both cases the post-graduation income flow is the same. It is clear that from a strictly economic point of view both the student and the State should be indifferent between the two specializations, since all extra-student costs, all returns, and the time and effort of the student are just the same. However, let us suppose that at any moment before graduation the wage available to the student were he to drop out from his studies is not invariant with his specialization. The reason does not matter, but one can imagine a partly trained mechanical engineer's income as greater than that of a partly trained astro-physicist. Evidently the income forgone rule indicates one completed career as more costly than the other, and there is tremendous competition for scholarships in astro-physics, a *reductio ad absurdum*, The conclusion is that income forgone should not include the forgone earnings on part-training.

Clearly the relation between part-training and the wage-rate in alternative employment is of interest, but it is appropriately dealt with by considering any course short of the full career as an alternative investment project and calculating separately its rate of return. As an extension of this the overall rate of return expected from initiating training amongst a body of undergraduates should be adjusted for the number who will probably leave the institution before taking their degree. In the example used above this would make *engineering not astro-physics* more attractive to both students and the State, yet this is nothing to do with costs, but with anticipated returns.

The other serious difficulty encountered in estimating human capital costs arises in defining what outlays are to be included, and this will be of particular importance at the university level. Expenditures on residential and dining-hall accommodation must certainly be excluded where the community would have had to have made them in any case. However if the food and living-space consumed by the student in these institutions does involve the economy in extra outlays, rather than the reallocation of the financing of a given level of expenditures, then these extra costs must be included. This is the case with Halls of Residence when accommodation within the student's family has zero marginal cost.

Research can be regarded as investment not in the transmission of knowledge but in its extension. Therefore it does not produce a "machine" indissolubly associated with the primary labor unit, but specializes in the production of external economies, so research outlays should be excluded from the cost estimate. This is not to deny the importance of research departments but simply to put them in another economic box. Intercollegiate athletics, in fact all Student Union activities, may be regarded as consumption, not "machine"-creating, and likewise excluded from costs. The distinction may be hard to make. How does one deal with research into structuralist inflation when it is embodied in a future course of lectures on the Latin American dilemma? How does one deal with a subsidized performance of "The Crucible" when it is instructive to a future lecturer on American literature?

What are the major problems involved in measuring the benefit stream? Most commentaries on the process of investment in education, usually with university education in mind, suggest that our measurements have the great weakness of ignoring both the consumption benefits the primary labor unit derives from extending his knowledge and intellectual capacity and the consumption benefits of holding graduate-occupations. This is a fair criticism, but totally misleading when it is posed as a problem specific to education. Returning to the original model, we can regard the individual receiving education as co-operating in the production of a "machine" and at the end of such a process working with the "machine" he has helped to manufacture. Now it becomes clearer that these study- and work-related benefits—the pleasure derived from mastering the intricacies of Robinson on the foreign exchanges, and the pleasure derived from extending the analysis of devaluation to include absorption affects—are conceptually in the same category as Marxian alienation, the consumption losses through inability to comprehend one's function in a factory, the powerlessness to change the pattern of production processes. Thus if alienation is looked on as a subject suitable to social psychologists rather than economists, so too are these study- and work-related benefits. What *has* been shown is how poor a measure of human sacrifice is provided by labor costs measured by wage and salary outlays. When, with the neo-classicists, labor was regarded as homogeneously distasteful to workers, their distaste being compensated by money payments, then labor costs did seem to perform a useful function. But surely the enormous heterogeneity of working activity has now been recognized. This is not compensated by money differentials, as Adam Smith held, since occupation groups broadly defined are non-competing through entry qualifications.[2] The neo-classical marginal compensation thesis must be abandoned. But, I repeat, this objection does not lie at the door only of education cost-benefit procedures, but any such procedure involving human activity.

A rather different objection is that education changes the nature of our leisure activities. (In the preceding paragraph I dealt only with pre- and post-graduation work-related pleasure.) This does seem to be a greater burden for investment in human capital than any other form of investment, since it is clearly one of the functions of education to produce qualitative changes in our tastes. This effect is simply outside the scope of economics and for this reason the use of the concept of human capital is justifiably criticized for the narrowness of its criteria.

How can one deal with the external economies of education? Since it has been suggested already that the extension of knowledge, in contrast to its transmission, is not relevant to the model nor therefore to the estimation of the rate of return, this most recalcitrant of problems is neatly side-stepped. But this still leaves the political, social, and psychological benefits of having an educated population, although as Balogh and Streeten have pointed out these benefits may be negative, by creating a revolutionary unemployed class of intellectuals, breeding contempt for manual labor, or setting up an *élite* whose ideals conflict with the needs of development.

The seriousness of this problem for the economist, especially with respect to the low-income countries, can be illustrated by the literacy campaign on the part of the Cuban Government in 1961, one of the main objectives of which was to instill in the people a common purpose, the enthusiastic construction of a socialist nation [9]. Success or failure in this endeavor would clearly have profound economic consequences, yet it was impossible to express the activity generated by the campaign in units, and therefore the product of the education process could have no price and no measureable return. At the moment external effects such as the creation of nice neighbors and informed electorates, the reduction of delinquency rates, and the re-structuring of people's attitudes toward economic growth and social change seem quite beyond the techniques evolved in the science of economics, and must be left to the other social sciences, in particular politics, psychology and sociology. For this reason calculating the rate of return to education is of much more limited value than calculating the rate of return to (say) electricity generation, since these immeasurable external economies are often the major objective of the education process.[3]

The most widely adopted method of predicting future earnings is through a cross-section by age of the population with given educational qualifications. Then, if we wish to know what the income will be in five or ten year's time of a 25-year-old student now graduating from high-school we take the average income of that sub-set of the population with the same level of education, and of age 30 and 35 respectively.

The use of cross-section material completely ignores the dynamics of sectoral and occupational structure. Historically, shifts in the demand and supply schedules for different types and levels of skills have been very great, and it seems that such an evolution is one of the mechanisms essential to the process of economic growth. Some valuable information in this respect has been set out for the case of the United States [14, p. 331]. In 1910 the proportion of the labor force who were white-collar workers, skilled and semi-skilled workers, laborers and service workers, and farmers stood at 21 percent, 26 percent, 36 percent and 17 percent respectively. By 1950 these proportions had changed to 37 percent, 35 percent, 21 percent and 7 percent.

The rates of return on the various types and levels of education required for different occupations and economic sectors may well indicate in any time-period that the mix of educational output is optimal, even in those cases where present price differentials between formally acquired skills can only remain constant in the future if our rate-of-return estimates show that large supply changes will be necessary from the education sector. That is, the relative prices derived from cross-section data are determined independently of future changes in the demand for different skills, but the rate of return which uses these relative prices should not be, otherwise it becomes useless as an instrument of social policy. For any government of the Third World intending to convert the country from an agricultural backwater to an industrial economy it would be extremely dangerous to adopt that set of prices reflecting the present situation. For one thing many occupation categories vital to the Development Plan's success might not yet exist.

Finally, even assuming no change in the occupation structure, there is every reason to believe that present prices will not equal future prices since, for the industrialized countries at least, *per capita* incomes have maintained an upward trend since the end of the Second World War. One knows that factor prices and therefore their residuals are influenced in many ways—the trade cycle, technical progress, the accumulation of capital, the international terms of trade. Therefore any prediction of the benefit stream needs to state the future conjuncture of the economy—stagnation, steady growth, the cycle fluctuating about an upward trend—whatever it may be. For the absolute income differential between two education groups will be greater in a growing economy than in a stagnant one, and in an economy cursed by the trade cycle unemployment rates will probably be lower amongst the better educated.

The figure eventually computed, the rate-of-return, is no more than a convenient way of summarizing two price-streams. If it is to have any meaning for public investment decisions, these prices must in some sense reflect factor productivities. But frequently this is not the case, as one can illustrate with several counter examples found in the literature on education and income.

The very fact that one has to go to great lengths in measuring student opportunity costs is because the primary labor unit does not receive a full wage reflecting his part in building the "machine." It might be argued that in this way students are paying the cost of their training. This cannot be so since even if they received a zero income they would be paying only the wage of the primary labor unit—by not receiving it themselves.

Machlup has complained that inadequate payments are made to university teachers, in comparison with lawyers, doctors, and dentists [10, p. 80]. In general there seems to be a feeling that the teaching profession as a whole receives less than its opportunity cost. As Eckaus has pointed out: "Is the low rate of return on teachers' education a signal to stop educating teachers? Or is that relatively low rate of return itself the consequence of a social decision which could and should be changed without recourse to the rate of return calculation?" [6, p. 183].

Balogh and Streeten in attacking the rate of return model have said: "If anybody attempted to use these models for calculating the returns to education in many underdeveloped countries he would discover even higher rates of return. All this would show, however, is that pay scales in the civil service, in universities and in the professions are still governed by the traditional standards of a feudal or colonial aristocracy and by natural or artificial restrictions. It would provide no clue as to how public money ought to be distributed between 'investment' in 'physical capital' and in 'people'" [1, p. 102].

Finally, in Miller's study of U.S. incomes it was pointed out that: "In the South, the proportion by which the average income of whites exceeded that of non-whites increased from 48 percent for grammar school graduates to 73 percent for high school graduates t o 85 percent for college graduates" [11, p. 45]. There were controls for age and residence. The proximate cause lay with occupation. "Behind the dissimilar relationships between education and income among white and non-white men lie differences in vocational opportunities, among other things. To illustrate, the proportion of white men between 45 and 54 employed as service workers and laborers (two occupation groups with low average incomes) decreases significantly for each successively higher education group. Among non-white men in the same age-group, on the other hand, the proportion employed as service workers or laborers decreases very little for successively higher education groups. Even a college education has not been a sufficient qualification to elevate a majority of the' non-white men above the occupational level of service workers or laborers" [7]. But there can be little doubt that the fundamental cause operating through occupation was color. In this case factor prices may have conceivably reflected productivities, but certainly did not reflect opportunity cost.

This leads to a different but associated question. Even when prices do reflect present productivities, this may provide a very poor basis for making public investment decisions. For low productivity and low prices may merely reflect an economy that is out of joint, badly structured. For instance, there may be little demand for agricultural engineers in some Latin American countries, not because they are unproductive, but because the system of latifundio and minifundio precludes their co-operation in enriching the soil.

In the final section of the paper I wish to discuss the econometric difficulties involved in measuring education's rate of return. The level of an individual's earnings is not wholly determined by education. A short list of other leading factors will include: location, occupation, sex, race, age, physical condition, drive, and intelligence, including both psycho-motor and intellectual skills. A simple bi-

variate analysis will always lead to an overestimation of the influence
of education on income. For men, whites, urban workers, the
ambitious and the intelligent tend to be more highly educated than
women, non-whites, rural workers, the sluggards, and the unintelli-
gent, and, *even when there is no difference in education* the first group
tends to earn more than the second. Only the association between age,
education, and income provides a counter-example. As a result in a
simple correlation between income and education the positive
association between the independent variable education, and all
these other non-computed determinants will lead to their effects
swelling the size of education's regression coefficient. In fact in any
society where progress to higher education levels depends on the
outcome of a selection process, inevitably the more educated will be
distinctive from the rest of their age-cohort in terms of the criteria of
that selection process. In order to pare down the gross bivariate
returns to a net differential, the obvious procedure is to use multiple
correlation analysis.

A sample is drawn from the population who have left the
formal education system; the $n$ members of the sample will vary in
terms of the explanatory variables chosen, say education and intelligence. An equation of the form

$$Y_i = \beta_1 + \beta_2 X_{2i} + \beta_3 X_{3i} \qquad (i = 1, ..., n) \qquad (1)$$

is then fitted to these observations by least-squares, where $Y$ equals
income, $X_2$ equals number of years of education and $X_3$ equals
measured intelligence. In this way we can arrive at the coefficient of
multiple determination, $r^2$, showing what proportion of the variance
of the dependent variable can be explained by the variance in the
values of the independent variables. And to each of the latter we can
assign a net regression coefficient, $\beta_2$ and $\beta_3$.[4]

Some econometric problems of lesser or greater difficulty are
bound to be met with. First, the right-hand side of the equation
contains one or more variables of a qualitative nature, such as sex and
occupation. To deal with this one can either adopt a numerative scale
or use dummy variables. In one case, the variable, occupation for
instance, although considered as ordinal in nature, is graded into a

number of subdivisions which are then ranked in order of the degree of skills supposedly required to carry them out, and each subdivision is then assigned a numerical value. The qualitative variable has been transformed into a quantitative variable. In the other case one uses dummy variables, so that each subdivision is regarded as a variable itself, with its own regression coefficient, taking the value 1 whenever an observation falls into that subdivision, and zero in all other cases. In this case the relation between income, education, and sex would take the following form:

$$Y_i = \beta_2 X_{2i} + \beta_4 X_{4i} + \beta_5 X_{5i}, \qquad (2)$$

where $X_4$ and $X_5$ are the dummy variables for sex such that

$$X_4 = \begin{cases} 1 \text{ for each male} \\ 0 \text{ for each female} \end{cases} \qquad X_5 = \begin{cases} 0 \text{ for each male} \\ 1 \text{ for each female} \end{cases}$$

$\beta_4$ is the estimation of the intercept, $\beta_1$, in equation (1) for an all-male sample and $\beta_5$ the estimate of the intercept for an all-female sample [8, pp. 221–28].

It has been pointed out already that a bivariate technique will have a bias to overestimation. The intercorrelation of the independent variables which caused this unfortunately reappears in the multivariate analysis under the guise of multi-collinearity. Since many of the variables are moving together it becomes extremely difficult to disentangle, so to speak, their independent effects. Whilst this brings about no systematic bias, it does increase the size of the standard errors.

The beta coefficients are measures of the net effect of each supposedly causal variable, excluding the influence of other associated variables contained in the equation. However, even a variable with a statistically significant beta coefficient may have in reality no causal relationship with the dependent variable income. This will be the case when there is an association between the independent variable in question and any other variables which are excluded from the equation and yet causally related to the dependent variable. Probably the most comprehensive attempt to discover the net relation between income and education was carried out by Morgan, David, Cohen, and Brazer [14]. They used 14 explanatory variables divided into 84 groups. Since they believed age and education did not hold an additive relation, the two variables were combined to give 21 age-education groups; each group was then treated as a dummy variable. These 21 groups accounted for the largest part of the explanation, the set having a beta coefficient of 0.234. Their analysis accounted for 35 per cent of the variance. However, with so much unexplained the possibility of spurious significance and errors in the size of the beta coefficients is inevitable, reducing the education coefficient's value in allowing us to pare down the gross income differentials.

Some of the explanatory variables which one needs to incorporate are difficult to define, let alone measure. This is true most obviously of intelligence and drive. In addition, "years of education" are quite clearly unsatisfactory units when one is dealing with different education sectors and with different generations of students. Measurement error and heterogeneity of the measurement unit will always give a bias toward underestimation. This can be illustrated in a two-variable case (Fig. 1).

Suppose the relation $Y_i = \beta_1 + \beta_6 X_{6i}$ in Fig. 1 is the relation when both income and drive are measured precisely. With a correlation coefficient of 1 all observations would be on the straight line representing that equation. Now suppose that although income is measured accurately, drive is mismeasured so that the scatter points lie horizontally about the true line as indicated. Least squares regression gives the result: $Y_i = \beta_1' + \beta_6' X_{6i}$, and clearly $\beta_6' < \beta_6$, so that the importance of drive in effecting income is understated. Intuitively one can see that mismeasurement in any of the variables will tend to underrate their significance. In addition, tests for multicollinearity can be spuriously *insignificant* through measurement errors.

Finally the original equation assumes additivity amongst the independent variables, that a coefficient can be assigned to each variable independently of the values of the other variables—we assume away interaction. If the answer to the following eight questions are in the affirmative one will be justified in assuming an additive relation between education and location, occupation, sex,

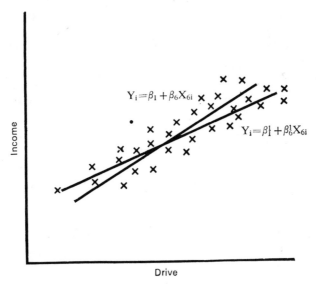

**Figure 1**

race, age, physical condition, drive and intelligence. "Will the increase in a person's annual income as a result of taking a university degree be independent of the fact that: (1) the graduate works in a rural backwater rather than a thriving metropolis? (2) the graduate enters an unskilled occupation rather than one of the professions? (3) the graduate is female rather than male? (4) the graduate is a Negro rather than an Anglo-Saxon? (5) the graduate is a young man rather than a mature student? (6) the graduate is frequently sick rather than in excellent health? (7) the graduate is lazy rather than hard-working? (8) the graduate has an intelligence quotient of 100 rather than 150?

Additivity seems an absurd assumption; it would imply for instance that there is no economic benefit to be derived from selecting the intelligent for university training. It seems plausible that initial advantages in variables other than education are likely to multiply up the benefits of education. As soon as we admit interaction amongst education and any or all of the other independent variables, then in order to define a regression coefficient for education alone, which is what we need, we have to control for these variables, perhaps as a result reducing the observations in each cell to a statistically useless number. Furthermore a whole series of regression coefficients will have to be calculated each applying to a set of values of the other variables.[5]

The complexity of a regression model which would be capable of dealing with all these econometric difficulties has been greatly underestimated in some recent studies. Blaug, using Henderson-Stewart's results, has quoted the private rate-of-return to the three years required to complete secondary school education in Great Britain in 1963 as about 13 per cent [3]. This statistic was derived from British data on income, age, and education by applying a "Denison coefficient" of 0.6 to the gross income differentials (controlled for age) between education groups to solve the multiple correlation problems. But Denison's coefficient itself was derived from a study of 2,759 high school graduates from Illinois, Minnesota, and Rochester in the U.S.A., who graduated thirty years ago, the great majority of whom were drawn only from those children who attained high I.Q.'s or were high in their class ranking, and for whom we have only crude data on their intelligence test scores, rank-in-class in high-school, and father's occupation [5].

The calculation of the rate of return to education, like any other piece of economic research, meets with a host of minor difficulties, such as the measurement of student opportunity costs, and the exclusion of expenditures on residential accommodation, research, and consumption activities from the cost estimate. However, in measuring the benefit stream these difficulties become really very ugly. At the conceptual level the economist seems unable to deal with psychic income, whether positive or negative, from study and graduate occupations; with changes in the nature of leisure activities; and with the measurement of external economies, a euphemism for shifts in the frame of reference and drive of the individual in the political, sociological, and psychological spheres. Yet those effects, along with the desire to create skilled personnel for the economic system, are the objectives of education. The human capital concept seems incapable of dealing with them. At the technical level it is wholly mistaken, in some societies, to assume factor prices are equal to productivity or opportunity cost. Large errors will probably be made in deriving the benefit stream as a residual from two income streams predicted with the use of cross-section data. Finally, in order to derive the net contribution of education to income one becomes engaged in a multi-variate analysis, using a large number of variables, both quantitative and qualitative, heterogeneous in their units, intercorrelated and holding non-additive relations.

The conclusion of this paper is that research into the rate of return on education should be discontinued. The most fruitful fields of future research in the economics of education seem to be the relation: between economic output, occupational structure, and educational qualifications; the efficiency of the education process in attaining its objectives; and the relation between education and socio-economic phenomena such as innovatory activity, work incentives, and social cohesion.

## APPENDIX

A variant on this theme has appeared in the work of Becker and Mincer essentially as an *ad hoc* means of coping with scarcity of data. Mincer wished to calculate the costs and returns to on-the-job training in the United States. The costs would normally consist of: the opportunity cost of training, that is the difference between what could have been produced and what is produced by the trainee; the time spent in supervision by experienced workers; increased maintenance costs and depreciation of machinery; higher inspection costs; and a higher accident rate. These may be borne by the firm or passed on to the worker by paying him a wage less than his marginal product.

There are some distressing lacunae in the data available. It is not known and impossible to estimate the fraction of total costs borne by worker and firm respectively. Data on total training costs are both scarce and unreliable. Finally: "A direct computation of forgone earnings of workers engaged in on-the-job training would be possible if data were available on their earnings during and after the period of training, and on earnings of a comparison group of workers who have the same amount of formal schooling and are otherwise similar to the trainees, but do not receive any on-the-job training. . . . Unfortunately, it is impossible to classify workers empirically into such comparison groups" [13, p. 53].

Nevertheless, the study arrives eventually, by indirect procedures, at an estimate of training costs borne by workers through lower earnings and rates of return estimates, the latter given to the nearest 0.1 per cent. This, if nothing else, shows a quite extraordinary degree of ingenuity. The ingenuity derives from Becker who demonstrates how costs, the rate of return *and* the investment period can all be calculated by knowing the "net earnings" streams of the two groups in question, one with and one without training. As Becker admits, the possibility of arriving at a total cost estimate depends on our ability to define the earnings stream of a comparable group with zero investment in training [2, p. 36].

The argument runs as follows. Take two earnings streams: one simply the wages of labor power, the other a "net earnings" stream composed of three elements. These elements are: receipts paid to the worker for his unadulterated labor power, receipts paid to the worker as a result of his "machine" investment in past periods, outlays by the worker in financing his share of current investment costs. Thus there is an apparently inextricable mixture in the "net earnings" stream of capital and income accounts, of costs and benefits over an unknown investment period.

However, if one assumes that the individual is indifferent between the two income streams, then their present values will be equal. But if this is true the rate of return on the investment stream will be that discount rate equating the present values of the two streams. Once given this, and assuming a constant rate of return period by period, it is easy to arrive at both the cost estimate and the length of the investment period. For instance, worker-borne costs in the initial period will simply equal the excess of non-investing workers wages over those investing. In the second period investment costs will equal the excess of what the investing worker *could* have earned in that period over his actual earnings. The former will equal unadulterated labor power plus the return on the investment of the first period. Costs are summed up from period to period, and the last period will be that in which actual earnings equal potential earnings. Mincer's estimates turn on the good sense of this method and permit him to utilize the comprehensive income data available in the United States census. Unfortunately the reliability of results using this "procedure under information constraints" is open to considerable doubt since the following assumptions must necessarily be made: perfect competition in the labor market, the rate of return is constant from period to period, trainees know both their potential income and cost streams, and that *trainees are indifferent between the two earnings streams*; additionally since Becker uses an inclusive definition of income forgone, in the sense that it includes the earnings on part-training, his analysis is invalid on these grounds also.

# F. H. HARBISON

# The Strategy of
# Human Resource Development
# in Modernizing Economies

*F*. *H. Harbison, Professor of Economics, Princeton University,
develops a broad strategy of manpower development for nations
now in the throes of early economic development. Capital accumulation,
whether for human or physical purposes, is an important prerequisite to
accelerated development. Several important constraints that retard
human capital formation and otherwise press upon less developed
countries are identified. Constraints such as rapid population growth,*

Reprinted from F. H. Harbison, "The Strategy of Human Resource Development
in Modernizing Economies," *Policy Conference on Economic Growth and Investment in Education* (Paris: Organisation for Economic Co-Operation and Development, 1961), pp. 9–33, with permission of the author and publisher.

Notes to this essay will be found on page 293.

*migration, immediate gratification, foreign aid, nationalistic fervor and independence, and resistance to innovation and change render accelerated development difficult. The stark realities for the developing nations also may include labor surpluses of either unskilled workers or underemployed intellectuals. Shortages of skilled human resources in relation to demand are problems that must be overcome by manpower planning. According to Harbison, the major ingredients of implementing human resource development plans center around incentives, training manpower, and rational educational programs.*

## INTRODUCTION

The newly developing nations of the world are in a state of revolt. They have rejected the notion that poverty, squalor, and disease are preordained. They want high-speed modernization and are resentful of those who caution that economic growth in the advanced Western countries was a gradual process. Even the forced-draft development of the Soviet Union is for them too slow. As Nehru once remarked, India must learn to run before she learns to walk. The newly developing nations are interested not just in economic growth: they are hoping and planning for *accelerated development*; they think in terms of leaps rather than steps in building a modern social, political and economic order.

Accelerated development is, of course, a goal rather than a firm prospect for the future. All of the newly modernizing nations may not be able to leap forward; some may stand still, and others may even fall backward. But the vast majority of the nations of Asia, Africa, and Latin America are increasingly engaging in deliberate planning to achieve it. They are groping for a *strategy* of accelerated development, and also for a strategy for getting aid from the economically advanced countries.

In this paper, I propose to list briefly some of the imperatives and also some of the constraints in devising a strategy for accelerated development. I then propose to concentrate on the elements of a strategy of human resource development, after first examining the patterns of manpower problems which seem to be emerging in the modernizing countries. Finally, I shall discuss the machinery for implementation of a strategy for human resource development. . . .

## THE IMPERATIVES AND CONSTRAINTS OF ACCELERATED DEVELOPMENT

### Imperatives

The country which commits itself to accelerated growth will find that it is imperative to do certain things. It must increase sharply its rate of savings by one means or another. It must place emphasis on industrial development, but at the same time it must modernize and increase the productivity of agriculture. It must invest wisely both in real capital and in people. In so doing, it must develop a sense of priority and timing, so that savings and manpower are directed into the most productive channels. All of this requires integrated planning and coordination of effort.

If the newly developing nations are to have accelerated growth —more rapid, more sweeping and more dramatic than the "historical development" of the advanced nations—they must take deliberate, unprecedented and sometimes drastic measures. They must quickly and sharply increase taxes; they must restrict the too rapid expansion of consumption particularly by the wealthier classes; they must compete successfully for available foreign aid; and they must be prepared to think in terms of long-range economic growth rather than short-term political expediency. Most countries have the capacity for rapid growth, but it is questionable whether some of them can develop the will to do the hard things which are necessary to bring it about. On this point, Arthur Lewis has sounded a rather pessimistic note:

> *Politics is exciting to young countries, and politicians in these countries have attracted to themselves all the glamour which was previously reserved for priests and kings, not excluding the military parades, the salutes of guns, the yachts and the country houses. We must resign*

> *ourselves to the fact that most of the new countries will be too pre-occupied with other matters to give to economic development the priority which it needs*[1]

I do not share completely Lewis' pessimism. Some, though certainly not all, young countries will find the road to accelerated development. In general, the successful countries will be those which are able to accumulate physical and human capital rapidly and to utilize both in high-priority, productive activities.

So much has been written about physical capital formation that no further elaboration is called for here. Let us assume that, on the average, a rapidly modernizing country may need to invest 20 percent or more of its national income each year in order to achieve something approaching the goal of accelerated growth, and that, through taxation, forced savings, foreign aid or other measures, it must accumulate savings at this rate. My contention then is that it must have a correspondingly high rate of human capital formation in the form of the skilled people and institutions which are indispensable for the modernization process.[2]

In the view of the prominent economists, less than one-third of the increase in national income of countries can be explained by quantitative increases in factor inputs—such as capital and labor.[3] The "residual" is explained by *qualitative* improvements in these inputs, such as more productive capital, more productive human resources, economies of scale and other factors. Though an accurate break-down of the residual has not yet been made, the most important factors appear to be the upgrading of human resources—through education, training, health improvement, etc.—as well as the development of knowledge and technology, which are, of course, closely associated with education. From this, it is reasonable to conclude that the wealth of a nation is at least as dependent upon the development of human resources as upon the accumulation of material capital.

There is, however, little to be gained by argument over which is the more important—physical or human capital. Both must be accumulated at high rates of speed if rapid growth is to be achieved. A country's capacity to utilize effectively physical capital is dependent

upon the availability of human capital, and *vice versa*. And it is
essential for politicians and planners to understand that any development plan which does not give high priority to human capital
formation is simply unrealistic and almost certainly destined to fail,
for experience has shown repeatedly that high-level manpower does
not appear automatically or magically as dams, roads, factories,
hospitals, radio stations, and airports come into existence.

## Constraints

In planning modernization, the leaders of the newly developing countries operate within a context of pressures which limit the
range of realistic policy alternatives. Try as they may, the planners
and politicians can neither escape these constraints, nor alter them
significantly.

The first is the rapidly rising policy growth. In nearly all of the
newly modernizing societies, birth rates tend to remain high, while
death rates decline as a result of the spread of public health measures
and medical services. Even if there are no religious or cultural resis-
tances to birth control, it is virtually impossible to have a fall in birth
rates commensurate with the drop in death rates in these countries.
Overpopulation in Asia and parts of the Near East is already a
serious problem. The high rates of population increase in Latin
America give cause for alarm. And even in the relatively uncrowded
areas of Africa, the population explosion is imminent. An increasing
population nearly always complicates the achievement of accelerated
growth. The problems of feeding and health are magnified; expenditures for education must be augmented. A new nation attempting to
achieve accelerated growth is like a man weighing over 250 pounds
training for a two-mile run!

Second is the problem of rural-urban migration. With the
spread of education, the development of transportation, and the very
success of the appeal of modernization, people seek an escape from a
"life-sentence" to traditional farming and flock to the cities much
faster than employment, houses, water supplies, and other public
services can be provided.

Third, as the idea of modernization takes root, so does the desire for immediate improvements in standards of living. The upper classes in particular will increase their consumption of such things as motor scooters, automobiles, refrigerators, radios, hi-fi sets, and television. The poorer classes will want more to eat and more to wear.

Men are told today by leaders and by international organizations such as UNESCO that education is a human right. As a result, the demand for education on the part of all classes becomes particularly strong. In Brazil, families will wait in queues for two or three days at the opening of schools in an attempt to get their children in only to be turned away because of insufficient places. In some countries, children who cannot get *into* schools seek to learn by standing outside at the windows, straining to hear what the teacher is saying *inside*. In the African countries, the building of a school in one village immediately results in pressure from surrounding villages for schools.

Universal primary education is a goal to which all political leaders today must be committed. The increase of primary education creates irresistible pressures for increase in secondary education, and the expansion of secondary education makes expenditures for higher education almost mandatory.

Fourth, practically all of the modernizing nations are dependent upon external aid of one kind or another. They must have financial help from the advanced countries; they must import, temporarily at least, high-level manpower from abroad in order to make use of accumulated knowledge and modern technology; in many cases they must count on foreign countries to maintain and stabilize the prices of raw materials which they sell in the world markets. Distasteful though it may be to the leaders of the modernizing countries, they are in significant respects at the mercy of the more advanced nations. They cannot go it alone.

Fifth, although inextricably dependent upon the services of foreigners, the modernizing countries are always under pressure to get rid of them as speedily as possible. In countries newly emerging from colonial status, the expatriates in the civil service must be replaced wherever possible by nationals. The foreign-owned industrial corporation must open the avenues to higher managerial positions to nationals as soon as they can qualify. The resentment against expatriates who cultivate the art of making themselves indispensable runs high. The newly educated elites are strongly convinced that they have a right to the foreigner's jobs. This is why so much store is placed upon "Nigerianization," "Africanization," or "Indianization," of high-level manpower. The foreigner is needed desperately. He may arrive through technical assistance, or with a new enterprise, or as a consultant. But, except in those countries (*i.e.*, Brazil, Argentina, Chile, Mexico, etc.) where he may remain to become a citizen, he is supposed to expedite his departure. No perceptive political leader rests easily when the top posts in government or industry are occupied by foreigners.

Sixth, the newly modernizing nations must above all maintain political independence while striving for economic independence. The desire to remain neutral in the East-West struggle is becoming ever stronger. Indeed, many nations look at the East-West competition as an opportunity to increase their demands for foreign aid.

Seventh, the leaders of modernizing nations always encounter some resistance to change. The extensive family system, traditional ethical valuations, and legal concepts often stand in the way of innovation. Vested interests, such as large rural landowners or organized religious powers, and their political allies may be expected to offer resistance to basic reforms which the modernization process demands. Such traditions and powerful groups are not easy to brush aside and, for many years to come, the developing countries will continue to have dual economies consisting of a modernizing sector and a vast traditional society responding very slowly to the need for change.

Finally, the *symbols* of modernization are important to the newly developing countries. To several African nations, an international airline is an imperative. In Egypt, the new steel mill is a tangible symbol of the commitment to industrialization. Brazil has built a fabulous new capital city in the heart of the country. Nigeria and Ghana have lavish new universities and more are planned. In most modernizing countries, there are likely to be impressive new government buildings, modern apartments, luxury hotels, and broad new boulevards. Television stations are appearing throughout Latin America and Africa. Everywhere there are new shining factories, huge dams and projects, and plans for big jet airports. These are tangible manifestations and concrete reminders of the commitment to modernization and accelerated growth. As such they are, in the minds of the modernizing elites, almost indispensable elements in any program of development.

The constraints listed above lend support to the view that economic development is as much a political as an economic process. At any rate, the politicians cannot be expected to follow the theoretical trails blazed by the economists. So, the planners and their technical supporters, while being fully aware of the imperatives for rapid growth, must help to design a strategy which will be viable under the cross-fire of practical constraints which throw obstacles in the path of development and narrow the range of rational choice.

## THE MANPOWER PROBLEMS
## OF MODERNIZING ECONOMIES

Most modernizing economies are confronted simultaneously with two persistent yet seemingly diverse manpower problems: *the shortage of persons with critical skills* in the modernizing sector and *surplus labor* in both the modernizing and traditional sector. Thus, the strategy of human resource development is concerned with the two-fold objective of building skills and providing productive employment for unutilized or under-utilized manpower. The shortage and surplus of human resources, however, are not separate and distinct problems; they are very intimately related. Both have their roots in the changes which are inherent in the development process. Both are related in part to education. Characteristically, both are aggravated as the tempo of modernization is quickened. And, paradoxically, the shortage of persons with critical skills is one of the contributing causes of the surplus of people without jobs. Although the manpower problems of no two countries are exactly alike, there are some shortages and surpluses which appear to be universal in modernizing societies.

## Manpower Shortages

The manpower shortages of modernizing countries are quite easy to identify, and fall into different categories:

1.  In all modernizing countries there is likely to be a shortage of highly educated professional manpower such as scientists, agronomists, veterinarians, engineers, and doctors. Such persons, moreover, usually prefer to live in the major cities rather than in the rural areas where in many cases their services are most urgently needed. Thus their shortage is magnified by their relative immobility. And, ironically, their skills are seldom used effectively. In West Africa and also in many Asian and Latin American countries, for example, graduate engineers may be found managing the routine operation of an electric power sub-station or doing the work of draftsmen. Doctors may spend long hours making the most routine medical tests. The obvious reason is that:

2.  The shortage of technicians, nurses, agricultural assistants, technical supervisors, and other sub-professional personnel is generally even more critical than that of fully qualified professionals. For this there are several explanations: First, the modernizing countries usually fail to recognize that the requirement for this category of manpower exceed by many times those for senior professional personnel. Second, the few persons who are qualified to enter a technical institute may also be qualified to enter a university, and they prefer the latter because of the higher status and pay which is accorded the holder of a university degree; and finally, there are often fewer places available in institutions providing intermediate training than in universities.

3. The shortage of top-level managerial and administrative personnel, in both the private and public sectors, is almost universal, as is the dearth of persons with entrepreneurial talents.

4. Teachers are almost always in short supply, and their turnover is high because they tend to leave the teaching profession if and when more attractive jobs become available in government, politics, or private enterprise. This shortage is generally most serious in secondary education, and particularly acute in the fields of science and mathematics. It is a "master bottleneck" which retards the entire process of human resource development.

5. In most modernizing countries there are also shortages of craftsmen of all kinds, senior clerical personnel such as bookkeepers, secretaries, stenographers, and business machine operators, and of other miscellaneous personnel such as radio and television specialists, airplane pilots, accountants, economists, and statisticians.

I shall use the term "high-level manpower," or alternatively "human capital," as a convenient designation for persons who fall into categories such as those mentioned above. The term "human capital formation," as used in this paper, is the process of acquiring and increasing the numbers of persons who have the skills, education, and experience which are critical for the economic and political development of a country. Human capital formation is thus associated with investment in man and his development as a creative and productive resource. It includes investment by society in education, investment by employers in training, as well as investment by individuals of time and money in their own development. Such investments have both qualitative and quantitative dimensions—*i.e.*, human capital formation includes not only expenditures for education and training, but also the development of attitudes toward productive activity.

As stressed earlier, a central problem of all modernizing countries is to accelerate the process of human capital formation. Now human capital may be accumulated in several ways: it may be *imported from abroad* through a variety of means such as technical assistance, expatriate enterprises, hiring of consultants, or immigration. It may be *developed in employment* through on-the-job training, inservice programs of formal training, management development seminars, part-time adult education classes, better organization of work, creation of appropriate attitudes and incentives, and better management of people. Finally, it is developed through *formal education* in schools, technical training centers, colleges, universities and other institutions of higher learning. The development process is assisted at all levels by improvements in public health and by better nutrition.

The analysis of human capital formation is thus parallel and complementary to the study of the processes of savings and investment (in the material sense). In designing a strategy for development, one needs to consider the total stock of human capital required, its rates of human accumulation, and its commitment to (or investment in) high-priority productive activities.

The rate of modernization of a country is associated with both its stock and its rate of accumulation of human capital. High-level manpower is needed to staff new and expanding government services, to introduce new systems of land use and new methods of agriculture, to develop new means of communication, to carry forward industrialization, and to build the educational system. *Innovation*, or the process of change from a static or traditional society, requires very large "doses" of strategic human capital. The countries which are making the most rapid and spectacular innovations are invariably those which are accumulating this kind of human capital at a fast rate. Here we may make two tentative generalizations:

First, the rate of accumulation of strategic human capital must always exceed the rate of increase in the labor force as a whole. In most countries, for example, the rate of increase in scientific and engineering personnel needs to be at least three times that of the labor force. Sub-professional personnel may have to increase six to nine times as fast. Clerical personnel and craftsmen usually should increase at least twice as fast, and top managerial and administrative personnel will normally need to increase at a comparable rate.

Second, in most cases the rate of increase in human capital will exceed the rate of economic growth. In newly developing countries which are already faced with critical shortages of highly skilled persons, the ratio of the annual increase in high-level manpower to the annual increase in national income may need to be as high as three-to-one, or even higher in those cases where expatriates are to be replaced by citizens of the developing countries.

The accumulation of high-level manpower to overcome skill bottlenecks is a never-ending process. Advanced industrial societies as well as underdeveloped countries are normally short of critical skills. Indeed as long as the pace of innovation is rapid, the appetite of any growing country for high-level manpower is almost insatiable.

## Labor Surpluses

The overabundance of labor is in most countries as serious a problem as the shortage of skills. Its more common manifestations are the following:

1.  In nearly all countries the supply of unskilled and untrained manpower in the urban areas exceeds the available employment opportunities. The reasons are not hard to find. First, large urban populations are likely to build up prior to, rather than as a consequence of, the expansion of industrial employment. Then, as industrialization gains momentum, the productivity of factory labor tends to rise sharply, and this limits the expansion of demand for general industrial labor. Indeed, modern industrialization may even displace labor from cottage and handicraft industries faster than it is absorbed in newly created factories. Again, government service is able to provide employment for relatively few people. And finally, unless development is extremely rapid, trade, commerce, and other services simply do not absorb those who cannot find jobs in other activities. But despite relatively limited employment opportunities and overcrowded conditions, the moderniza-

tion process impels people to migrate from the rural areas to the cities. And, as progress is made toward universal primary education, nearly every modernizing country is faced with the problem of mounting unemployment of primary school leavers.

2. In overpopulated countries, such as Egypt or India, the rural areas are also overcrowded resulting in widespread underemployment and disguised unemployment of human resources. Indeed, in many countries it is evident that total agricultural output could be increased if fewer people were living on the land and the size of agricultural units was increased. Thus, surplus labor in rural areas in most cases is no asset and in some cases is definitely a liability for increasing agricultural output.

3. The "unemployed intellectual" constitutes an entirely different kind of surplus. In many countries there would seem to be too many lawyers or too many arts graduates, and there may be instances also of unemployed or under-employed engineers, scientists, economists, and even agronomists. The unused intellectual, however, is unemployed only because he is unwilling to accept work which he considers beneath his status or educational level. In particular, a university education creates very high employment expectations. In some countries, a university degree may be looked upon almost as a guarantee of a soft and secure job in the government service, and in most it is assumed to be a membership card of the elite class. But, even in rapidly modernizing countries, the purely administrative jobs in the government service become filled fairly rapidly; the demand for lawyers is certainly not as great as, for example, the demand for technically trained personnel. And in some societies where large enterprises are owned and managed by members of family dynasties, even the opportunities for professionally trained engineers and technicians may be limited, at least in the early stages of development. Rather than accept work beneath his status

or employment in remote rural areas, the university graduate, and sometimes even the secondary school leaver as well, may prefer to join the ranks of the unemployed. A sizable quantity of unused human capital of this kind reflects a wasteful investment in human resource development and poses a serious threat to a country's social and political stability.

4. There are other miscellaneous kinds of surplus labor. For example, the introduction of new processes and automated machinery may throw skilled labor out of work. And, in some countries, immigrants and refugees swell the ranks of the unemployed.

Unfortunately, there is no reason to believe that accelerated growth will by itself solve the problems of labor surplus such as those described above. In part they are the inevitable consequence of a too rapid population growth over which planners and politicians may have little or no control. In part, they are diseases inherent in the modernization process itself, and are directly related to rising aspirations. Some are aggravated and others alleviated by rapid growth.

Some labor surpluses, however, can be eliminated and others reduced substantially by a well-conceived and balanced program of economic growth. A strategy of human resource development, therefore, must make an attack on surpluses as well as shortages.

### Manpower Analysis

As indicated above, no two countries have exactly the same manpower problems. Some have unusually serious surpluses, and others have special kinds of skill bottlenecks. Politicians and planners, therefore, need to make a systematic assessment of the human resource problems in their particular country. Such assessment may be called "manpower analysis."

The objectives of manpower analysis are:

1. The identification of the principal critical shortages of skilled manpower in each major sector of the economy, and an analysis of the reasons for such shortages.
2. The identification of surpluses, both of trained manpower as well as unskilled labor, and the reasons for such surpluses.
3. The setting of targets for human resources development based upon reasonable expectations of growth.

Such targets are best determined by a careful examination, sector by sector, of the utilization of manpower in a number of countries which are somewhat more advanced politically, socially, and economically.

Manpower analysis need not be based on an elaborate or exhaustive survey. It involves no precise calculation of the numbers of people needed in every occupation at a future period. Nor is it a projection of past trends. The purpose of manpower analysis is to give a reasonably objective picture of a country's major human resource problems, the interrelationships between these problems, and their causes, together with an informed guess about probable future trends. It is both qualitative and quantitative, but it is based more upon wise judgment than upon precise statistics. In countries where statistics are either unavailable or clearly unreliable, the initial manpower analysis may be frankly informed guesswork. Indeed, detailed manpower surveys and precise projections are likely to be misleading, because they give a false impression of accuracy.

In conclusion, the major shortages and surpluses of manpower in most countries are easy to identify. Many of them are common to all modernizing societies. Manpower analysis, based on relevant comparisons with other countries at different stages of development, is useful in assessing particular problems and probable future trends. To be sure, there is need for research in manpower supply and demand as related to economic growth. But those who are responsible for the planning of accelerated growth cannot and need not wait for the completion of definite studies before designing a realistic strategy for human resource development.

## THE COMPONENTS OF A STRATEGY
## OF HUMAN RESOURCE DEVELOPMENT

A strategy of human resource development then is one of the imperatives of any program for accelerated growth. And to be viable, it must be realistic and take into consideration the constraints which were mentioned earlier. The planners can do little to stem the increase in population; the politicians cannot go back on their promises of rapid achievement of universal primary education; they can rely only temporarily on expatriate manpower as a source of human capital. The resources which they can allocate to education are limited by competing demands for investment in roads, factories, dams, and irrigation systems; and nothing can be done which is inconsistent with the bolstering of economic and political independence.

What then are the feasible policy alternatives? What instruments are available for policy implementation? What obstacles lie in the path of development of a sound strategy? These are the central questions posed in this paper.

A strategy of human resource development has three essential components: the building of appropriate incentives, the promotion of effective training of employed manpower, and the rational development of formal education. These three parts are interdependent: the country's leaders cannot concentrate on only one or two of them at a time; they must plan an integrated attack on all three fronts at once.

### The Building of Incentives

The purpose of building incentives is to encourage men and women to prepare for and engage in the kinds of productive activity which are needed for accelerated growth. To accomplish this, the compensation of an individual should be related to the *importance of his job in the modernizing society*. It should not depend upon his level of formal education, the number of degrees held, family status, or political connections. And the relative importance of jobs should be based not on tradition or heritage from colonial regimes but on an assessment of the manpower needs of the developing economy.

If, for example, agricultural officers or village workers are desperately needed in rural areas to carry out a program of modernizing agriculture, their pay may have to exceed that of professionally trained people who have desk jobs in the cities. If a technician with limited education can perform work normally assigned to an engineer, he should receive the same pay as the engineer on that job. If science and mathematics teachers are urgently needed in secondary schools, their rates of remuneration should be higher than that of other less urgently needed teachers (whether university graduates or not) and perhaps higher also than that of professionally trained people in some other less essential activities. If technicians, nurses, and foremen are in very short supply (as is the case in most modernizing countries), their rates of pay may need to be higher than those of some university graduates holding administrative jobs which many other persons could do. In some cases, the medical technician or the agricultural assistant who is willing to live in the bush deserves to be paid as much as the doctor or the agronomist who insists upon living in the city. And the manager of an enterprise who may have had only a limited secondary education is entitled to higher remuneration than the university graduate who is subordinate.

Large outlays for education are unlikely to produce the kind of high-level manpower needed if the proper incentives are lacking. In many developing countries, any university degree is looked upon almost as a right to employment in the government service. Thus, a university graduate is also strongly motivated to prefer work in the large urban areas. The idea that a university education is a "permanent escape from the bush" is widespread, for example, in Africa. In Nigeria the reason for the critical shortage of agricultural specialists of all kinds is not the lack of places in agricultural schools but rather the reluctance of students to go into them.[5] Obviously, in the minds of young people, the employment opportunities are not as attractive in agriculture as in some other fields which are less vital for the country's development. For the same reasons, technical education, particularly at the intermediate level, has had little appeal in Nigeria. As the Ashby Commission pointed out:

> . . . *the literary tradition and the university degree have become*
> *indelible symbols of prestige in Nigeria; by contrast technology,*
> *agriculture and other practical subjects, particularly at the sub-*
> *professional level, have not won esteem*[6]

I would argue most strongly that situations of this kind will
not be corrected by publicity, exhortations of prime ministers, and
the building of more educational institutions. They will be changed
only when the system of rewards and status values in a modernizing
society are changed and the initiative in making changes must come
from the government itself in the form of a complete revision of the
entire system of reward of government employees. The failure of
politicians and planners to come to grips with this problem will
produce in the newer countries, as it has already done in Egypt and
India, an army of unemployed intellectuals.

By the same token, the problems of rural-urban migration and
the unemployed primary school leavers are not likely to be alleviated
substantially by mere changes in the curriculum of primary and
secondary schools. In this age of rising aspirations and spreading
mass communication, the sons of farmers are not going to sentence
themselves to *traditional agriculture* if they can possibly avoid it.
The only fundamental solution is the *modernization of rural life*. This
calls for sweeping measures such as land reform, agricultural research
and extension services, widespread rural community development
programs, the effective utilization of rural labor in the building of
roads, irrigation systems, houses, and schools, and other programs
aimed at making rural life more productive and attractive. If people
see a positive reason for remaining in the rural areas and a promise
of a better life there, the problem of revision of curricula in the
schools is relatively easy to handle.

A detailed discussion of the need to develop agriculture lies
beyond the scope of this paper. It is necessary only to point out that
none of the modernizing countries are likely to solve many of their
most pressing human resource problems unless they find the means
of revolutionizing rural life. Industrialization by itself will never
solve the problem of surplus labor in most of today's underdeveloped

countries; government employment, petty trade, and domestic services will not soak up the teaming masses in overcrowded cities; and the retention of surplus human resources in traditional agriculture, even if it were possible, would simply result in more disguised unemployment. Again, to quote Arthur Lewis, "If˝ agriculture is stagnant, it offers only a stagnant market, and inhibits the growth of the rest of the economy. The core of the doctrine of "unbalanced growth" is that neglect to develop agriculture makes it more difficult to develop anything else." Similarly, the failure to develop effective measures for productive utilization of human resources in rural areas will make it infinitely more difficult to solve the manpower problems in any other part of the economy.

Thus, a primary condition for the solution of all manpower problems whether they be critical skill bottlenecks in the modernizing sector or mounting labor surpluses throughout the nation, is the building of appropriate incentive. Lacking this, massive expenditures on training and education will contribute little to accelerated development. The notion that there is always a direct relation between the development of education and economic growth can be misleading, and planners should be wary of accepting it without careful scrutiny.

The leaders of the modernizing nations probably have the means to influence the structure of wages and salaries if they have the courage to do so. In most cases, the government is by far the largest employer of manpower, and private employers are strongly influenced by the patterns which it sets. But, being bound by tradition and constrained by established interests bent on preserving the *status quo*, some politicians and planners think that it would be rather arbitrary suddenly to gear remuneration to the relative importance of occupations as determined by development objectives. Yet, it is equally arbitrary and even politically dangerous to cling to an archaic system of reward which may have been inherited from a past era of colonialism. In committing themselves to planned, accelerated development, the modernizing nations are charting a revolutionary course. And if they are to follow it successfully, they must discard traditional and orthodox ideas, many of which they have borrowed from the advanced nations which never had to face the same kinds of problems.

## The Training of Employed Manpower

The potentialities of fully utilizing government agencies, private employers, expatriate firms and foreign technical experts as trainers and developers of manpower are enormous, but this is seldom fully realized by the leaders of most modernizing countries. Human resource development is usually equated with investments in formal education, and government, business, and education leaders for some reason cling to the notion that schools and universities can prefabricate the skills needed. They may be quick to see the need for technical training but, unfortunately, just as quick to assume that the system of formal education must be given the responsibility for it.

At this point, it is important to understand that training and education are two quite different processes, and planners should draw a sharp distinction between them. Training involves the development of specific skills which are needed to perform a particular job or series of jobs. Education involves the acquisition of general knowledge and the development of basic mental ability. Both training and education are involved in human capital formation. Education is, of course, a prerequisite for various kinds of training. But this does not mean that the *responsibility* for training and the *responsibility* for education are inseparable.

The strategy of modernizing nations should be to shift as much responsibility as possible for *training* onto the major employing institutions—government ministries, public or quasi-public enterprises, private industry and commerce, and foreign-owned and managed firms. At the same time, the strategy should aim to exploit more systematically the training possibilities of technical assistance.

The government, as the largest employer, should take the lead in shouldering this responsibility. Most of the arts of public administration can be developed effectively by a well-conceived and organized program of in-service training. It is likewise practical for the appropriate employing ministries to train craftsmen, senior clerical employees, and even certain categories of sub-professional technical personnel. Each major government ministry, therefore, should have an organization responsible for on-the-job training, in-service

programs of instruction, supplementary off-the-job programs of
training in cooperation with educational institutions, periodic
examination of accomplishment, and certification of qualification
for promotion and advancement. The techniques of in-service
training of this kind are available but the idea that the government-as-
employer should assume responsibility for such training is completely
strange and unorthodox to most leaders in newly developing countries.

At the same time, pressure should be exerted upon private
employers to assume a corresponding responsibility for training. The
larger enterprises should be expected to have foreman training and
manager development programs. They should also be required to
assume major responsibility for training their own craftsmen,
clerical workers, and some categories of technicians as well as
semi-skilled production workers. In short, the development of human
capital through in-service training should be accepted as an integral
part of business operations.

The small employer can also carry some of the burden of
training, and in practice he often carries more than his share. In
Nigeria, for example, most lorries and automobiles are repaired in
small shops consisting of an owner and several apprentices, who may
even pay him for the opportunity of learning a trade. The handicraft
industries in most countries are completely dependent upon an
informal apprenticeship system. The planners in the modernizing
countries will be well advised not to replace such systems with costly
vocational schools, but rather to try to improve them by providing
programs of technical assistance in apprenticeship and on-the-job
training.

The foreign-owned enterprise can be a powerful instrument of
human capital formation if it is handled properly, because its training
capacity is usually greater than that of the local enterprises. The host
country should allow the foreign firm to bring in as many expatriates
as it wishes, *provided* that it guarantees to train local nationals to take
over their jobs within a reasonable specified time. In most instances,
the foreign firm trains more people than it uses itself. For example,
craftsmen and mechanics trained by an expatriate oil company may
take jobs in other local industries; or service station attendants may
soon become independent dealers. A well-trained foreman in a

foreign-owned truck assembly plant may be a future organizer of a locally managed parts factory. Unquestionably, a more deliberate and carefully planned policy of using expatriate firms as training institutions could greatly accelerate the process of human capital formation in many countries, and politicians should be more concerned with exploiting this asset to the maximum than in placing arbitrary restrictions on the employment of expatriate personnel.

Finally, the newly developing countries should fully exploit the potentialities of technical assistance as a training medium. The purpose of technical assistance should be to train one or more nationals to do work which was previously done by a foreigner, or not done at all. It is shortsighted to invite foreign technical experts to a country to handle operations or merely to make studies or surveys. In whatever activity they are engaged, the responsibility of foreign experts should be to train counterparts—to transmit knowledge by training people.

The advantages of utilizing employers and technical assistance as trainers and developers of manpower would appear to be blindingly obvious. But the failure to do so is almost universal in newly developing countries. Outside technical experts are employed in operations, and often no local counterparts are assigned to them for training. Government ministries are too busy to spend time on in-service training, and complain when vocational schools and universities send them poorly trained recruits. The idea that training is a continuous process of human resource development rather than a simple pre-employment indoctrination seems to escape politicians, planners, and public and private employers alike. The solution here is relatively simple. The employing enterprises should be given the *responsibility* for a considerable amount of training and also the incentives to provide it. If they have the incentives, the means of carrying out this training will not be lacking.

## Formal Education

No one would argue, of course, that all training activity can or should be undertaken by employers. Teachers, engineers, scientists,

agronomists, doctors, and many kinds of sub-professional personnel
are not likely to be effectively trained in employment. And some
kinds of crafts are learned better in schools than through apprenticeship or on-the-job training.

In the main, however, the essential function of formal
education is to prepare people for training rather than to train people
for particular occupations. In other words, the principal output of
formal education should be "trainable" people. Like a photographic
film, the capacities of people are developed after exposure to productive activity. Pre-employment education, as in the coating of the film,
determines the future sensitivity of man for understanding and
continuous learning.

Nearly all modernizing countries have rejected the idea of
*gradual* elimination of illiteracy; they are determined to have
universal primary education in record time. This must be accepted as
a major objective in any program of accelerated development. But in
many countries particularly in Africa and parts of Asia, universal
primary education cannot be achieved in the next ten to fifteen years
if the educators insist on the same teacher-student ratios and teacher
qualifications as those in the advanced countries. More often than
not, the developing countries are being forced to sacrifice quality to
quantity in their mass attack upon illiteracy.

It is unquestionably true that the cost of primary education
must be held down; otherwise it will consume most of the resources
which are more urgently needed for secondary and higher education.
Most of the developing countries currently spend less than 4 percent
per annum for formal education of all kinds, and, in view of competing demands for funds for development purposes, it is doubtful
whether many of them will be able to raise this to 5 or 6 percent in the
next decade or two. And the need for high-level manpower is such
that most modernizing countries will have to devote well over
two-thirds of total educational expenditure to secondary and post-
secondary institutions.

Consequently, developing countries should concentrate their
attention on finding new techniques of education which can be
utilized effectively by large numbers of teachers who themselves have

had little more than primary education and which can maximize the strategic services of a very small group of more highly trained personnel. The application of new teaching techniques—visual aids, programmed learning, instruction by radio and television, revised and simplified curricula and texts—offer a real challenge both to the developing countries and the assisting countries. The discovery of new techniques for primary education will be given much more serious consideration once it is understood by politicians, planners, educators, and outside experts alike that under conditions of accelerated growth it will be impossible to raise substantially either the pay or the qualifications of teachers in the near future.

The main purpose of primary education is to make people literate and to make them more effective citizens in the modernizing society. It is not and should not be vocational education, and indeed most educators in advanced as well as underdeveloped countries are united in opposing such an orientation. It must, however, provide a means of selecting and preparing those who are to proceed to secondary level education.

One of the consequences of rapid introduction of universal primary education is to raise aspirations of people more rapidly than places in secondary schools and jobs can be provided. This is one of the penalties of rapid modernization. In time, however, the social and political pressure for more secondary education will assist the rapid accumulation of high-level manpower.

If a country demands accelerated development, the proportion of students in secondary education must rise sharply. The secondary school leavers constitute the main reservoir from which "trainable" high-level manpower must be drawn. Its size and quality, therefore, are critical for human capital formation. As in the case of primary education, streamlined methods of instruction and new educational techniques are needed. But, at the secondary level, the main consideration is not to keep costs from rising; it must be to provide high-quality education for an ever-increasing minority of the school-age population.

The proportion of the school-age population in secondary education will depend upon the stage of development. In the least developed countries less than one percent of the normally eligible age groups (12–18 years) are in secondary schools. Some of the more advanced African countries have been able to raise this proportion to 4 or 5 percent. Egypt, India and some of the Latin American countries have ratios as high as 15–20 percent. In most of the industrially advanced countries, it is already in excess of 50 percent. Thus, in most modernizing countries there is underinvestment in secondary education and need for an immediate and sharp increase. The Conference of African States on the Development of Education recommended that the tropical African countries as a whole increase the proportion of school-age population in secondary schools from an average of 3 percent in 1961 to 23 percent in 1981, during which period universal primary education would also be achieved.[8]

The major mission of secondary education is to give students firm grounding in verbal and written communication skills, mathematics, foreign languages, history, social studies and science. In this process, some attention should be given to development of manual skills as well. In most cases, the aim should be breadth of education rather than specialization at an early stage, and especially if a large part of occupational skill development is to be left to later training in employment or to post-secondary educational institutions.

Vocational training at the secondary level presents particular problems. It is expensive, and competent teachers are very difficult to find. Modernizing countries often waste large sums of money in misplaced emphasis on primary and secondary vocational schools. In some countries, for example, students who prove to be unfit for higher academic training are sent to vocational schools, and as a consequence these become the catch-basins for incompetents. And, in many instances, the training received tends to be of poor quality and not sufficiently relevant to the occupations which the students later enter. As stressed above, the policy of newly developing countries should be to place more responsibility on employers to train workers for specific occupations, and to this end funds might better be channelled into the training of trainers in employing institutions than into the proliferation of poorly equipped and poorly staffed vocational schools.

There is a need, however, for teacher training institutions at the secondary level (primarily to provide elementary school teachers). In addition, a limited number of well-staffed and well-equipped craft training centers are undoubtedly necessary, as are certain kinds of secretarial schools and agricultural training institutions. But plans for these should be carefully made after analysis of expected manpower requirements and the training potentialities of the employing enterprises.

The mission of higher education is two-fold:

1. to provide liberally educated persons for positions of leadership in the modernizing society.
2. to develop high-level technical manpower.

The newly developing countries are keenly aware of the importance of higher education, and except in rare cases, they are not likely to underinvest in it; but, in terms of development objectives, they are prone to place the wrong emphasis on the investments which they make.

It is probably reasonable to assume that, on the average, the newly developing countries can and will provide higher education for about 20 percent of those who complete secondary education. The crucial questions then are: what proportion should have university level education and what proportion should take intermediate training? what proportion should concentrate on technical studies and what proportion should devote themselves to academic studies? and, of those who should have university-level education, what proportion should be educated at home and what proportion should be sent to study abroad? In each country these issues are likely to be resolved partly by logical analysis and partly by political expediency.

The logical answers may be found in part by a manpower analysis. Typically, a manpower analysis might suggest that 2–4 students should pursue studies at the intermediate level (two or three years beyond secondary) for every one who takes a full university course (ranging from four to six years). It would probably also suggest that, in a country committed to accelerated growth (with emphasis on industrialization and modernization of agriculture), at least half of the students at both the intermediate and university level should concentrate on subjects such as science, engineering, medicine, agriculture, veterinary medicine, or pharmacy. Another 25 percent should go to intermediate-level teacher-training colleges, and the remainder should concentrate on law, letters, social sciences, and business administration.[9]

From an economic standpoint, the logical course for the typical country would be to build institutions at home to take care of practically all students at the intermediate level, and to send a substantial portion of those qualified for university level work to foreign institutions, at least until the country is rich enough to afford first-class university level education without cutting into the high-priority need for investment in secondary and intermediate higher education.

The politicians, however, will have difficulty in accepting such a rationalized program for higher education, even if it is based upon a quite reliable manpower assessment and even if it can be demonstrated to be the more rapid and least expensive way of producing trainable high-level manpower. The reasons are obvious.

As the number of secondary school graduates increases, the government will be under pressure from students and irate parents to provide *more places* in universities. And as long as university degrees determine in large measure the starting salaries for the better jobs (irrespective of what subjects have been studied), students will want to by-pass the intermediate institutions. Moreover if *numbers* are important to the politicians the universities will tend to offer more places in the non-scientific areas than are needed. Because the cost of educating an engineer or scientist is 3–4 times that of educating a lawyer or a man of letters and arts.

But this is not all. From the standpoint of national grandeur and prestige, a university is a much more impressive symbol of modernization than a teacher-training college, an intermediate technical training institute, or a "junior college of arts and sciences." A university along with an international airline, a steel mill, and television stations, is important in the eyes of the leaders of newly developing nations. Finally, too much reliance on sending university level students abroad for study is often considered to be inconsistent with bolstering economic and political independence.

Modernizing countries will therefore probably commit themselves to spend more money on universities than they should and tend to neglect the development of intermediate education; and they are likely, in the interest of providing the maximum number of places for university students, to understress scientific and engineering education. This leads eventually to the lowering of standards of the university, reliance on professors who teach only part time because of poor salaries, and the development of obstacles to innovation in the form of professors who have a vested interest in the *status quo*.[10] In the end, the education and training offered in universities may sink to a level below that of a good teacher training institution or technical or junior college, and the curriculum is likely to be unrelated to the needs of a rapidly modernizing society.

In view of these pressures, how can modernizing countries give the needed emphasis to intermediate-level training and to science and engineering studies in the universities? As already stressed above, it is rationally desirable and politically feasible to gear remuneration of jobs, particularly in the government service, to their relative importance for the country's development rather than to formal degrees or educational levels. If this were done, the artificial value of the traditional academic university degree would soon disappear and students would have an incentive to enter the intermediate technical training institutions, secondary teachers' colleges, and scientific and engineering faculties in the universities. These would become the new avenues to positions of high pay and status; and parents and students would then exert pressure to expand and improve these avenues. In this way, the adaptation of the system of higher education to the needs of a rapidly modernizing society would become politically more feasible. And, this need not conflict with the university's mission of providing liberally educated persons for positions of service and leadership in the nation. The modernizing society will always have an important and highly-paid positions for the well-educated lawyer, arts graduate, and social scientist. But, it should not allow large numbers of poorly educated university graduates to use their degrees to claim high-level positions for which they are not well prepared.


# THE IMPLEMENTATION OF THE STRATEGY

## The Strategy in Summary

Only the bare skeleton of a strategy of human resource development has been presented above. It is admittedly over-simplified; many important questions have been passed by; and some elements of the strategy have been implied but not mentioned specifically. However, the strategy as a whole has a consistent rationale, and it has been presented primarily to stimulate serious discussion among those who are committed to accelerated development.

It has been argued that investments in formal education alone are not likely to solve either critical skill shortages or persistent labor surpluses in modernizing societies. Investments in education are likely to contribute effectively to rapid growth only:

1. if there are adequate incentives to encourage men and women to engage in the kinds of productive activity which are needed to accelerate the modernization process.
2. if appropriate measures are taken to shift a large part of the responsibility for training to the principal employing enterprises.

The building of incentives and the training of employed manpower, therefore, are necessary both as a means of economizing on formal education and as a means of making the investment in it productive.

In the building of incentives, a cardinal principle is that the status and remuneration attached to occupations should be related to their importance as measured by the high-priority needs of a developing society, and not to arbitrary levels of education, degrees, family status or political connections. This is essential for the accumulation of human capital and for its most effective utilization. The surpluses of labor, particularly those connected with rural-urban migration and the unemployment of primary school leavers, may be reduced in part by a far-reaching program of modernization of agriculture and rural life as a counterpart to a program of industrialization. Because of rapidly increasing populations and the emphasis on an early universalization of primary education, however, there will still be large numbers of unemployed or underemployed persons in most modernizing societies.

The potentialities of fully utilizing government agencies, private employers, expatriate firms and technical experts as trainers and developers of manpower, though very great indeed, are seldom exploited fully. Thus, a key element in the strategy of human resource development is to shift as much as possible the responsibility for training to the major employing enterprises, and to provide the necessary technical guidance to enable them to develop in-service training programs along modern lines.

The third component of the strategy is wise judgment and prudent investment in building the system of formal education. This calls for giving priority to investment in and development of broad secondary education. It requires that the costs of universal primary education be kept as low as possible by applying new techniques which can make effective use of relatively untrained teachers, the contribution of a very small but strategic group of highly-trained personnel. Finally, in the area of higher education, the strategy stresses the need for giving priority to investment in intermediate-level training institutions and the scientific and engineering faculties of universities. But this does not mean that the production of graduates in other faculties should be neglected.

The three essential components of the strategy are interdependent and call for a well designed and integrated attack on all three fronts at once. And it is imperative that the strategy of building and utilizing human resources be an integral part of a country's national development program.

The strategy assumes that the politicians of the country are firmly committed to the goal of accelerated development, and that they have the will to do the things which are imperative for its attainment. It recognizes, however, that there are certain constraints over which the leaders have little or no control and which narrow their choice of policy alternatives.

Such strategy ought to provide a logical framework for the formulation of policies to govern manpower utilization and development. It should identify the major sectors where foreign technical assistance is required, and provide the criteria for determining priorities. It should be instrumental in integrating fragmented activities into a well coordinated effort.

## Some Obstacles to be Overcome

Quite apart from the constraints listed earlier in this paper, there are other obstacles to the implementation of such a strategy. The most formidable, perhaps, is traditional thinking. Those who are accustomed to traditional methods of elementary education are suspicious of new techniques. Most of the leaders of the underdeveloped countries are unaware of the great strides made recently in the methodology of in-service training in the advanced countries. The thought of overhauling the wage and salary structure of government ministries is frightening. The idea of tampering with higher education to turn out larger proportions of sub-professional personnel is not consistent with the kind of indoctrination one may have had at Oxford, Cambridge or the Sorbonne. And the very thought that there is a strategic relationship between incentive, in-service training and formal education is strange and difficult to grasp. Yet those who preach the revolutionary doctrine of planned, accelerated growth—more rapid and more sweeping than anything before— must be prepared to reject outworn concepts and employ the most modern techniques available. In their approach to development, they must be more modern in many respects than the advanced nations from which they seek aid and advice.

The governmental structure of the developing countries is another obstacle. Thinking and planning tend to be in compartments.

The ministries of education deal only with formal education, and some do not even have jurisdiction over technical education. Ministries of labor are concerned with employment standards and some aspects of training skilled and semi-skilled labor. The ministries of industry, commerce and agriculture are likely to be preoccupied with technical and financial questions. The economic development ministries or development boards, if they exist at all, are generally concerned with physical capital formation, the balance of payments, and other urgent economic questions. They are likely to assume that trained manpower will appear magically as soon as factories, dams, roads, and ditches are completed. The traditional economic planners are likely to banish human resource development to that "no-mans'-land" of social welfare. Thus, no ministry or board is in a position to see the problem as a whole. Each grasps rather blindly for some program of manpower development, and in justification makes wild claims for its indispensable role in promoting rapid growth.

Until recently, moreover, foreign technical experts have added to the confusion and fragmentation of effort in this field. Each has a particular package to sell; each normally deals with only one ministry; each with tireless zeal tries to "educate the top leadership" on the importance of a particular project. There is "competition among the givers." In the developing country, offers of help may be forthcoming from the United Nations, UNESCO, I.C.A., the West German Government, the Soviet Union, and other governments as well as several private philanthropic foundations and a host of church missions and other voluntary organizations. Each essentially offers assistance in a specialized field.

This "competition among givers" is desirable in many respects. It offers the developing countries a range of choice. It puts pressure on the givers to do as good a job as possible. It gives the recipient countries a feeling that many nations and many institutions are concerned with their welfare. And it makes it easier for them to maintain a position of neutrality. But there are obvious drawbacks. Aid is given without regard for broader, underlying problems. The energies of the recipient governments are consumed by a proliferation of scattered and unrelated projects. Often the best qualified local manpower is lured away to foreign countries on fellowships, study tours and other exciting ventures, leaving virtually no one at home to handle the day-to-day work of project development. And, worst of all, in some countries the politicians are tempted to use some of the givers as scapegoats by asking for "a survey by experts" as a convenient means for postponing action on a thorny problem.


## Implementing Machinery

The design of a strategy calls for integrated rather than compartmentalized planning. The implementation of a strategy requires coordinated activity. What machinery then is necessary for this implementation?

Since manpower problems are the concern of many ministries, the program of human resource development must be implemented by an inter-ministerial board. In addition to members of the government, this board should normally include representatives from the non-government employers and from organized labor. It is essential, however, that such a board have a secretariat. And this board and its secretariat should be integrated with whatever machinery is established for general economic development planning. Among its key functions are:

1. Coordination and approval at the national level of *all requests* for external and technical assistance involving manpower and human resource development.
2. The determination of priorities in the strategy of human resource development, and the continuous re-assessment of these priorities as the program progresses.
3. The assessment of human resource problems through periodic manpower analysis.
4. The promotion and stimulation of planning activity by the ministries represented on the board, as well as by employer and labor organizations.
5. The co-ordination of the above planning activities.

6. The integration of human resource development strategy with other components of the country's plans of economic and political development.
7. The general review of all activity connected with human resource development, and periodic evaluation of the work of the various agencies which assume responsibility for it.
8. The selection and design of research projects which may be useful for the formulation, implementation, and evaluation of the strategy of human resource development.

Formal machinery such as that suggested above is not difficult to establish. Its effectiveness, however, will depend upon the calibre of its leadership and its secretariat, and also upon the effective use of the right kind of foreign experts as consultants; in short, upon the quality of the people concerned.

A human resource strategy board should be neither a statistical agency, nor a study commission, nor a long-range planning organization. Though primarily concerned with policy formulation, it may also have executive responsibilities. The top staff, therefore, should be neither statisticians, nor professional educators, nor economists as such. They should be *strategists*—persons who combine political insight with a rational understanding of the processes of modernization, and who are able to comprehend the inter-relationships between the component parts of an intricate program for accelerated development.

So far advanced countries have been unable to send such strategists to the newly developing countries. This has been partly because the need for a coherent strategy has not been recognized; partly because the recipient countries have been wary of foreigners who want to "master-mind" their development; but mainly because the type of strategists needed are in rare supply.

Here then lies the crux of the problem: *the training of strategists in human resource development.* This is a task which calls for joint effort by both givers and recipients of technical assistance. And indeed no other task is more important to the future of developing nations.

# PHILIP H. COOMBS

# The Adjustment of the Educational Structure to the Requirements of Economic Development

*E* conomic development increasingly requires educational planning,
*as Philip Coombs, Director of Research of the International
Institute for Educational Planning (Paris), points out. As an embryonic
field, educational planning is groping for its direction, a search which
embodies both philosophy and methodology. Coombs suggests that
educational planners must deal with the total human resource process.
Manpower forecasting techniques amd mathematical models, valuable
though they are, are but one of many dimensions of educational planning that require the integration of social, economic, and educational
variables. It is also important that imbalance within various educational*

Reprinted from Philip H. Coombs, "The Adjustment of the Educational Structure
to the Requirements of Economic Development," *International Review of Education* 10 (March 1964), pp. 53–70, with permission of the author and publisher.

*levels be avoided in the educational system. Evaluation of the qualitative facets of education as well as a realistic assessment of capabilities to implement human resource development schemes are important features of educational planning. Comprehensive educational planning must also concern itself with institutional change and innovation in education, a task which demands that planning be pragmatic.*

## THE PRESENT SITUATION

Strictly speaking, of course, educational planning, and the idea that education contributes to a society's form and growth, are not new. They are as old as civilization's earliest efforts to instruct the young. Plato and Aristotle dealt with these notions with conspicuous effect, as did the great teachers and philosophers of other ancient societies. Over the centuries those responsible for managing school systems or universities, or even individual classrooms, have practiced educational planning of a sort, if only to get the next day's lesson ready or to provide enough seats for the students. Such practical educators, I suppose, would be surprised to learn that they were planners, just as the man who discovered to his amazement that he had been talking prose all his life.

There are some quite new things about educational planning as we conceive of it today, compared to the past. For one, it takes a much broader view, embracing a nation's entire educational establishment, not merely an individual school or university or some particular slice of the educational enterprise.

Also new is the conscious effort to make education a major force and an integral part of economic and social development. Thus, educational planning, seen in this broader frame, embraces both the *internal* affairs of education and its *external* relationships to the rest of society and the economy.

One further new feature is that educational planning and development has lately become a respectable and challenging subject for scholarly research and analysis. This past summer, for example, there were some half dozen European conferences on the economics of education, including one sponsored by the International Economic Association. This would have been inconceivable only five years ago.

One does not have to look far to explain this heightened interest in educational planning. It reflects the fact that virtually all nations today—regardless of their age, stage of development or type of social system—are preoccupied with economic growth and social improvement, not only for themselves, but in many cases, for others as well.

To a great extent this new interest of economists and others in development was a response to the actions of political leaders, rather than the reverse. After World War II, public policy in this area stole a march on scholarship and theory. Such measures as the Marshall Plan, Point Four, and the Colombo Plan, launched by statesmen and practical politicians, prompted professional economists to turn their attention to the processes of development. Since then a substantial new literature on development has flourished. At first it focused largely upon the *physical* components of development—industrial plants, power dams, railroads and the like—which have an obviously important role in a modern economy's growth. It also focused upon the Gross National Product as the main yardstick of development progress.

As practical experience was gained with the complex realities of the development process, however, two further important insights emerged. One was that the development of a viable modern society involves much more than *economic* factors, important as these are. It involves also a host of social, administrative, political and psychological factors. Therefore, terms such as "infra-structure" and "social development" crept into the language of scholars and development practitioners alike. At the same time the gross national product, though admittedly a handy yardstick of economic growth, came to be seen as an incomplete and inadequate measure of the goals and progress of societies. Faced with these realities, some economists became interested in sociology, political science and social psychology in order to have a better understanding of the development process *as a whole* and to discover ways to break stubborn bottlenecks.

The second insight involved recognition of the fact that the *human factor* in development—as distinct from physical plant and physical resources—played a more central role than had earlier been appreciated. Educational deficiencies and the resulting shortages of qualified manpower came to be seen as major obstacles to economic and social development. Accordingly, more and more economists turned their attention to education.

Only a few years ago the "conventional wisdom" of economists held that education was a *consumption* expenditure, whereas *investment* expenditures were obviously the prime movers of economic growth. In these circumstances, education budgets were at a competitive disadvantage. Rather suddenly economists forsook this conventional wisdom and agreed that education, in addition to being a consumption good, was an indispensable *investment* in national growth. It should be so regarded, they felt, in national accounting and in national investment decisions. This, in my experience, was an important turning point in economic thought. Conventional wisdom and the theory of economic development have never been quite the same since.

In the ensuing years many important changes have occurred, both in theory and in practice. International and bilateral aid programs, for example, have given greater emphasis to the development of human resources. The United Nations Special Fund is today investing a large fraction of its pre-investment funds in education and training. UNESCO has been doing a land-office business in sending educational planning missions to less-developed Member States at their urgent request. And what would have been unthinkable only a few years ago, the World Bank has adopted a policy of making IDA "soft loans" available to educational projects and, more recently, World Bank "hard loans" as well. To sum up, *education is the new girl in town,* as the President of the Carnegie Corporation, Dr. John Gardner, put it, *and all the old boys are eager to dance with her.*

Professional educators, whose girl she was in the first place, have been somewhat bewildered by all this new attention. Their reactions have been somewhat mixed, a fact which deserves brief comment here in the interest of mutual understanding. Educators naturally welcomed the added support provided by their newfound allies. The economists' fresh arguments were especially useful at budget time for persuading reluctant finance ministers and legislatures of the virtue of larger educational expenditures, now that they were an "investment." On the other hand, these new allies, the economists, are, after all, a very materialistic group, always talking about increased production, efficiency, higher incomes and that sort of thing. These are strange words in education circles, though certainly educators would be the last to deny the importance of higher incomes. But higher incomes and greater material affluence, they insist, are not the only stuff of which the "good life" is made. From Aristotle onward, educators have been devoted also to non-material values, which, even though they are hard to measure, seem no less important than the gross national product. There was thus a fear among some educators that the economists might pervert the educational enterprise to simply an instrument of economic growth.

Educators, moreover, are deeply interested in people as *individuals*, not simply as manpower statistics. Thus they tend to be nervous about such impersonal aggregates, used by the economist, as the "labor force" and "human resources." Equally alarming has been the economist's talk of education as an "industry"—just as if producing educated people were the same as producing steel or fertilizer. Some educationists, even now, bristle with rage when such cold-blooded terms as "efficiency," "waste" and "productivity" are applied to education. Others, however, have come to see the relevance and usefulness of such concepts, applied to education.

In all fairness, it should be noted that the economists, too, have had their troubles understanding the educators' specialized concepts and semantics. Economists become especially frustrated when they try to get educators to define just what "product" it is that they were trying to produce, in sufficiently specific terms to be able to determine whether in fact they are producing it, and if so how much. To the horror of economists, it seems that educators are inclined to assess their output mainly by the inputs—things such as the pupil-teacher ratio, expenditures per pupil, or the number of hours a student spends in a classroom, rather than by the performance of the product. How, asks the economist, can one appraise the efficiency of resource use or compare the advantages of alternative systems of production under such circumstances? These two sub-cultures—economics and pedagogy—having lived apart for a long time, naturally have found some initial difficulty learning to live together, as the pressures of history have now obliged them to do. As one who has dwelt happily for some years in both sub-cultures, however, I am convinced that their differences are not irreconcilable. Indeed, educators and economists, as their recent dialogues have demonstrated, have much to teach each other, and once each has learned they make an agreeable and powerful team.

All this recent talk about education being a good investment in economic growth has, in any event, now reached epidemic proportions, all over the world. Seldom in history have the ideas of scholars been so quickly reflected in public policy and action. Last year, in a world survey of educational planning, conducted by the International Bureau of Education, 45 percent of the 75 responding governments said they were engaged in *general* educational planning (though not surprisingly their responses implied quite different definitions of educational planning). Had the same question been asked ten years ago, it would surely have brought far fewer positive answers, and if asked a year from now it would reveal a still larger number of nations attempting to apply educational planning.

By now the majority of less developed nations are taking at least the preliminary steps toward orderly and comprehensive education planning. And increasingly the advanced countries are doing the same, however reluctantly. The recent report of the Robbins Commission on the future of higher education in the United Kingdom is a notable case in point.

This new enthusiasm for educational planning and human resources development, however, has brought in its wake some serious problems and challenges, to which the scholarly world must now respond. The rapid shift of public policy toward educational planning has outdistanced the supply of knowledge and of qualified experts in this field. Indeed, at the moment, there still remains

confusion among the experts themselves as to just what educational
planning means. Much remains to be learned, and much of it can only
be learned through systematic research into the process of educational,
economic and social development, and the role which planning can
play in accelerating such development.

But what specific research topics, we must then ask, are most
urgently in need of attention? In other words, where, intellectually,
should the field of educational planning go from here? The answer
depends upon how one conceives educational planning, narrowly or
broadly. Let us turn to this matter briefly.


## A BROAD VIEW OF EDUCATIONAL PLANNING

There are, if I may oversimplify slightly to make the point,
two extremely different conceptions of educational planning in vogue
today.

One is very narrow. It sees planning as ending in a model of
the future, on paper. It focuses upon the analytical techniques and
methodologies involved in designing such a model, with heavy emphasis on the quantitative dimensions. The educational planner—the
architect of this model—is seen as a specialist who possesses special
techniques, largely statistical and mathematical in character, which
are mysterious to most mortals. In the extreme the planner is viewed
as a new kind of medicine man, a worker of miracles—at least until
the miracles fail to materialize (in which case he can always blame the
politicians).

The other conception is as broad as the first is narrow. It sees
educational planning as a *total* process, in which the "plan" on paper
is but one stage. The accent here is on *action* and *results*, and planning
is seen as an instrument for getting the *best* results possible in the
circumstances; there is really no such thing under this view as *the*
"educational planner," for everyone involved in the total process
along the way must in some measure participate in planning and
thus be a planner, if the effect is to succeed.

Both these views have obvious merit, but if educational

planning is to come of age they must be harmonized. I should say that the first—the manpower concept—must be subsumed within the larger one and certainly not abandoned. And it is inevitable that this will happen.

Anyone sharing responsibility for shaping his nation's educational future will certainly be well served by rigorous analytical concepts, tools and methods, such as those associated with mathematical models, for which the Netherlands Economic Institute is so justly renowned. The exercise of formulating such models has the obvious virtue of bringing many relevant variables into clearer focus, of calling attention to the alternatives and choices available, forcing hidden assumptions into the open, and providing a visible test of the economic feasibility and internal consistency of any given set of proposed targets and actions.

But statistical methods and mathematical models also have their limitations. They cannot, for one thing, take adequately into account the qualitative factors and the curriculum changes required to advance education. Moreover, they must necessarily abstract from many earthy realities which, though often immeasurable, unpredictable and sometimes even unmentionable, are important determinants of any plan's success or failure.

No one, of course, knows these limitations better than the builder of a model. The trouble comes when he or others forget that the model is, inevitably, a gross oversimplification of reality. But if it ignores too much of reality and is taken seriously, the model can do more harm than good. Miracles may be expected that never occur, and in their stead frustration and disillusion proliferate.

It is quite evident, I think, from the varied experience which numerous countries have had in recent years with educational planning and development, that those responsible for such matters, up and down the line—call them planners, administrators, policy-makers, politicians, or what you will—must constantly view the whole landscape through a wide-angle lens. What they will see will differ greatly, of course, from one country to another, or at different periods in the same country. Each nation must shape its educational goals, and the means and strategy for achieving them, to fit its own peculiar conditions. There is no one formula to fit them all, and only those who have never left home would dare to think that there is.

Taking this broad approach to educational planning, and recognizing the differences between countries, one can still identify a few basic guidelines that would serve all countries well that turn to educational planning.

First, as far as possible educational planning should try to view the educational system *as a whole*, from bottom to top, and laterally as well, to include those important training and educational activities which go on outside the formal educational structure. Only with such a broad view can rational choices be made in allocating available educational resources to different parts of the whole system.

If wasteful imbalances are to be avoided, then, for example, higher education must be planned with a careful eye to the secondary schools that supply their students and to whom higher education must supply teachers and intellectual content. Likewise, enthusiasm for achieving universal primary education must not be allowed to obscure the fact that, without adequate teachers supplied by secondary schools and colleges, hundreds of new elementary school buildings can prove to be a hollow educational mockery.

A second guideline is that if education is to make a maximum contribution to society, its own development must be well integrated with economic and social development generally. Attention must be given, for example, to future manpower requirements and to other priority needs, both economic and non-economic. Likewise attention must be given to the nation's economic limitations, to what is feasible and what is not. One has the uneasy feeling that many of the educational expansion targets that have been boldly proclaimed in recent years, in the name of educational planning, may be economically and politically impossible of attainment, at least in the time allotted. This would have to be called not planning but misplanning. Education is no more exempt than any other enterprise from the obstinate constraints imposed by a nation's economic resource limits.

There is wide agreement in principle today on the importance of integrating educational planning with overall development, but, of course, it is far easier said than done. This is one of the many practical areas requiring more analysis and research, and more experience.

The third suggested guideline is that educational planning should look well beyond the purely *quantitative* dimensions of educational development. Without criticism of those who have pioneered courageously in this field, it must be said that the overwhelming emphasis of most educational plans to date, judging from those I have seen, have been upon expanding the educational *status quo* into substantially a large version of itself.

This early emphasis on quantitative expansion is understandable. There has yet been time and skill for little else. But it would be a dangerous illusion to assume that any developing nation, or any advanced one for that matter, can successfully meet its long range educational needs simply to do what it is already doing educationally but on a larger scale. Virtually every educational system in the world, I dare say, needs internal *change* and improvement fully as much as it needs expansion—changes in structure, content, and what I would broadly call the technology of education itself. Even if it were economically feasible to achieve a vast and rapid expansion of the educational *status quo* (which it usually is not), this still would fail to meet today's and especially tomorrow's educational needs. We must face the fact candidly that today's educational systems are in many important respects seriously obsolete. Education must run fast at this stage of history even to stand still, relative to fast changing needs and conditions, and almost nowhere has it run that fast. It is not too much to say, I believe, that education is as much in need of an internal revolution of methods as industry and agriculture were fifty years ago.

Here again, of course, there are no easy short cuts. These changes are far easier to advocate than to attain. Not only are educational systems all over the world notoriously resistant to innovation, but education lacks sufficiently strong and creative internal institutional mechanisms to provide a continuing critical appraisal of its prevailing processes and products, and to invent and foster new and better ones. The pioneer educators who approach their work with a scientific spirit—who are not afraid of constructive criticism and new ideas—constantly complain of being frustrated by a deep-rooted and stubborn folklore. Educational planning must pave the way and provide support for these pioneers and innovators.

Finally, it seems increasingly evident that educational planners must be at least as concerned with the *implementation* of a plan as with designing it in the first place. Indeed, for maximum success, the feasibility and strategy of implementation must be considered from the outset, in the very process by which a plan is produced, so that those who must play a role in carrying it out have a voice in formulating it. In short, a "good" educational plan—if by that one means, among other things, that it has a reasonable chance of success—is one which contains the seeds of its own implementation. What is possible in one situation will not be in another. But educational planning can be of significant use in virtually *all* situations, provided it is regarded as being, like politics, the art of the possible, not a counsel of perfection.

If the practical constraints in any given country—the hard economic, administrative, political, psychological and sociological facts of life which inevitably define the limits of feasibility—are not kept in view by educational planners, they run the risk of becoming not only frustrated but discredited. Most of these constraints cannot be easily measured, diagnosed, or predicted. And most of them lie beyond the normal professional competence of both educators and economists. Therefore other social scientists, as well as practical administrators, statesmen and politicians, must be looked to for guidance on these matters. Though their arithmetic may seem poor, their intuition is often good. They are perhaps as important to the planning team's success as the skilled statistician, economic analyst, or the educator himself. Each has a special and important contribution to make, but somehow they must make it jointly.

## ILLUSTRATIVE RESEARCH NEEDS

If one accepts this broad and flexible view of educational planning, it is evident that important research needs exist today across a wide spectrum of very practical and intellectually challenging problems. Indeed, the urgent current needs for research in this field exceed the world-wide research capabilities to meet them. There is more than enough work for all of us, and a great need exists to build a stronger international research community on this subject, fortified by better communication and collaboration. Likewise there is need for closer cooperation between the "producers" and the "consumers" of research. And while such research is most imperatively needed by the developing countries of Asia, Africa and Latin America, the benefits would also be great, I suspect, for the more advanced countries, for they too, without exception, are in need of educational reform and advancement.

From the preliminary interchange which our new International Institute for Educational Planning has had with various producers and consumers of research in this field, a great variety of useful suggestions for future research have already emerged. Some concern the *external* relations of education—its linkages with economy and growth, for example—while others concern the *internal* affairs of education. Many relate to the techniques and implementation of educational planning and development, while some especially important ones involve its international aspects. Let me mention just a few to illustrate the variety and scope of what is needed, cutting across a number of academic disciplines and professions.

1. One of the more basic needs initially is for a series of systematic case studies which would reveal how a cross-section of nations have fared with educational planning and development efforts to date. This would make possible a comparative analysis of typical problems encountered, though in different forms, in various countries, to see how they have been dealt with in each, and with what success. Such a systematic inventory of practical experience would build a valuable foundation for more research endeavors and for advancing the body of theory. It would also provide excellent practice in interdisciplinary field research. Since the task is a very large one, it would be desirable, and a good means of welding together a stronger research community, if several research institutions (universities and others), capable of team research, could cooperate in carrying out this series of case studies on a comparable basis.

2. A second category of research required relates to the methodological techniques of formulating educational plans. It would be useful, for example, to review the experience of various countries that have sought to use manpower projections and statistical models, to appraise their practical feasibility, their values and their limitations. One likely conclusion would be, I suspect, that the degree of sophistication of the techniques which are appropriate to use varies enormously from country to country, depending upon their stage of development and a variety of other factors. While this generalization is no doubt valid, it would be of greater practical value if someone would sort out more specifically the kinds of techniques most appropriate to different classes of situations.

A related question needing study is just what, in practice, it means to integrate educational and economic planning and development. What are the main points of linkage between the two and how in practice can these linkages be forged? Two of them, obviously, are manpower requirements and educational financing. A third and, the real nexus between education and society's needs, is the curriculum itself. In my judgement, the most crucial and yet most difficult issue of all, is how to define the *learning objectives* of an education development plan, as distinct from *quantitative objectives* of education, at each level, in sufficiently specific terms and with sufficient selectivity and priority, to provide practical criteria for curriculum choices. Despite all the talk of fitting education to the needs and priorities of the individual and society, the curriculum continues to be made much more by tradition and prejudice than by rigorous analysis of real needs.

It is not enough to proclaim curriculum goals in such broad terms that they are little more than slogans—such as "we want to produce good citizens" or we want to produce "modern men for a free society." Educators with the help of others must peel off these easy outer layers and define much more precisely the specific characteristics and capabilities the schools and universities should seek to develop in individuals, if there is to be any rational basis for formulating a curriculum and for evaluating its effectiveness.

Until further progress is made in tailoring the curriculum to priority needs and in appraising its results, educators and economists will be seriously handicapped in trying to discover the relationship (and efficiency) between educational inputs and outputs, or in judging the relative merits of alternative systems of instruction. Meanwhile, also, a good many important problems will continue to be swept under the rug.

Another question much on the mind of responsible development officials today is how to select specific priority projects within the general context of a well conceived educational plan. It is one thing to determine, for example, that 40,000 additional secondary teachers will be needed annually by 1970, but it is yet another to determine precisely how and where they are to be produced. And it is a still different matter to get the action required and to bring the projects to reality. The planner who calculates targets cannot ignore the means for achieving them. The criteria and techniques of project selection, and for determining their practical feasibility, are among the most urgent problems facing educational development today.

Turning to still another question of planning technique, one of the fatal weaknesses of many recent educational plans—preoccupied as they have been with setting quantitative expansion targets, such as the proportion of the youth population that should be attending elementary or secondary school by 1975—is that they have not considered the financial feasibility of carrying out the plan or, worse still, the feasibility of obtaining a sufficient supply of teachers and administrators. Such plans are often so unrealistic as to constitute little more than dreams. There are, of course, sophisticated techniques of constructing plans which take account of all this, but it is often not possible to apply them in practice. What is needed is some relatively simple, self-administered technique for testing the economic and manpower feasibility of plans devised under relatively rudimentary circumstances, and for testing likewise whether the program proposed is internally consistent and provides for the balanced development and mutual reinforcement of the different sectors and levels of education.

Another important question in the area of planning techniques concerns making choices among alternative ways of investing limited educational resources. What should be the division of effort, for example, between elementary, secondary and higher education, or between technical and general education at the secondary level, and how much should be earmarked for out-of-school education? While one can construct an elaborate cost-benefit theory for treating these questions, such theories are impossible to apply in most practical situations. If research is to have practical value, it must provide simpler techniques which practising educational developers can apply on the spot with the hope of achieving considerably better results than are likely to be obtained otherwise, even though they may fall considerably short of theoretical perfection.

3. From the problems of planning techniques, let us turn briefly to a third category of research question relating to the *implementation* of plans. The first could be put this way: what are the pre-conditions for effective planning? Some nations, convinced that planning is important, have adopted the forms and rituals of planning with no discernible results. What was missing in these situations? And in other cases where successful action flowed from planning, what were the conditions that made this action possible? Research is needed which will enable individual countries to diagnose their general situations to determine whether they are really ready for effective planning and if so what kind? Such factors as the state of popular attitudes toward planning, of political leadership and the level of priority given to education, the strengths and weaknesses of the administrative infra-structure, the availability of essential information needed even for the most rudimentary forms of planning, and the possibility of achieving clarification and a reasonable consensus on educational objectives—all these are among the practical constraints which a country should assess before it embarks on a planning effort. But we know too little about how to assess them, and how to create the conditions conducive to successful planning. An examination of the actual experience of a number of nations would shed useful light on the matter.

In this matter of implementation there is need also for fuller study of the organizational and administrative conditions which assist or frustrate implementation, and of the *process* by which plans can be evolved so as to give them the best chance of success. Here again a wealth of practical experience is waiting to be examined.

4. A fourth research category covers a fascinating variety of major special problems confronting most nations in the realm of educational development. One concerns the educational and economic aspects of reforming the curriculum and introducing structural and methodological innovations. What kinds of *institutional* innovations are needed to create these other innovations, to develop and test them out, and then to get them incorporated on a large scale? What are the most effective strategies for inducing change in education? It might be most profitable to examine on a comparative basis a variety of past cases in which educational changes were attempted, both successfully and unsuccessfully. I suspect that a study of innovations in agriculture—where resistance to change has also been notoriously strong—might provide some useful clues for educational innovators.

Another special topic that deserves intensive investigation is education's own manpower problem, which is usually the heart of the problem of any educational expansion plan. There should be comparative studies in several countries, by manpower economists and educators, of the factors affecting teacher supply and utilization, including the whole range of incentives and dis-incentives, with resulting suggestions for policies and program alternatives to meet the situation more adequately.

Research needs should be directed also at the often ignored matter of meeting out-of-school training and educational requirements. It is important to break down the very vague and general concept of "adult education" into more specific groups with specific needs, and to examine the best ways of meeting these needs, including their economy feasibility.

A closely related problem, affecting the large majority of people in developing regions, is that of rural education, integrated with comprehensive rural development. The needs in rural areas are typically much different than in urban areas, though often school programs largely ignore these differences. In hundreds of thousands of villages in Asia, Africa and Latin America, it will be many years before there are conventional schools and teachers. Yet the educational needs are urgent. Therefore, unconventional but economically feasible means must be sought to meet them. This is a challenging area for research and development which could, if successful, make it possible to include much more ambitious provisions for rural education in educational plans.

Another special problem for virtually all developing areas lies in technical training, particularly at the secondary level. There has been a strong tendency to import technical school patterns from more advanced countries, but these are often a poor fit, both for meeting the peculiar needs of the country and its resource limitations. It is patently absurd to start with a fancy and expensive imported model which cannot be duplicated on a large scale, and should not be even if it could. There is the question, too, of how much and what kinds of training can best and most economically be done in formal schools, and of what can be better done outside—on the job, for example. Satisfactory educational plans need satisfactory answers to these questions.

Finally, there are two extremely important special topics for research having to do with the international aspects. One is how foreign aid can more effectively be fitted into a receiving country's educational development plan, to reinforce it rather than to push it off the track. What are the criteria for selecting forms of foreign aid that will give it maximum leverage, even though foreign aid will be at best only a small fraction of the developing country's total educational outlay? And to what extent can educational planning serve to coordinate and harmonize the efforts of numerous external aid agencies, all seemingly "going it alone" in different directions in a given country? What changes of policy and practice would be required in order for these aid agencies to make their aid more effective.

The other international problem concerns the bewildering flow of people from less advanced to more advanced countries for education and training. Overseas study is unquestionably of great importance and is doing much good. Even so, great wastes are also involved in the present situation. Too often the wrong student goes, or the right one goes to the wrong country, or to the wrong institution or studies the wrong thing in terms of what can help him and his country most. Too many students whose talents are needed at home fail to return, or if they do return they fail to find a position which utilizes their newly acquired knowledge. This whole flow and re-cycling of manpower across national lines need to be examined, in the large and close up, in search of ways in which improvements can be made.

These are some of the very practical topics for research which today are troubling those concerned with educational planning and development, and to which the research community will hopefully give greatly increased attention in the immediate future.

Two points should be stressed in conclusion:

First, if educational planning, integrated with economic planning, is to be a genuinely useful instrument of development, as I am convinced it can, then it must not only involve rigorous analytical methods and concepts but it must also take a very comprehensive view of education itself, of the processes of implementation, and of the whole living context in which educational development must take place.

Second, to be effective, educational planning must be realistic. It must aim to do the possible, not the impossible. In each country the techniques of planning employed, and the targets and means adopted, must be fitted to the conditions which prevail. If this is done, there should be no grounds for anyone to claim, as many do today, that educational planning is too vague, too theoretical and too impractical. And if this is done, even though imperfectly, it will be better than flying blind.

Finally, it is abundantly clear that this field is still in its infancy, and to mature it must have the concerted attention of competent research scholars in a wide range of disciplines, working hand in glove with practicing educational developers. I know of no field that holds greater challenge and opportunity for young people of high intellectual ability and an equally high desire to serve mankind.

# references

REFERENCES TO PAGES 23–41:
*Investment in Human Capital*
BY THEODORE W. SCHULTZ
(*Notes* to this essay are on pages 273–276.)

[1] G. S. Becker, preliminary draft of study undertaken for Nat. Bur. Econ. Research. New York 1960.

[2] ——, "Underinvestment in College Education?," *Proc., Am. Econ. Rev.*, May 1960, *50*, 346–54.

[3] P. R. Brahmanand and C. N. Vakil, *Planning for an Expanding Economy*. Bombay 1956.

[4] H. F. Clark, "Potentialities of Educational Establishments Outside the Conventional Structure of Higher Education," *Financing Higher Education, 1969–70*, D. M. Keezer, ed. New York 1959.

[5] Solomon Fabricant, *Basic Facts on Productivity Change*, Nat. Bur. Econ. Research, Occas. Paper 63. New York 1959. Table 5.

[6] Irving Fisher, *The Nature of Capital and Income*. New York 1906.

[7] Milton Friedman and Simon Kuznets, *Income from Independent Professional Practice*, Nat. Bur. Econ. Research. New York 1945.

[8] B. Horvat, "The Optimum Rate of Investment," *Econ. Jour.*, Dec. 1958, *68*, 747–67.

[9] H. G. Johnson, "The Political Economy of Opulence," *Can. Jour. Econ. and Pol. Sci.*, Nov. 1960, *26*, 552–64.

[10] Simon Kuznets, *Income and Wealth in the United States*. Cambridge, England 1952. Sec. IV, Distribution by Industrial Origin.

[11] Alfred Marshall, *Principles of Economics*, 8th ed. London 1930. App. E, pp. 787–88.

[12] H. P. Miller, "Annual and Lifetime Income in Relation to Education: 1939–1959," *Am. Econ. Rev.*, Dec. 1960, *50*, 962–86.

[13] Jacob Mincer, "Investment in Human Capital and Personal Income Distribution," *Jour. Pol. Econ.*, Aug. 1958, *66*, 281–302.

[14] S. J. Mushkin, "Toward a Definition of Health Economics," *Public Health Reports*, U. S. Dept. of Health, Educ. and Welfare, Sept. 1958, *73*, 785–93.

[15] J. S. Nicholson, "The Living Capital of the United Kingdom," *Econ. Jour.*, Mar. 1891, *1*, 95; see J. S. Mill, *Principles of Political Economy*, ed. W. J. Ashley, London 1909, p. 8.

[16] T. W. Schultz, "Investment in Man: An Economist's View," *Soc. Serv. Rev.*, June 1959, *33*, 109–17.

[17] ———, "Agriculture and the Application of Knowledge," *A Look to the Future*, W. K. Kellogg Foundation, Battle Creek, 1956, 54–78.

[18] ———, "Capital Formation by Education," *Jour. Pol. Econ.*, Dec. 1960, *68*, Tables 3 through 7.

[19] ———, "Education and Economic Growth," *Social Forces Influencing American Education*, H. G. Richey, ed. Chicago 1961.

[20] H. von Thünen, *Der isolierte Staat*, 3rd ed., Vol. 2, Pt. 2, 1875, transl. by B. F. Hoselitz, reproduced by the Comp. Educ. Center, Univ. Chicago, pp. 140–52.

[21] Morton Zeman, *A Quantitative Analysis of White-Nonwhite Income Differentials in the United States*. Unpublished doctoral dissertation, Univ. Chicago, 1955.

REFERENCES TO PAGES 196–213:
*The Rate of Return to Education: A Critique*
BY STEPHEN MERRETT
(*Notes* to this essay are on pages 292–293.)

[1] Balogh, T., and Streeten, P. P., "The coefficient of ignorance," *Bulletin of the Oxford University Institute of Economics and Statistics*, May 1963, pp. 99–107.

[2] Becker, G. S., "Investment in human capital: a theoretical analysis," *Journal of Political Economy* (Supplement), October 1962, pp. 9–49.

[3] Blaug, M., "The rate of return on investment in education in Great Britain," *Manchester School*, September 1965. [Includes an Appendix by D. Henderson-Stewart, "Estimate of the rate of return to education in Great Britain."]

[4] Blitz, R. C., "A calculation of income foregone by students," in S. J. Mushkin (Ed.), *Economics of Higher Education*, U. S. Department of Health, Education and Welfare, 1962.

[5] Denison, E. F., "Proportion of income differentials among education groups due to additional education: the evidence of the Wolfle-Smith Survey," *The Residual Factor and Economic Growth*, J. Vaizey (Ed.), O.E.C.D. Paris 1964.

[6] Eckaus, R. S., "Economic criteria for education and training," *Review of Economics and Statistics*, May 1964, pp. 181–90.

[7] Glick, P. C., and Miller, H. P., "Educational level and potential income," *American Sociological Review*, June 1956, pp. 307–12.

[8] Johnston, J., *Econometric Methods*, 1963.

[9] Jolly, Richard, "Education," in Dudley Seers (Ed.), *Cuba, the Economic and Social Revolution*, 1964.

[10] Machlup, F., *The Production and Distribution of Knowledge in the United States*, Princeton, 1962.

[11] Miller, H. P., *The Income of the American People*, New York, 1955.

[12] —— "Annual and lifetime income in relation to education: 1939–1959," *American Economic Review*, December 1960, pp. 962–87.

[13] Mincer, J., "On-the-job training: costs, returns and some implications," *Journal of Political Economy* (Supplement), October 1962, pp. 50–79.

[14] Morgan, J. N., David, M. H., Cohen, W. J., and Brazer, H. E., *Income and Welfare in the United States*, New York, 1962.

[15] —— ——, "Education and income," *Quarterly Journal of Economics*, August 1963, pp. 423–37.

[16] Schultz, T. W., "Capital formation by education," *Journal of Political Economy*, December 1960, pp. 571–84.

[17] Vaizey, J., *The Economics of Education*, London, 1962.

# notes

part one

**Education, Human Capital,
and Economic Growth**

*Introduction*

1. M. Debeauvais, "The Concept of Human Capital," *International Social Science Journal* 14 (December 1962): 662.

2. Two excellent papers that trace the historical contributions of early economists to the human capital concept are B. F. Kiker, "The Historical Roots of the Concept of Human Capital," *Journal of Political Economy* 74 (October 1966): 481–499; and W. J. Miller, "The Economics of Education in English Classical Economics," *Southern Economic Journal* 32 (January 1966): 294–309. Also see John Vaizey, *The Economics of Education* (London: Fabernel Faber, 1962), chapter 2.

3. Kiker, "Historical Roots," p. 481; and Miller, "Economics of Education," p. 308.

4. J. S. Nicholson, "The Living Capital of the United Kingdom," *Economic Journal* 1 (March 1891): 95–107.

5. See S. J. Strumlin's "The Economic Significance of National Education" in M. J. Bowman, M. Debeauvais, V. Komarov, and J. Vaizey, eds., *Readings in the Economics of Education* (Paris: United Nations Educational, Scientific and Cultural Organization, 1968), pp. 413–451.

6. J. R. Walsh, "Capital Concept Applied to Man," *Quarterly Journal of Economics* 49 (February 1935): 255–85.

7. Richard F. Young, "Educational Expenditures in the United States," *Monthly Review*, Federal Reserve Bank of Kansas City (September-October 1967): 5.

8. United States Department of Health, Education, and Welfare, Office of Education, *Digest of Educational Statistics* (Washington, D. C.: Government Printing Office, 1968).

9. Theodore W. Schultz, "Capital Formation by Education," *Journal of Political Economy* 68 (December 1960): 580.

10. ———, *The Economic Value of Education* (New York: Columbia University Press, 1963). A review of the problems and alternative approaches used to estimate the stock of human capital is carefully described in a paper by Mary Jean Bowman, "Human Capital: Concepts and Measures," in Selma J. Mushkin, ed., *Economics of Higher Education*, United States Department of Health, Education, and Welfare (Washington, D. C.: Government Printing Office, 1962), pp. 62–92. Health and medical care investments in human capital in the United States are estimated by S. J. Mushkin and B. A. Weisbrod, "Investment in Health: Lifetime Health Expenditures on the 1960 Work Force," *Kyklos* 16 (April 1963): 583–99.

11. Two frequently cited efforts in this direction are those of Nicholson and Walsh, above. Estimates have been made more recently by B. A. Weisbrod, "The Valuation of Human Capital," *Journal of Political Economy* 69 (October 1961): 425–36.

12. Odd Aukrust clearly postulated the significance of the "human factor" and its strong implications for the then conventional approach to theories of economic growth that placed heavy reliance on physical capital formation in his "Investment and Economic Growth," *Productivity Measurement Review* 16 (February 1959): 35–50. Also see R. M. Solow, "Technical Change and the Aggregate Production Function," *Review of Economics and Statistics* 39 (August 1957): 312–20; and Z. Griliches, "Research Expenditures, Education, and the Aggregate Agricultural Production Function," *American Economic Review* 54 (December 1964): 425–36.

13. See John Kendrick, *Productivity Trends in the United States*, Appendix A (Princeton: Princeton University Press, 1957); E. F. Denison, *The Sources of Economic Growth in the United States and Alternatives Before Us* (New York: Committee for Economic Development, 1962), p. 30; R. M. Solow, "Technical Progress, Capital Formation, and Economic Growth," *American Economic Review* 52 (May 1962): 76–86; and Kenneth

J. Arrow, "The Economic Importance of Learning by Doing," *Review of Economic Studies* 29 (June 1962): 155–74.

14. National income ignores numerous factors that affect the welfare of society, including changes in output quality, unaccounted for output (*e.g.*, a housewife's production), and welfare changes emanating from changes in the composition of consumed output. Growth in total or per capita income can be used, although measures of per capita income growth may confuse matters, since population change and income distribution enter as variables. Economic growth at full employment represents growth in *potential* national income that may not be realized unless full employment is achieved. Full employment growth is of most immediate concern because growth due to utilization of previously underemployed factors of production is short term in nature and does not represent changes in the potential long-run welfare of the economic community. Finally, interest typically centers upon real growth and not growth in the money value of output (*i.e.*, prices are held constant with the passage of time).

15. Assume there is no technological change and no change in the stock of capital ($R = 0$ and $Kg = 0$). Then

$$Yg = XLg; \; \frac{\Delta Y}{Y} = X \frac{\Delta L}{L}; \; X = \frac{\Delta Y}{Y} \div \frac{\Delta L}{L}; \text{ or } X = \frac{\Delta Y}{\Delta L} \times \frac{L}{Y}$$

The percentage change in output ($\Delta Y/Y$) divided by the percentage change in the quantity of labor ($\Delta L/L$) is the elasticity of output with respect to labor. Assuming a competitive market, the real price of labor ($W/P$) equals labor's marginal product ($\Delta Y/\Delta L$). Thus, we can substitute in the equation above as follows:

$$X = \frac{W}{P} \times \frac{L}{Y} = \frac{\text{Labor's income}}{\text{Total income}}$$

16. See Kendrick, *Productivity Trends*, or Denison, *Sources of Economic Growth*. We are assuming the production function to be homogenous with degree 1. Therefore, equal proportionate increases in both inputs generate a like increase in output.

17. Denison, *Sources of Economic Growth*, p. 148.

18.
$$Yg = XLg + ZKg + R$$
$$Yg = \tfrac{3}{4} \times .9\% + \tfrac{1}{4} \times 5\% + 0$$
$$Yg = .68\% + 1.25\%$$
$$Yg = 1.93\%$$

19. The oversimplified view of economic growth that follows should be supplemented by additional readings. See E. D. Domar, "Expansion and Employment," *American Economic Review* 37 (March 1947): 34–55; R. F. Harrod, "An Essay in Dynamic Theory," *Economic Journal* 29 (March 1939): 14–33; or R. F. Harrod, *Toward A Dynamic Economics* (London: Macmillan Co., 1948).

20. Equilibrium output in time period $t$ is $Y_t = \sigma K_t = \frac{1}{s}\Delta I_t$, where $\Delta I_t$ represents investment expenditures in the current time period; *i.e.*, net increments to the capital stock ($\Delta K_t$):

$$\sigma K_t = \frac{1}{s}\Delta K_t$$

$$\sigma s = \frac{\Delta K_t}{K_t}$$

$$\frac{Y_t}{K_t} \times \frac{\Delta S_t}{Y_t} = \frac{\Delta K_t}{K_t}$$

$$\frac{\Delta S_t}{K_t} = \frac{\Delta K_t}{K_t},$$ or current savings and investment are equal.

21. Equilibrium growth in output $Yg$ (or $\Delta Y^c/Y = \Delta Y^d/Y$) in percentage terms is:

$$Yg = \frac{I\sigma}{Y} \text{ or } \frac{sY\sigma}{Y} = s\sigma.$$

22. Robert M. Solow, "Technical Progress, Capital Formation, and Economic Growth," *American Economic Review* 52 (May 1962): 76–86.

23. Arrow, "Economic Importance of Learning by Doing."

24. Nicholas Kaldor, *Essays on Value and Distribution* (New York: The Free Press, 1960); and Joan Robinson, *Accumulation of Capital* (New York: Macmillan Co., 1956).

25. Additional information on benefit-cost analysis which supplements the brief explanation that follows can be obtained from Robert Dorfman, ed., *Measuring Benefits of Government Investments* (Washington: D. C., The Brookings Institution, 1965); A. R. Prest and R. Turvey, "Cost Benefit Analysis: A Survey," *Economic Journal* 75 (December 1965); Gary Becker, *Human Capital* (New York: Columbia University Press, 1964); Jack Hirshleifer, "On the Theory of Optimal Investment Decision," *Journal of Political Economy* 66 (August 1958); and Arthur Maass,

"Benefit Cost Analysis: Its Relevance to Public Investment Decision," *Quarterly Journal of Economics* 80 (May 1966).

26. See W. J. Baumol, "On the Social Rate of Discount," *American Economic Review* 58 (September 1968); and United States Congress, Joint Economic Committee, Subcommittee on Economy in Government, "Interest Rate Guidelines for Federal Decision-Making," *Hearings*, 90th Congress, 2nd Session, 1968.

27. This condition is identified by equation (5) in Selection 5 written by Jacob J. Kaufman, Teh-wei Hu, Maw Lin Lee, and E. W. Stromsdorfer, from *A Cost Effectiveness Study of Vocational Education*, The Pennsylvania State University Institute for Research on Human Resources (1969), pp. 6–19.

28. Excellent discussions of measurement problems are contained in Burton A. Weisbrod, "Education and Investment in Human Capital," *Journal of Political Economy*, Supplement 70 (August 1962): 106–23; Giora Hanoch, "An Economic Analysis of Earnings and Schooling," *Journal of Human Resources* 2 (Summer 1967): 310–29; and Becker, *Human Capital*.

29. Among the useful additional readings which explain the discounting process and public investments in more adequate detail see Prest and Turvey, "Cost Benefit Analysis."

30. T. Balogh and P. P. Streeten, "The Coefficient of Ignorance," *Bulletin of the Oxford University Institute of Economics and Statistics* 25 (May 1963): 99–107; Neil W. Chamberlain, "Some Second Thoughts on the Concept of Human Capital," *Industrial Relations Research Association*, Twentieth Annual Winter Proceedings (1967), pp. 1–13; and Jack Wiseman, "Cost-Benefit Analysis in Education," *Southern Economic Journal* 32 (July 1965): 1–14.

31. See Becker, *Human Capital*.

## Investment in Human Capital

1. This paragraph draws on the introduction to my Teller Lecture [16].

2. Based on unpublished preliminary results by Joseph Willett in his Ph.D. research at the University of Chicago.

3. I leave aside here the difficulties inherent in identifying and measuring both the non-human capital and the income entering into estimates of this ratio. There are index number and aggregation problems aplenty, and not all improvements in the quality of this capital have been accounted for, as I shall note later.

4. Even so, our *observed* return can be either negative, zero or positive because our observations are drawn from a world where there is uncertainty and imperfect knowledge and where there are windfall gains and losses and mistakes aplenty.

5. In principle, the value of the investment can be determined by discounting the additional future earnings it yields just as the value of a physical capital good can be determined by discounting its income stream.

6. Health economics is in its infancy; there are two medical journals with "economics" in their titles, two bureaus for economic research in private associations (one in the American Medical and the other in the American Dental Association), and not a few studies and papers by outside scholars. Selma Mushkin's survey is very useful with its pertinent economic insights, though she may have underestimated somewhat the influence of the economic behavior of people in striving for health [14].

7. For instance, the income elasticity of the demand for food continues to be positive even after the point is reached where additional food no longer has the attribute of a "producer good."

8. Based on comments made by Harold F. Clark at the Merrill Center for Economics, summer 1959; also, see [4].

9. Based on observations made by a team of U. S. economists of which I was a member, see *Saturday Rev.*, Jan. 21, 1961.

10. Becker has also noted still another implication arising out of the fact that the income and capital investment aspects of on-the-job training are tied together, which gives rise to "permanent" and "transitory" income effects that may have substantial explanatory value.

11. Had other things stayed constant this suggests an income elasticity of 3.5. Among the things that did change, the prices of educational services rose relative to other consumer prices, perhaps offset in part by improvements in the quality of educational services.

12. This of course assumes among other things that the relationship between gross and net have not changed or have changed in the same proportion. Estimates are from my essay, "Education and Economic Growth" [19].

13. From [19, Sec. 4]. These estimates of the stock of education are tentative and incomplete. They are incomplete in that they do not take into account fully the increases in the average life of this form of human capital arising out of the fact that relatively more of this education is held by younger people in the labor force than was true in earlier years; and, they are incomplete because no adjustment has been made for the improvements in education over time, increasing the quality of a year of

school in ways other than those related to changes in the proportions represented by elementary, high school and higher education. Even so the stock of this form of human capital rose 8.5 times between 1900 and 1956 while the stock of reproducible nonhuman capital increased only 4.5 times, both in constant 1956 prices.

14. In value terms this stock of education was only 22 percent as large as the stock of reproducible physical capital in 1900, whereas in 1956 it already had become 42 percent as large.

15. Several comments are called for here. (1) The return to high school education appears to have declined substantially between the late 'thirties and early 'fifties and since then has leveled off, perhaps even risen somewhat, indicating a rate of return toward the end of the 'fifties about as high as that to higher education. (2) The return to college education seems to have risen somewhat since the late 'thirties in spite of the rapid influx of college-trained individuals into the labor force. (3) Becker's estimates based on the difference in income between high school and college graduates based on urban males adjusted for ability, race, unemployment and mortality show a return of 9 percent to total college costs including both earnings, foregone and conventional college costs, public and private and with none of these costs allocated to consumption (see his paper given at the American Economic Association meeting, December 1959 [2]). (4) The returns to this education in the case of nonwhite urban males, of rural males, and of females in the labor force may have been somewhat lower (see Becker [2]). (5) My own estimates, admittedly less complete than those of Becker and thus subject to additional qualifications, based mainly on lifetime income estimates of Herman P. Miller [12], lead to a return of about 11 percent to both high school and college education as of 1958. See [19, Sec. 5].

Whether the consumption component in education will ultimately dominate, in the sense that the investment component in education will diminish as these expenditures increase and a point will be reached where additional expenditures for education will be pure consumption (a zero return on however small a part one might treat as investment), is an interesting speculation. This may come to pass, as it has in the case of food and shelter, but that eventuality appears very remote presently in view of the prevailing investment value of education and the new demands for knowledge and skill inherent in the nature of our technical and economic progress.

16. The returns on this consumer capital will not appear in the wages and salaries that people earn.

17. Real income doubled, rising from $150 to $302 billion in 1956 prices.

Eighty-nine billions of the increase in real income is taken to be unexplained, or about 59 percent of the total increase. The stock of education in the labor force rose by $355 billion of which $69 billion is here allocated to the growth in the labor force to keep the per-worker stock of education constant, and $286 billion represents the increase in the level of this stock. See [19, Sec. 6] for an elaboration of the method and the relevant estimates.

18. In percent, the lower estimate came out to 29 percent and the upper estimate to 56 percent.

19. I am indebted to Milton Friedman for bringing this issue to the fore in his comments on an early draft of this paper. See preface of [7] and also Jacob Mincer's pioneering paper [13].

## Converging Concerns of Economists and Educators

1. Two other approaches frequently characterize efforts of economists to deal with one or another aspect of investment in education. One of these is analysis of production functions over time; growth in the national income is "explained" by a statistical analysis of changes in inputs of various production factors. Edward F. Denison has gone further than anyone else in applying this approach to analysis of the role of education in economic growth; see Chapter 7 and the conclusion of his *The Sources of Economic Growth in the United States and the Alternatives Before Us* (New York: Committee for Economic Development, 1962). T. W. Schultz combines elements of this approach with rate-of-return analysis when he plugs the latter into a time series of human capital "stock carried" in an attempt to identify the role of education in American economic growth; see his "Education and Economic Growth" in *Social Forces Influencing American Education*, edited by Nelson B. Henry (Chicago: University of Chicago Press, 1961), pp. 46–88. The writer has also made use of elements of this type of analysis in two articles: M. J. Bowman, "Human Capital; Concepts and Measures" in *The Economics of Higher Education*, edited by Selma J. Mushkin (Washington, D. C.: U. S. Department of Health, Education and Welfare, Office of Education, 1962), and "Social versus Private Returns to Education," in the *International Social Science Journal* (forthcoming). Though analysis of production functions over time has been a central interest to many economists, it opens few if any points of contact at which economist and educational researcher could join for constructive endeavor.

Manpower analysis is in a different category. Thus far manpower studies have been planning instruments. They have assumed the answers to the basic questions about economic structure and process, rather than seeking answers. However, as this work becomes more sophisticated it must perforce lead to more fundamental investigations of the role of education in long-term economic growth, including the basic structural changes that such growth entails. For a useful critique of manpower orientation, see Bert F. Hoselitz, "Investment in Education and Its Political Impact in Developing Countries," mimeographed paper for the Conference on Education and Political Development at Lake Arrowhead, California, June 25–29, 1962, sponsored by the Committee on Comparative Politics, Social Science Research Council.

2. As readers will discover, the position taken in this paper differs substantially from that taken by John Vaizey primarily in the stress laid on the value of this allocative approach, although there are also some disagreements on other points. See John Vaizey, "Education as Investment in Comparative Perspective," in the October 1961 issue of *Comparative Education Review*, 5: 97–104.

3. Child labor laws prohibiting work for children under, say, fourteen years would of course make opportunity costs of schooling below that age zero, apart from uncovered jobs such as helping on the family farm.

4. See Vaizey, *op. cit.*, p. 99.

5. For a more complete discussion of social returns see the writer's "Social and Private Returns to Education," previously cited, and Burton A. Weisbrod, "Education and the Investment in Human Capital," *Journal of Political Economy*, LXX (supplement), August 1962.

6. A study just completed by Lee Hansen suggests that, contrary to common assumption, there is not a "shortage" of doctors in the United States today. Neither, by the same token, is there evidence of monopolistically high returns to investment in medical training. (Typescript.)

7. Vaizey appears to take this position (*op. cit.*, p. 97).

8. This is a matter of application of the analysis to a wide range of public decision problems, not to education in particular. The earliest attempt to treat education in something like this kind of analytical framework was apparently the work of a Russian, Stanislas Strumiline, who developed his ideas in the 1920's, though these were not accepted by the Soviet rulers at the time. Rate-of-return measurement has been coming back gradually as the need for the interest-rate concept in national planning has been increasingly recognized.

9. Monopolistic pricing of human services does not imply deviation of private incomes from social contributions, though it does imply restrictions of opportunity and enters into the discrepancies among true private rates. The distortions involved in group 5 arise from controls on the demand

side of the market for skills; in the illustration given here the problem is the power of a group in control to coerce payment for their services. An opposite effect, in which incomes may be depressed below the value of services rendered, arises when buyers are in a position to exercise "monopsonistic" controls over the wages of a particular group; situations in which this can be of significance are more limited than is commonly supposed by the noneconomist.

10. There is a peculiar twist to this situation when viewed from a structural change as well as a rate-of-return orientation. While analysis of the distortion in the measured rate-of-return because of elitist controls indicates that the true rate is a lower one, socioeconomic considerations suggest that the best way of boring from within to break open a situation that is blocking progress may nevertheless be expansion of education on a large scale. Global social returns may deviate significantly from partial social returns in such a situation because explosive structural change is called for if economic growth is to occur.

11. The most systematic and careful empirical work that the writer has been privileged to see for either of these kinds of comparisons is contained in two articles just completed by Lee Hansen and not yet submitted for publication.

12. See Gary S. Becker, "Investment in Human Capital: A Theoretical Analysis," and Jacob Mincer, "On the Job Training: Costs, Returns and Some Implications," both in *Journal of Political Economy*, LXX (supplement), August 1962.

## Investing in Human Capital

1. *Economics of Public Health* (Philadelphia: University of Pennsylvania Press, 1961), p. 84.

2. *Ibid.*, p. 83.

3. U.S. Department of Labor, "Educational Attainment of Workers, March 1962," Special Labor Force Report No. 30 (1963), p. A–5.

4. *Statistical Review of Canadian Education, Census* (1951), p. 69.

5. Estimated from the data in the *1961 Census of Canada, Labour Force*, Bulletin 3.1–13, pp. 19–1, 2.

6. *The Role of the Federal Government in Financing Higher Education* (Washington: Brookings Institution, 1961).

7. U.S. Department of Health, Education and Welfare, *Health, Education, and Welfare Trends, 1963* (Washington: GPO, 1963), p. 60.

8. T. W. Schultz, "Capital Formation by Education," *Journal of Political Economy*, LXVIII (December 1960), 583.

9. *Ibid.*, p. 580.

10. Estimates by G. S. Becker, as reported in T. W. Schultz, "Education and Economic Growth," in *Social Forces Influencing American Education* (Chicago: National Society for the Study of Education, 1961), p. 78. See also G. S. Becker, *Human Capital* (New York: National Bureau of Economic Research, 1964).

11. W. J. Swift and B. A. Weisbrod, "On the Monetary Value of Education's Intergeneration Benefits," *Journal of Political Economy*, LXXIII (December 1965), 643–49.

12. Tax implications of the existence of intertemporal education returns have been discussed by R. Goode, "Educational Expenditures and the Income Tax," in S. J. Mushkin, ed., *Economics of Higher Education* (Washington: GPO, 1962).

13. See, for example, C. F. Schmid, V. A. Miller, and B. Abu-Laban, "Impact of Recent Negro Migration on Seattle Schools," in *International Population Conference Papers* (Vienna: Union International pour l'étude scientifique de la population, 1959), pp. 674–83.

14. V. O. Key, Jr., *Public Opinion and American Democracy* (New York: Knopf, 1961), pp. 324–25; Angus Campbell, Gerald Gurin, and Warren Miller, *The Voter Decides* (White Plains: Row, Peterson, 1954), pp. 194–99.

15. Key, *op. cit.*, Table 13.3, p. 325. These data were compiled from Survey Research Center studies in 1952 and 1956. See Campbell *et al.*, *op. cit.*, Table B.2, p. 197; and A. Campbell, W. Miller, P. Converse, and D. Stokes, *The American Voter* (New York: John Wiley, 1960), Table 17–5, p. 480.

16. *External Benefits of Public Education* (Princeton: Princeton University, Industrial Relations Section, 1964), pp. 96, 98.

## Theory of Public Expenditures for Education

1. Joint Economic Committee, Congress of the United States, *Federal Programs for the Development of Human Resources*, Vol. I., December 1966, p. 8.

2. The most important contribution in this area is T. W. Schultz, *The Economic Value of Education* (New York: Columbia University Press, 1963).

3. For example, Robert Solow, "Technical Change and the Aggregate Production Function," *Review of Economics and Statistics*, August 1957, pp. 312–323.

4. For example, Gary S. Becker, *Human Capital* (New York: Columbia University Press, 1964), pp. 7–66.

5. See Burton Weisbrod, *External Benefits of Public Education* (Princeton: Princeton University), 1964.

6. Jacob Mincer, "Investment in Human Capital and Personal Income Distribution," *Journal of Political Economy*, August 1958, pp. 281–302.

7. For a detailed discussion see Howard R. Bowen, *Toward Social Economy* (New York: Rinehart & Co., 1948), Chapter 17.

8. Nels Hanson, "Economy of Scale as a Cost Factor in Financing Public Schools," *National Tax Journal*, March 1954, pp. 92–95.

9. John Riew, "Economies of Scale in High School Operation," *Review of Economics and Statistics*, August 1966, pp. 280–287.

10. Weisbrod, *op. cit.*, p. 23.

11. Schultz, *op. cit.*, p. 51.

12. Edward F. Denison, "Education, Economic Growth, and Gaps in Information," *Journal of Political Economy, Supplement*, October 1962, pp. 124–129.

13. Milton Friedman, "The Role of Government in Education," in his *Capitalism and Freedom* (Chicago: University of Chicago Press, 1962), pp. 83–107.

14. While this general discussion is couched in terms of comparing vocational-technical with academic secondary education, the actual cost-benefit analysis . . . is done on the basis of comparisons between the graduates of vocational-technical and comprehensive senior high schools.

15. A. C. Pigou, *The Economics of Welfare*, 4th Edition (London: MacMillan Co., 1950), p. 183.

16. Charles J. Hitch, *Problems of Application of the Planning-Programming-Budgeting System to Education*, a paper prepared for the Stanford Research Institute, Conference on Vocational-Technical Education, Airlie House, Virginia, April 10–12, 1967.

17. The method of "program-budgeting" was proposed by David Novick of the RAND Corporation who in 1954 presented a systematic exposition of how the technique could be applied effectively to military spending. See his RAND study, *Efficiency and Economy in Government Through New Budgeting Procedures*, 1954.

18. For detailed discussions, see Jack Hirshleifer, *et al.*, *Water Supply: Economics, Technology, and Policy* (Chicago: The University of Chicago Press, 1960), Chapters 6 and 7.

19. See for example J. V. Krutilla and Otto Eckstein, *Multiple Purpose River Development* (Baltimore: Johns Hopkins University Press, 1958).

20. Charles J. Hitch and R. N. McKean, *Economics of Defense in the Nuclear Age* (Cambridge: Harvard University Press, 1960).

21. For detailed discussions of these fields see Robert Dorfman, Editor, *Measuring Benefits of Government Investments* (Washington: Brookings Institution, 1965).

*part two*

**Returns from Investment in Education**

## *Underinvestment in College Education?*

1. Presumably, the difference between the return to whites and nonwhites partly results from discrimination against nonwhites.

2. A woman receives indirect returns from college if it enables her to marry a man with a higher income than she would have married if she did not go to college. These returns may be substantial and should be considered when a woman decides whether to go to college. It is not obvious that the total return to women graduates is much less than that to men; such a comparison would require data on the family incomes of the average male and female college graduates rather than on their personal incomes.

3. If all persons working on military technology were employed by the government and if salaries measured expected (or actual) military contribution, there would be no external military effects since the full marginal productivity would be directly measured by salaries. This argument clearly holds for all government employees regardless of their speciality.

4. Business had about 14 percent, education about 20 percent, and humanities and social sciences about 25 percent of all first degrees.

5. Few systematic studies have been made of the return to different college specialities. According to the 1950 Census the average income of engineers was about $5,100, much lower than the $6,600 average income of college graduates. This seems to indicate that the direct money return to engineering graduates is less than that to other graduates. But about 40 percent of the Census engineers are not college graduates, and they may receive less income than graduate engineers simply because they have less training. Moreover, even if they have the same total amount of training—received

on the job rather than in college—they would tend to report lower incomes because their incomes would be net of training costs, while the reported incomes of graduate engineers (and other college graduates) would be gross of training costs.

6. I have abstracted from the increase in administrators, teachers, etc., that would accompany a 50 percent increase in scientists. This omission partly offsets the upward biases in the estimate.

7. Thus about 14 percent of high school graduates ranked in the top 20 percent of their high school class, while 59 percent of college graduates ranked below the top 20 percent of their high school class.

8. Let $Y = f(A,E)$, where $Y$ is the income of a person with an education equal to $E$ and ability equal to $A$. Education and ability would be substitutes if

$$\frac{\partial(\partial Y/\partial E)}{\partial A} = \frac{\partial^2 Y}{\partial A \partial E} = \frac{\partial(\partial Y/\partial A)}{\partial E} < 0$$

complements if the inequality were reversed, and independent inputs if equality held.

9. To a first approximation

$$g = iC,$$

where $g$ is the average gain per unit time from college training, $C$ is the cost of college, and $i$ is the internal rate of return on college costs. If these costs were the same for all (actually they would be larger for able persons since opportunity costs would be greater for them), then

$$g_1 \gtrless g_h \text{ as } i_1 \gtrless i_\lambda,$$

where $g_1$ and $g_h$ are the gains and $i_1$ and $i_\lambda$ are the rates of return to persons of low and high ability, respectively.

10. They may also receive less nonpecuniary income from college education than do children from upper strata families.

## Education and Income

1. U.S. Bureau of the Census, *U.S. Census of Population 1950*, Vol. IV, Special Reports, Part 5, Chapter B, "Education" (Washington, 1953).

1a. This source has always been used by Paul C. Glick and Herman P. Miller of the U.S. Bureau of the Census. See Paul C. Glick, "Educational Attainment and Occupational Advancement," *Transactions of the Second World Congress of Sociology*, Vol. II (London, 1954), 183–93; and Paul C. Glick and Herman P. Miller, "Educational Level and Potential

Income," *American Sociological Review*, XXI (1956), 307–12. Unfortunately I did not learn of the existence of these useful papers until the calculations here presented were completed, though I was familiar with Mr Miller's Census Monograph, *Income of the American People* (New York, 1955), which surveys the basic data. In any case the duplication is not large, for Glick and Miller had a different starting age for life-time income (22 rather than 14 years); they did not take income taxes into account, nor did they apply discount factors. Moreover they used a different procedure for estimating mean income (see below).

2. Apart from questions of accuracy, for which see especially Miller, *op. cit.*, I have made no attempt to correct numerically for any biases to which the data may be subject.

3. Glick took the midpoint of each interval as its mean, a practice which leads to bias if the distribution is skew. It may be noted that the mean incomes for age-education groups as estimated by Glick are nearly all lower than in my Table 1, though this is partly attributable to the difference in the next footnote.

4. Miller, *op. cit.*, 153, notes that income tax returns of families and unrelated individuals for 1944 to 1949 with adjusted gross incomes over $10,000 had a mean of between $21,000 and $22,000, but that this figure would overstate the mean income of persons (to which the Census data refer). He therefore uses a mean of $20,000. I have nevertheless preferred a figure of $22,000 mostly because in the more highly educated groups, where relatively many incomes over $10,000 are to be found, the distribution is more unequal, so that a still larger mean would have been appropriate for those groups. In the groups where high incomes are few it makes less difference what mean is used.

5. The not inconsiderable groups with "income not reported" and "school years not reported" had to be left out of account.

6. It does not conform to any of the well-known distribution functions, such as the normal, the log-normal, or (except in the right-hand tail) the Pareto distribution.

7. From U.S. Treasury Department, Internal Revenue Service, *Statistics of Income for 1949*, Part 1 (Washington, 1954); both taxable and non-taxable returns were considered.

8. Glick, *op. cit.*, and Glick and Miller, *op. cit.*, start at age 22, this being the age at which for nearly all people school attendance is completed. In doing so, however, they leave out of account the lack of earnings of the better-educated while at school, and consequently overstate the latter's advantage in life-time income. Although perhaps more satisfactory in this

respect, my procedure also fails to provide a complete picture, for it does not allow for income received while at school. On the other hand it does not consider tuition either, thereby introducing a wholly or partly compensating error.

9. From U.S. Department of Health, Education, and Welfare, National Office of Vital Statistics, *United States Life Tables, 1949–51*, Special Reports, Vol. 41, No. 1 (Washington, 1954).

10. Glick and Miller, *op. cit.*, p. 310.

11. It is regrettable that the Census tabulations do not distinguish between those who completed four years of college and those with more than four years.

## Total and Private Rates of Return to Investments in Schooling

1. Herman P. Miller, "Annual and Lifetime Income in Relation to Education: 1929–1959," *American Economic Review*, L (December, 1960), 962–86.

2. H. S. Houthakker, "Education and Income," *Review of Economics and Statistics*, XLI (February, 1959), 24–28.

3. Theodore W. Schultz, "Capital Formation by Education," *Journal of Political Economy*, LXVIII (December, 1960), 571–83.

4. Gary S. Becker, "Underinvestment in College Education?" *American Economic Review*, L (May, 1960), 346–54; and Theodore W. Schultz, "Education as a Source of Economic Growth" (Economics of Education Research Paper, August 15, 1961) (Mimeographed), and "Education and Economic Growth," *Social Forces Influencing American Education*, ed. H. G. Richey (Chicago, 1961). It should be noted that Schultz uses a short-cut method to derive his rate of return estimates.

5. United States Bureau of the Census, *1950 Census of Population, Special Report*, P.E. No. 5B, *Education*, Table 12.

6. The mean income figures used in this study were estimated by weighting the mid-values of each income size class by the numbers of income recipients in each size class, for each age-level-of-schooling category. A value of $20,000 was used for the mid-value of the open-ended class. Houthakker used a "representative" income in his weighting, in order to take account of the skewness. However, such a procedure superimposes the skewness of the entire distribution upon each age-level-of-schooling category; this leads to serious problems, particularly at the younger age levels, where the resulting mean income values will substantially overstate the "correct" values.

7. This is an oversimplification, but it did not seem worthwhile to deal with this in a more detailed fashion.

8. It is unfortunate that such data are not collected since the earnings of male workers below age fourteen are assuredly not zero. Thus opportunity costs are understated to some extent.

9. "Capital Formation by Education," *op. cit.*

10. These opportunity cost figures tend to be slightly lower, on a per student basis, than those of Schultz, which average $583 for high school and $1,369 for college, on an annual basis.

11. *Ibid.*

12. Average college tuition and fees amounted to $245 in 1949 (see Ernest V. Hollis, "Trends in Tuition Charges and Fees," *Higher Education*, XII [June, 1956], 70). Actually, a figure of $245 was used; this figure was estimated from data on tuition and fees collected, reported for 1949–50 in *Biennial Survey of Education, 1955–56* (Washington: Government Printing Office, 1957), chap. iv. See sources to Table 2.

13. Schultz simply assumed that these costs were 5 percent of income foregone at the high-school level and 10 percent of income foregone at the college level. The absolute figures derived from Schultz's work were used in these calculations even though the income foregone figures differed somewhat.

14. Calculated from U.S. Department of Health, Education and Welfare, National Office of Vital Statistics, *United States Life Tables, 1949–51* (Special Reports, Vol. XLI, No. 1 [Washington, 1954]). No attempt was made, however, to adjust for the incidence of unemployment, largely because of the difficulty of disentangling unemployment from non-labor-force status in the data, which show all males classified by the receipt or non-receipt of income rather than by labor-force status.

15. Houthakker, *op. cit.*, calculated from Tables 1 and 2, pp. 25–26.

16. Several of the education-age categories were adjusted for taxes by applying the average effective tax liability by size of income group to the midpoint of the size group to determine the mean tax paid. In general, the average effective tax rate derived for an education-age category was almost identical with that calculated by Houthakker.

Admittedly, the use of the average tax liability ignores the effects of age differences, family size, and so on, but it did not seem worthwhile to adjust for these factors, even to the limited extent that such adjustments could be attempted.

17. The main criticisms of this whole approach have been expressed most fully and forcefully by Edward F. Renshaw, "Estimating the Returns to

Education," *Review of Economics and Statistics*, XLII (August, 1960), 318–24.

18. Becker, *op. cit.*, has made some adjustments for differences in ability, but his method of doing so is not yet available. Differences in intelligence at different levels of schooling are given in Dael Wolfe, *America's Resources of Specialized Talent* (New York: Harper & Bros., 1954), pp. 142–49.

19. This point is discussed in T. W. Schultz, "Investment in Human Capital," *American Economic Review*, LI (March, 1961), 1–17.

20. For another dissenting note see John Vaizey, *The Economics of Education* (London: Faber & Faber, 1962), chap. iii.

21. It is interesting to note that most states require compulsory school attendance at least to age fourteen (in effect, to the end of Grade 8).

22. *Op. cit.*

23. *Op. cit.*

24. The differences shown here differ somewhat from those that are derived from Miller and Houthakker because of differences in the assumed shapes and levels of the age-income profiles.

25. Opportunity costs are reflected in the figures showing "additional" lifetime income inasmuch as the income of the person in school is set at zero while his income-earning counterpart receives a positive income; the difference appears in the cost-return stream and measures opportunity costs. However, the other private costs of schooling are omitted in this calculation.

26. The differences shown here differ somewhat from those derived from Houthakker because of differences in the assumed shapes and levels of the age-income profiles.

27. For a fuller treatment of this point see J. Hirshleifer, "On the Theory of Optimal Investment Decision," *Journal of Political Economy*, LXVI (August, 1958), 329–52.

28. For an excellent analysis of some of the conceptual differences between private and social returns see Mary Jean Bowman, "Social Returns to Education," *International Social Sciences Review* (forthcoming), and Burton Weisbrod, "Education and Investment in Human Capital," *Journal of Political Economy: Supplement*, LXX (October, 1962), 106–23.

## Some Benefit-Cost Considerations of Universal Junior College Education

1. The Educational Policies Commission, *Universal Opportunity for*

*Education Beyond the High School* (Washington, D.C.: National Education Association, 1964), pp. 5–6.

2. *Ibid.*, p. 27.

3. For a more complete account of education cost elements see Werner Z. Hirsch, Elbert W. Segelhorst, and Morton J. Marcus, *Spillover of Public Education Costs and Benefits* (Los Angeles: University of California, Institute of Government and Public Affairs, 1964), 465 p.

4. The use of 8 percent as the estimator of capital costs from capital value follows the practice of Robert Rude as used by T. W. Schultz and cited by Rudolph C. Blitz, "The Nation's Education Outlay," in *Economics of Higher Education*, Selma J. Mushkin, ed. (Washington: Office of Education, Bulletin 1962, No. 5, OE-50027), pp. 160–61.

5. Closer to the present is the private return to the woman if her college education enables her to marry a male with higher earning potential. Gary Becker in his *Human Capital* (New York: National Bureau of Economic Research, 1964) p. 101, suggests that part of the wives' earnings should be considered in the private returns of the husbands'. Measurement of these benefits would be as difficult as for any second party effect. However, since this factor is reflected in the earnings of the second party, it is included in *national* education benefit estimates.

6. The assumption that the student finds employment at the median level and that the differential income by age and education level remains constant over time may not be bad for a single student who takes the existing distribution of employment as given. However an assumption of no changes in the demand and supply conditions under universal junior college education is more serious. Herman Miller has argued that a cross-section approach fails to account for increases in earnings due to economic growth which an individual may expect over time. Miller uses a cohort method for 1950–1960 to demonstrate the downward bias of the cross-section approach. See Herman P. Miller, "Lifetime Income and Economic Growth," *American Economic Review*, LV (Sept. 1965), pp. 834–844; also see H. S. Houthakker, "Education and Income," *Review of Economics and Statistics*, XLI (February 1959), pp. 24–28.

7. U.S. Bureau of the Census and Department of Agriculture, *Factors Relating to College Attendance of Farm and Nonfarm High School Graduates: 1960* (Washington: June 15, 1962), Series P-27, No. 32, p. 17.

8. The capital outlay per student of technical institutes, as reported by McLure, *op. cit.*, is $3,000. To maintain pace with technological change,

we assume a 10-year depreciation period for these institutes, or an annual capital cost of $300 per student.

9. In the liberal arts college and technical institute cases the assumption was made that students did not change their occupations as a result of college attendance, but merely moved to a different income stream associated with a higher level of education. This assumption was not made in the first three cases. 1960 census data (*Educational Attainment, op. cit.,* pp. 136–37.) indicate that a college education can provide the opportunity for occupational mobility. In addition to the income possibilities of this shift, there is opportunity for the individual to obtain a different station in life and the chance to experience the stimulation of more challenging activities. These aspects of a college education can be of consequence to the individual in his decision calculus, although for society-at-large the income differential tends to indicate the value placed upon each occupation, and the prestige of the position is likely to follow the relative pecuniary advantage.

10. *Op. cit.*, p. 22.

11. This follows the spirit of proposals made by Fritz Machlup, *The Production and Distribution of Knowledge in the United States* (Princeton: Princeton University Press, 1962), 416 p.

12. We assume here that the positive income differential between high school graduates and persons with one to three years of college begins at age 18 rather than in the mid-twenties. The median income for males at age 18 to 24 with four years of high school exceeds that of males with one to three years of college by as much as $1,100. The reasons are that high school graduates are able to earn more as they gain experience, discharge their military obligations, secure permanent positions, and, chiefly, work full-time during these years.

13. Address to A Symposium on Employment sponsored by the American Bankers Association, Washington, D.C., February 25, 1964, pp. 15–16.

14. Robert A. Gordon, "Has Structural Unemployment Worsened?" *Industrial Relations* (May 1964), Table 8, p. 73.

15. See "Employment Projections, by Industry and Occupation, 1960–1975," *Monthly Labor Review* (March 1963), pp. 240–50.

16. Such remedial programs are part of the Master Plan for Higher Education In California. See Arthur D. Little, Inc., *The Emerging Requirements for Effective Leadership for California Education* (Sacramento: California State Department of Education, November 1964), p. 34.

17. Machlup, *op. cit.*, pp. 127–30.

18. James W. Thornton, Jr., *The Community Junior College* (New York: John Wiley & Sons, 1960), p. 35.

19. A recent California study found that 37 percent of the junior college students were 22 years of age or older and 22 percent over age 28. See J. Edward Sanders and Hans C. Palmer, *Financial Barriers to College Attendance*, Preliminary Report for California State Scholarship Commission (unpublished, 1965), p. 28.

20. Leland D. Medsker, *The Junior College: Progress and Prospect* (New York: McGraw-Hill, 1960), pp. 91–95 and 135.

## When Should Vocational Education Begin?

1. T. W. Schultz, "Education and Economic Growth," *Social Forces Influencing American Education* (Chicago: National Society for the Study of Education, 1961), Ch. III.

2. For a complete discussion of the option value of education, see B. Weisbrod, *External Benefits of Public Education: An Economic Analysis* (Princeton Industrial Relations Section, Princeton University, 1964), p. 20.

3. *Ibid.*, p. 20.

4. For an empirical study dealing with the problem of marginal returns, see W. Lee Hansen, "Total and Private Rates of Return in Investment in Schooling," *Journal of Political Economy*, LXXI (April 1963), pp. 128–40.

5. For a complete discussion of the average and marginal returns to education, see F. Machlup, *The Production and Distribution of Knowledge in the United States* (Princeton: Princeton University Press, 1962), p. 120.

6. The vocational high school student puts in a longer school day than the regular high school student in order to complete both basic academic work and shop work.

7. Machlup, *op. cit.*, p. 134.

8. Note, since the vocational high school student does take *all* basic academic courses, these extra general education courses would have to be additions to the core courses given *all* high school students.

9. All data in this paper referring to the Worcester school system were supplied by school officials.

10. The placement procedure was quite informal. One man was officially in charge of all placement for both groups. In reality, each department head helped place graduates in that trade area. Hence, the actual ratio of placement officers to students would vary with the size of the enrollments in each department.

11. A comparison of the salaries of vocational trade graduates with the salaries of technical course graduates is somewhat suspect, since we could argue that, from the individual's point of view, the two training choices are not substitutes for each other.

*part three*

**Selected Issues in the Economics
    of Education**

## Education and Income

1. To focus on the return to the individual, one would also have to take account of income taxes, further reducing the benefits; but for the individual the added freedom from unemployment cannot be ignored.

2. Several estimates have been made of differences in lifetime earnings of those with different amounts of education. Some have discounted future earnings; others have calculated the internal rate of return on the investment in education implied by the increased future earnings, and compared it with the rate of return on alternative investments. For recent contributions, see Herman Miller, "Annual and Lifetime Earnings in Relation to Education, 1939–1959," *American Economic Review*, L (Dec. 1960), 962–86; Theodore Schultz, "Investment in Human Capital," *Journal of Political Economy*, LXIX (Oct. 1961), 225–36; and H. Houthakker, "Education and Income," *Review of Economics and Statistics*, XLI (Feb. 1961), 24–28.

3. See Daniel Suits, "Use of Dummy Variables in Regression Equations," *Journal of the American Statistical Association*, Vol. 52 (Dec. 1957), pp. 548–551; and for an example and more theoretical discussion, see T. P. Hill, "An Analysis of the Distribution of Wages and Salaries in Great Britain," *Econometrica*, Vol. 27 (July 1959), pp. 355–81.

4. See M. G. Sirken, E. S. Maynes, and J. A. Frechtling, "The Survey of Consumer Finances and the Census Quality Check," *Studies in Income and Wealth*, Vol. 23 (Princeton: Princeton University Press, 1958).

5. They can be found together with more methodological detail in James Morgan, Martin David, Wilbur Cohen, and Harvey Brazer, *Income and Welfare in the United States* (New York: McGraw-Hill, 1962).

6. A beta coefficient is a measure of the number of standard deviations the dependent variable moves for a movement of the independent variable of one standard deviation. It is thus independent of the units of measurement of both variables. See note to Table 2.

7. It would be nice to be able to present a table showing the intercorrelations among the explanatory factors. Unfortunately, when we are dealing with classifications such as education and occupation, there is no really acceptable measure of correlation. If one asks to what extent one's ability to predict an individual's educational class is improved by knowing his occupational class, one is led to Goodman and Kruskal's lambda measure. See Leo A. Goodman and William H. Kruskal, "Measures of Association for Cross Classification," *Journal of the American Statistical Association*, Vol. 49 (Dec. 1954), pp. 732–64.

But when, as is common with survey data, there is one modal educational class within each occupational class, for instance, any very great concentration in the modal class makes this measure very insensitive, because it has no stochastic properties. If one assigned a dummy variable to each educational class, and one to each occupational class, and computed a canonical correlation between the sets, the size of that correlation would be an excellent measure of association. This is too much work. Suffice it to say that examination of the tables shows that education is correlated with occupation, with age, with race, with achievement motivation, with supervisory responsibility, and to a lesser extent with the various forms of mobility.

8. Of those under twenty-five and with less than a high school diploma, 57 percent reported that they had been unemployed at least once during the last five years. Even between twenty-five and thirty-four years of age, 39 percent of those who did not finish high school reported that they had been unemployed sometime during the last five years.

Other data have been reported indicating that those who start college but do not finish have IQ's the same as or lower than those who merely finish high school, but are more likely to have fathers in professional, semi-professional, or managerial occupations. See Dael Wolfle, *America's Resources of Specialized Talent* (New York: Harper and Brothers, 1954), pp. 314–25, 160, 162.

9. Herman P. Miller, "Annual and Lifetime Income in Relation to Education. 1939–1959," *American Economic Review*, L (Dec. 1960); see note 2.

10. Harry G. Shaffer, "Investment in Human Capital: Comment," *American Economic Review*, LI (Dec. 1961), 1026–35.

11. Shaffer, *op. cit.*, p. 1031.


*Education and Income: A Comment*

1. *Qtrly. J. of Economics*, LXXVII (Aug. 1963), 423–37.

2. For a fuller report, see Katona, Lininger and Mueller, *1963 Survey of Consumer Finances* (Ann Arbor, Survey Research Center, 1964).

## The Rate of Return to Education: A Critique

1. Glick and Miller have produced some evidence on this association [7] *1949 increase in income per year of schooling for men 45–54 years old.*

| Elementary | None | Base |
|---|---|---|
| | 1–4 years | $136 |
| | 5–7 years | $165 |
| | 8 years | $303 |
| High School | 1–3 years | $238 |
| | 4 years | $466 |
| College | 1–3 years | $477 |
| | 4+ years | $974 |

However, Miller has shown that a positive correlation does not always hold. [12]. In the United States in 1958, 2.7 million men with college degrees had incomes per annum under $7,000, whilst 1.9 million high school graduates recived more than this amount.

2. For instance in the United States: "Education first influences the career of an individual at the time he enters the labor force. Very few spending unit heads without a college degree entered the labor force in professional and technical work. Few without a high school diploma entered in clerical and sales work. More than 70 percent. of all spending unit heads with less than high school education entered in semi-skilled and unskilled occupations" [14, p. 349].

3. Blaug, in his defence of calculations of the rate-of-return to education, has provided a useful catalogue of types of external economy [3]. It is a curious anomaly in his article that after pointing out that such studies have been made in the Soviet Union in 1924, and more recently in the U.S.A., Mexico, Chile, Venezuela, and Israel, Blaug tries to demonstrate objections to rate-of-return calculations are not convincing, but explicitly limits his frame of reference to "advanced industrialized economies" [3, pp. 205–6].

4. Since the size of the net regression coefficient is not invariant with the units in which the variable is expressed, the ranking of such coefficients is best achieved by converting them to beta coefficients. A beta coefficient of +0.5 for $X_2$ would indicate that for each increase in education by one standard deviation of its distribution, there will be an increase in income by 0.5 of *its* standard deviation.

5. Morgan and David report that in their multivariate analysis they tested for interaction effects between education and race, sex, being a farmer. Such effects were said to exist, but were negligible [15, p. 426]. The first result, in particular, is curious in the light of Glick and Miller's findings

that even a college education is not "a sufficient qualification to elevate a majority of the non-white men above the occupational level of service workers or laborers" [7].

## The Strategy of Human Resource Development in Modernizing Economics

1. W. A. Lewis, "Problems of New States," paper delivered at the Weizman Institute, Rehovoth, Israel. August, 1960.

2. Some of the 20 percent investment, of course, may be in institutions contributing to human resource development as discussed later.

3. See Theodore W. Schultz, "Capital Formation by Education," *Journal of Political Economy*, vol. LXVIII, no. 6. For estimates as low as 10 to 25 percent, see H. M. Phillips, "Education as a Basic Factor in Economic and Social Development," *Final Report* of Conference of African States on the Development of Education in Africa, Addis Ababa, May, 1961.

4. The Inter-University Study has developed some working papers on manpower assessments and human resource development which treat this matter in greater detail. It is also working on comparisons of manpower utilization in countries at various stages of development.

5. See *Investment in Education*, The Report of the Commission on Post-School Certificate and Higher Education in Nigeria, Federal Ministry of Education, Lagos, 1960, p. 21.

6. *Investment in Education, Ibid.* p. 5.

7. W. Arthur Lewis, "Reflections on the Economic Problem," paper delivered to the Oxford Conference on Tensions in Development, New College, Oxford. September, 1961.

8. Conference of African States on the Development of Education in Africa, Addis Ababa, 15–25 May, 1961: *Outline of a Plan for African Educational Development*, Unesco, Paris, 1961.

9. In practice, of course, manpower assessments in individual countries will show a wide variation from this "typical model." The Inter-University Study is engaged in research and hopes to have available shortly more empirical evidence on this subject.

10. The Inter-University Study is involved in studies in a number of countries aimed at analysis of the university as a stimulating or retarding force in economic development and the factors which make for adaptability of the system of higher education to development needs.

# Index